MARKET DEMAND-BASED
PLANNING AND PERMITTING

Arthur C. Nelson, John Travis Marshall,
Julian Conrad Juergensmeyer, and James C. Nicholas
Foreword by Dwight Merriam

AMERICAN BAR ASSOCIATION
Defending Liberty
Pursuing Justice

Cover design by Anthony Nuccio/ABA Design

Library of Congress Cataloging-in-Publication Data
Names: Nelson, Arthur C., author.
Title: Market demand-based planning and permitting / Arthur C. Nelson [and three others].
Description: Chicago, Ill. : American Bar Association, [2017] | Includes bibliographical references and index.
Identifiers: LCCN 2017018007 | ISBN 9781634258906 | ISBN 1634258908
Subjects: LCSH: Real estate development—United States. | Real estate development—Law and legislation—United States. | Land use—United States—Planning | City planning—United States.
Classification: LCC HD255 .N453 2017 | DDC 333.73/150973—dc23 LC record available at https://lccn.loc.gov/2017018007

Printed in the United States of America.

21 20 19 18 17   5 4 3 2 1

Discounts are available for books ordered in bulk. Special consideration is given to state bars, CLE programs, and other bar-related organizations. Inquire at Book Publishing, ABA Publishing, American Bar Association, 321 N. Clark Street, Chicago, Illinois 60654-7598.

www.shopABA.org

*To James C. Nicholas
Mentor, Colleague, and Friend*

Contents

Foreword

You wouldn't want your grandmother to be trapped in a decrepit nursing home that is headed into bankruptcy because too many companies have developed too many beds. You would demand she receive the care she needs and you expected. You wouldn't want to see your regional hospitals battling for patients by establishing more open-heart surgery centers than may be needed, because you know that the quality of care and the competency of those providing the treatment is at risk of being substandard if there are too many hospitals and too many surgeons all trying to do the same thing.

No, health care is important enough that we are justifiably concerned about the potential for a highly dysfunctional oversupply of services and equipment. We do not want to leave the decision-making to the private market with independent, self-serving, uncoordinated operators. While competition is often good, and may be so in many instances of medical care, the stakes are too high—it's life and death, you know—to not consider the need for medical services and equipment before allowing them to come online. Indeed, thirty-seven states have some form of "Certificates of Need" requiring providers of medical services and equipment to demonstrate the need for them before going forward.[1] At least one of these thirty-seven states regulate thirty-plus different services and equipment, ranging alphabetically from acute hospital beds to ultrasound.

From the onset of the Great Recession in 2007, real gross domestic product (GDP) per capita declined from $49,000 to $47,000, not

---

[1] See www.ahpanet.org/matrix_copn.html.

recovering prerecession levels until 2013.[2] The civilian employment ratio declined 5 percent, from 63 percent to 58 percent.[3] By the middle of 2017, it had not fully recovered, at 60 percent.[4]

Most people have focused on the housing bubble, and rightly so. From 2007 through 2015, lenders commenced over 22 million foreclosure actions.[5] The bursting of the housing bubble not only ruined the lives of tens of millions of Americans, but it also brought down the rest of our economy, as those addressing the asymmetric recovery have noted: "Recent macroeconomic views emphasize the burst of the housing bubble and its effects on financial institutions, firms, and households as the main culprit for these developments [decline in GDP and employment]."[6]

For example, here is how Rognlie, Shleifer, and Simsek characterize what happened:

> *[There is] a third channel, which we refer to as the investment hangover, which could help explain the asymmetric recovery. Our key observation is that the housing bubble was an investment bubble as much as an asset price bubble. Overbuilding during the bubble years created excess supply of housing capital by 2007, especially certain types of capital such as owner occupied housing. Between 1996 and 2006, the share of US households living in their own homes rose from about 65% to about 69%. The homeownership rate fell back below 65% in 2014,[7] suggesting that the housing capital might have been in excess for many years after 2007. The excess housing capital lowers residential investment and slows down economic activity.[8]*

Do you get that? It's interesting and important, and for me it is a new way of looking at what happened. It was as much an investment bubble as an asset price bubble. We let too much money get over into

2   Matthew Rognlie, Andrei Shleifer & Alp Simsek, *Investment Hangover and the Great Recession*. Working Paper, 2017, www.economics.cornell.edu/sites/default/files/files/events/Alp.Simsek.pap_.pdf.
3   *Id.*
4   See https://fred.stlouisfed.org/series/EMRATIO.
5   See www.statisticbrain.com/home-foreclosure-statistics/.
6   *Supra* note 2, at 1.
7   Falling to less than 63 percent in mid-2016. See https://fred.stlouisfed.org/series/RHORUSQ156N.
8   *Supra* note 2, at 2.

residential development. Overbuilding wasn't just a factor among many in the Great Recession; it was a driving factor profoundly and adversely impacting investment in other sectors, and because residential capital is durable, depreciation is slow to reduce the overbuilt capital, resulting in a long lag time for residential recovery, heaping more pain and suffering on millions of people. It's all bad, and as a matter of social justice, we can't stand by idly and let this happen again.

Is preventing this type of damage to people and the economy not as important as the welfare of our grandparents in nursing homes or what care we will get in having open-heart surgery? Of course it is, and the authors of this astonishing book courageously (I say "courageously" because I foresee brickbats from all sides) offer up an approach to land development that has the potential to even out some of the capital allocation and market fluctuations that benefit few and injure many.

When it comes to managing development permitting, there are two views of thought, it seems. One is headed by Alan Greenspan, former chair of the Federal Reserve Board. In this view, regulation of markets is not needed because they are self-regulating. For instance, lenders would not lend to those who cannot repay home loans because the source of money for those loans—investors—would stop making such investments. In the case of housing, because oversupply would flood the market with excess supply, thereby eroding equity, buyers would retrench and builders would cut back production until prices returned to locally competitive levels. (Of course, one way in which to increase the supply of affordable housing is to destroy home equity by flooding the market with homes that cannot be sold.) Based on this view, advanced especially by Greenspan, the financial sector has been deregulated steadily since the 1970s. And in many ways the remaining regulations were not implemented vigorously.[9] It was on his watch that financial institutions poured trillions of dollars into the American home-building industry and essentially induced otherwise unqualified buyers to buy homes they could not afford. In his now famous mea culpa, Greenspan laments, as reported in the *New York Times* in 2008:

"Those of us who have looked to the self-interest of lending institutions to protect shareholders' equity, myself included, are in a state of shocked disbelief. . . .

---

[9] See MARK THOMA, *Why Self-Regulation of the Financial System Won't Work*, CBS MONEY WATCH (April 17, 2009), http://www.cbsnews.com/news/why-self-regulation-of-the-financial-system-wont-work/

*... "You had the authority to prevent irresponsible lending prac-
tices that led to the subprime mortgage crisis. You were advised
to do so by many others," said Representative Henry A. Wax-
man of California, chairman of the committee. "Do you feel that
your ideology pushed you to make decisions that you wish you
had not made?"*

*Mr. Greenspan conceded: "Yes, I've found a flaw. I don't know
how significant or permanent it is. But I've been very distressed
by that fact."*[10]

The rest is history. The U.S. government spent more than $1 tril-
lion to bail out financial institutions that lent more money for the
construction of homes ostensibly to be purchased by home buyers
than the market could absorb. Homeowners collectively lost trillions
of dollars in equity; millions lost their homes through the foreclosure
process. Millions of workers lost their jobs as the unemployment rate
rose to the highest levels since the Great Depression. Local governments teetered on bankruptcy in part as billions of dollars in infrastructure bonds sold to finance new facilities to accommodate new
development in excess of demand became difficult to pay. In part to
meet these and other financial obligations, hundreds of thousands of
government workers were let go or their jobs not replaced, including
teachers and first responders.

The cynical perspective is that markets did regulate themselves,
eventually, but only after imposing what could be considered uncon-
scionable damage on the American economy and its people.

The other view, the one that champions social justice and is what this
book is all about, is that it is up to local governments through regional
collaborations to engage in market demand–based planning and permitting. Market demand–based planning identifies the development
needs over a planning horizon and then choreographs land-use allocations along with infrastructure investments to ensure that development
occurs when and where needed and at the right scale among other factors consistent with market demand. To ensure that development is in
accordance with the plan, local governments would not permit more
development than the market could absorb as reflected in it.

Just imagine. Using tools readily available, if local governments
and their regions in the 1980s refused to permit more development

[10] Edmund Andrews, *Greenspan Concedes Error on Regulation*, N.Y. Times, Oct. 23,
2008, www.nytimes.com/2008/10/24/business/economy/24panel.html.

than needed, the savings-and-loan industry might not have collapsed. Moreover, if local governments and their regions refused to permit millions more homes than needed, the Great Recession might never have happened and all the financial damage and personal pain it did would be but a bad storybook.

Some might argue that what the authors of this book propose does not appear to be needed as we assess the continuing recovery. By the time of final editing of this book in 2017, the unemployment rate was near prerecession levels and incomes were rising, though gradually. More to the point: post–Great Recession regulations on financial institutions seemed to prevent excessive lending thereby preventing excessive development. For their part, lenders raised underwriting criteria, meaning that only qualified buyers could buy homes, though resulting in declining home ownership rates. The dollar once again climbed back into the position of being among the planet's strongest currencies.

But recall that we continue to suffer from an asymmetric recovery as reflected in the lagging improvement in home prices and residential sales in many areas of the country because of the prerecession overallocation of capital to the residential market and the difficulty in reallocating that capital. One unexpected consequence, or maybe it should have been expected, of the postrecession recovery with the reallocation of development capital to commercial real estate is the potential for a commercial real estate bubble that seems to concern Federal Reserve Chair Janet Yellin.[11]

It is also worth noting that the political party holding the House, Senate, and presidency (as of this writing) appears committed to reducing regulation and that may lead to uncontrolled flows of capital back into both commercial and residential development.

So, for these two reasons—the promise of federal deregulation of the financial sector and the potential for a new real estate bubble—it is essential to consider what action might be taken locally and within regions.

We need to bring what the authors propose to a wide audience and start implementing measures at the local and regional levels to protect all of the stakeholders—lenders, developers, purchasers, investors, and future generations of taxpayers. Tying development approval to what the market demands is critical in promoting social equity and in stabilizing and growing our economy in an orderly manner.

Dwight Merriam, FAICP

---

[11] See www.bloomberg.com/news/articles/2017-02-02/yellen-eyes-commercial-real-estate-froth-as-fed-weighs-17-risks.

About the Authors

Arthur C. Nelson, PhD, FAICP, is professor of planning, real estate development, and geography at the University of Arizona. His prior academic service includes the Georgia Institute of Technology (where he was also adjunct professor of Law at Georgia State University), Virginia Tech, and the University of Arizona, where he is emeritus presidential professor. Nelson's doctorate is in regional science and planning from Portland State University. He has authored nearly 30 books and more than 300 other publications. Recent books include *Foundations of Real Estate Development Financing, Reshaping Metropolitan America, The TDR Handbook* (with Juergensmeyer and Nicholas), and the critically acclaimed *Megapolitan America.* Nelson's research has been supported by the: National Science Foundation; National Academy of Sciences; U.S. Departments of Housing and Urban Development, Commerce, and Transportation; Environmental Protection Agency; Urban Land Institute; Brookings Institution; National Association of Realtors; and scores of other agencies, firms, nonprofits and foundations. His expert testimony helped frame urban sprawl as a legal concept in Florida, guide the Georgia Supreme Court to establish affordable housing case law, and provide rationale for the "rough proportionality" development exaction doctrine in *Dolan v. City of Tigard*, 512 U.S. 374. Nelson has nearly 50 years' experience in planning, real estate development, and policy analysis.

John Travis Marshall is an Assistant Professor at the Georgia State University College of Law, where he teaches Environmental Law and Land Use Law. From 1999 to 2007—just before the Great Recession— he was an associate and then partner in the Tampa office of Holland & Knight LLP, where he specialized in land use and zoning matters as well as real estate litigation. In 2007, Marshall received a Rocke-feller Foundation fellowship to join the New Orleans Redevelopment Authority (NORA) and advise the agency on creation and imple-mentation of its post-Hurricane Katrina neighborhood revitalization initiatives, including land acquisition, development, and disposition programs. From 2011 to 2013 he served as the Ludwig Community Development Fellow and Clinical Lecturer at Law at Yale Law School. He is co-editor of *How Cities Will Save the World,* and has written a number of articles and book chapters examining urban disasters and the steps that cities have taken—or might take—to bounce back from crisis. Marshall is admitted to practice in Florida and Louisiana. He received his JD from the University of Florida Levin College of Law.

Julian Conrad Juergensmeyer, a BA and JD graduate of Duke Univer-sity, and a member of the Ohio Bar, is currently Professor and Ben F. Johnson, Jr. Chair in Law at Georgia State University where he serves as Co-Director of the Center for the Comparative Study of Metropol-itan Growth and Editor in Chief of the *Journal of Comparative Urban Law and Policy.* He is also Adjunct Professor in City and Regional Planning at the Georgia Institute of Technology and Professor of Law emeritus at the University of Florida. For more than 50 years, he has taught property and land development regulation law at GSU and other schools including the University of Florida, Tulane, Hastings, British Columbia, LSU, Indiana (Bloomington), Duke, and universities in South America, Europe, Asia, and Africa. He is the co-author of the widely cited *Land Use Planning and Development Regulation Law; Impact Fees: Principles and Practice of Proportionate Share Devel-opment Fees* (with Nelson and Nicholas); and over 100 other books and articles. A specialist in infrastructure finance, Juergensmeyer has consulted with local governments and attorneys in regard to impact fee and other infrastructure finance issues in twenty-nine states.

James C. Nicholas, PhD, is emeritus professor of urban and regional planning and emeritus professor of law at the University of Florida. Nicholas has written widely on the subject of land, environmental policy and growth management. He has authored eight books, three monographs, and over sixty articles in the professional literature dealing primarily with growth and local governmental finance of infrastructure. He is author of *A Guide to Impact fees and Housing Affordability* (with Juergensmeyer and Nelson), editor of *The Chang-ing Structure of Infrastructure Finance* and author of *State Regulation* *and Housing Prices.* In addition to his academic duties, he has worked with hundreds of national, state, regional, and local governments. Nicholas has developed growth management and infrastructure funding programs for over 100 local governments in the states of Maine, Massachusetts, Maryland, Virginia, Georgia, Florida, Illinois, Iowa, New Mexico, Colorado, Nevada, California, and Hawaii. Together with Juergensmeyer and Nelson, he pioneered the *Rational Nexus Test* which has become the guiding principal for development exactions such as impact fees in the United States. Nicholas received a doctorate in economics from the University of Illinois in 1970 and has nearly 50 years' experience in economics and issues of public finance.

Acknowledgments

Our research for this book benefited enormously from the insights offered by an astute group of scholars and experts. In particular, we wish to thank Andrew Verstein, Stephen Villavaso, Linda Jellum, Jeremy Kidd, David Oedel, Scott Titshaw, Mark Jones, Marc Roark, Terrell Arline, Mary Robinson, Gary Kramer, Caitlin Cerame, Maria Cahill, Ira Goldstein, Katherine Porter, Daniel Jerrett, Bill Mealor, Tom Butsch, Michael Carnathan, Tim Reardon, Paul Waddell, Ezra Rapport, Frank Duke, Don Roe, Miriam Chion, and Dan Immergluck.

We also benefitted greatly from the insights offered by engaged audiences at the Rocky Mountain Land Use Institute (2014 and 2015), the Growth & Infrastructure Consortium (2014 and 2015), the Southeast Association of Law Schools (SEALS), and the Mercer University Walter F. George School of Law.

Students were immensely helpful. Students in Georgia State Law School's 2016 Advanced Land Use Law Seminar studied and critiqued the draft: Patrick J. Anderson, Gordon T. Glass, Jennifer N. Hamrick, Catherine Tracy (Katie) Neel, Rachel M. O'Toole, Yathurshi U. Rajendra, Randolph B. Russell, and Danielle E. Weit. Many students offered additional help beyond the class.

The authors are particularly indebted to those students who provided research and editorial assistance, including Peter Watson, Joseph Collins, Baxter Randolph, Corbin Aiken, and Katie Neel at Georgia State University and Laura Jensen from the University of Arizona.

Finally, the authors wish to thank the University of Arizona, the University of Florida, and the Georgia State University College of Law. Julian Juergensmeyer and John Marshall are especially grateful to Dean Steven Kaminshine for his generous support of their work through research grants.

Abbreviations of Terms

ARM = adjustable rate mortgage
BPF = British Property Federation
CBO = Congressional Budget Office
CDO = collateralized debt obligation
COGs = councils of government
DCA = Department of Community Affairs
DOT = Department of Transportation
DRI = Development of Regional Impact
ERTA = Economic Recovery Tax Act
FHWA = Federal Highway Administration
FSLIC = Federal Savings and Loan Insurance Corporation
FTA = Federal Transit Administration
GDP = gross domestic product
GIS = geographic information systems
GMA = Growth Management Act
GSEs = government-sponsored enterprises
HUD = Housing and Urban Development
LDIS = land development information system
LIHTC = low-income housing tax credit
LUBA = Land Use Board of Appeals
MBS = mortgage-backed securities
MDBPP = market demand–based planning and permitting
MPOs = metropolitan planning organizations
OTS = Office of Thrift Supervision
PD = planned development
PUD = planned unit development
RDA = regional development agency
RLIS = regional land information system

RPA = regional planning agency
RTC = Resolution Trust Corporation
RTPO = regional transportation planning organization
SCPEA = Standard City Planning Enabling Act
S&L = savings and loan
SPVC = special purpose vehicle corporation
SZEA = Standard Zoning Enabling Act
TARP = Troubled Asset Relief Program
TAZ = transportation analysis zone
TDR = transferable development rights
UGB = urban growth boundary

Renewed Appreciation for the Role of Planning to Make Markets More Efficient

The presidency of Ronald Reagan saw the collapse of an entire financial services industry—the savings and loan (S&L) institutions. There are many reasons for this, but the key one is that S&Ls financed more commercial development than the market could absorb. Overpermitting itself was stimulated in large part by federal tax policies producing after-tax profits on real estate investments that otherwise lost money. Lending more money to development than the market could absorb was also induced by "moral hazard," where lenders and other decision-makers in the financial industry knew it would be American taxpayers who would bail them out in the end. The Reagan era S&L collapse cost the American economy more than $1 trillion (in 2015 dollars) and helped trigger the 1990–1991 recession.

Yet, losses varied by state: those states where local governments were required to manage development permitting to minimize overpermitting relative to market demand lost far less money. They did so through market demand–based planning and permitting (MDBPP), where future development is estimated, plans are made to accommodate that demand, and permitting is allowed only where it is in accordance with a plan. Unfortunately, in most states there is little if any requirement to identify future development needs or planning to accommodate them, and there is little connection between permitting and plans—in effect, permitting occurs regardless of the plan. In a perverse outcome, taxpayers in MDBPP states subsidized losses in states without MDBPP.

Two decades later, under the presidency of George W. Bush, America entered into the largest economic downturn since the Great Depression. The Great Recession of 2007–2009 was fueled in large part by lax federal oversight of financial institutions, many of which lent more funds for home mortgages than borrowers could afford to repay. It was also fueled by local governments permitting millions more new homes than the market could absorb. The reason is that those communities did not engage in MDBPP.

Whereas the financial collapse of the 1980s was caused largely by the overpermitting of commercial development, two decades later the financial collapse of the 2000s was caused largely by the overpermitting of residential development. It was as if we did not learn the lessons of the 1980s. Since residential development is a far larger share of the economy than commercial development, the collapse of the residential mortgage market harmed Americans even more than the collapse of the S&Ls. Millions of workers lost their jobs; homeowners lost trillions of dollars in equity, including, in millions of cases, all their down payments and more; millions of homes were foreclosed or otherwise disposed through short-sales; and financial institutions received more than $1 trillion in bailouts because many were "too big to fail" or otherwise were exercising the same "moral hazard" behavior that collapsed the S&Ls two decades before. The economy lost at least $6 trillion and as much as $15 to $30 trillion (see Epilogue).

If history is a guide to the future, a future recession will also be attributable to overpermitting real estate development. Moral hazard will continue to induce financial institutions into underwriting excessive development—especially those too big to fail. Americans will once again be called upon to spend hundreds of billions or trillions of their dollars to bail out overpermitted development and the financial institutions underwriting it. Millions of Americans will lose their jobs and even their homes.

There is a better way. The federal government, including all its financial resources, should not have to bail out financial institutions. Instead, local governments must permit only that development for which there is a market demand, and in accordance with a plan. But local governments cannot act in isolation. Local-regional collaborations are needed to craft plans that anticipate market demand–based development needs and implement those plans through development permitting that is in accordance with them. Juergensmeyer and Nicholas[1] put it best:

> *Prior to the Great Recession, the prevailing thought had been that land use planning and implementation should be confined to matters of environmental impact and infrastructure availability; that matters of market were private and only the developers or builders were at risk. The recession of 2007–09 demonstrated that this thought is simply wrong. The public sector, at all levels, was left to pick up the pieces and pay the costs of the "excessive exuberance." Following the old adage, "he who pays the piper calls the tune," should not the public, which suffers the pains and pays the costs, have something to say about the pace at which new development occurs? We call for a different kind of land use planning system driven by market demand driven planning and permitting.*

The theme of our book is that new real estate development should be approved only when based on a demonstrated market demand for it and in accordance with a plan. We subscribe to the position of the eminent land economist Marion Clawson,[2] who wrote that local land-use plans should include just enough land to meet projected needs and no more. We also subscribe to the position of Charles Haar[3] that development permitting must be "in accordance with a comprehensive plan." Written in the middle of the last century, these are not new principles. Nor were they new then, as they are imbedded in the planning and permitting approaches advanced in the 1920s by then commerce secretary Herbert Hoover.

Market Demand–Based Planning and Permitting is divided into two parts:

Part 1: The Need for Market Demand–Based Planning and Permitting In Chapter 1, we review the big picture arguing the need for MDBPP. Chapter 2 explores the rich history of planning as a way in which to anticipate and meet market demand

---

[1] JULIAN C. JUERGENSMEYER & JAMES C. NICHOLAS, *Loving Growth Management in the Time of Recession*, URB. LAW. 42(4)/43(1), 417–423 (2010) at 422.

[2] MARION CLAWSON, *Urban Sprawl and Speculation in Suburban Land*, LAND ECON. 38, 99-111 (1962) at 109.

[3] CHARLES M. HAAR, *In Accordance with a Comprehensive Plan*, HARV. L. REV. 68(7), 1154-1175 (1955).

for development while ensuring that permitted development is in accordance with a plan. In Chapter 3, we illustrate what can happen when permitted development exceeds market based demand, using the Savings and Loan collapse in the late 1980s as our example. As if those lessons were not learned, we remind readers in Chapter 4 that, contrary to former Federal Reserve Board Chairman Alan Greenspan's faith in financial institutions to protect the economy, the evidence suggests they seem incapable of actually doing so—after all, they underwrote the financing of more development than the market needed which led in large part to the Great Recession of the late 2000s. It seems that Adam Smith's "invisible hand" is trumped by moral hazard whereby financial institutions know their losses will be covered by American taxpayers. Chapter 5 concludes this part of our book noting that while there will always be economic cycles, MDBPP can often reduce the downward slope of the cycle if not perhaps remove the role of excessive permitting as a cause for future recessions altogether.

Part 2: The Role of Institutions in Advancing Market Demand–Based Planning and Permitting, and its Legal Context While Part 1 lays out the argument for MDBPP, Part 2 addresses various planning and legal approaches to implement it. Chapter 6 summarizes how modern technologies can be used to create the maps and databases that are crucial for informing the market of the demand for certain kinds of development as well as the supply, and that merely having this information widely available can by itself reduce the risk of permitting more development than the market can absorb. Chapter 7 outlines the existing opportunities to create local-regional collaborations to craft market demand–based plans and implement them through market demand–based permitting that is in accordance with those plans. In Chapter 8 we argue that MDBPP can advance smarter planning leading to such benefits as more economic development and more resilient economics, more stable local fiscal structures, and improved social equity among others. Are the concepts underlying MDBPP new? In Chapter 9 we show that the concept of using market demand–based analysis to permit many kinds of development already exists, such as for energy facility siting, health care facility certificates of need, farm commodity quotas, and federal environmentally related acts. The key objective of these and other existing policies is to prevent excess development and thereby protect taxpayers from covering losses. Furthermore, Chapter 10 shows that many of the legal conditions needed to implement MDBPP already exist and its overall effectiveness may be advanced through modest changes in existing laws, rules, and procedures.

Lest one thinks our only concern is about permitting more development than is needed, we also worry about permitting *less* development than is needed to meet market demand. Part and parcel of any MDBPP system is to identify *all* development needs and accommodate them through planning. But since over permitting led substantially to the last two of three recessions, and cost the nation's economy dearly, our book focuses on preventing over development in the future.

If we can "right-size" development permitting, America's economy will flourish. In our epilogue, we assess what could have been had our MDBPP approach been in place since at least the early 1980s. We use data to estimate the economic benefits America could have reaped from market demand–based planning and permitting. Trillions of dollars would have been saved by not overpermitting, tens of millions of households would not have lost their homes or their savings, and America's economy would have been much more robust now despite the inevitable economic cycles. Looking ahead, we find that only through MDBPP may America's great economy be sustainable.

Finally, throughout the book, we use MDBPP as the acronym for market demand–based planning and permitting. However, in several contexts, we address only the planning or permitting elements, so in those cases we spell out the term.

The Need for Market Demand–Based Planning and Permitting

In Part 1, we establish the need for market demand–based planning and permitting (MDBPP). Chapter 1, "What Is Market Demand–Based Planning and Permitting and What Are Its Groundings in the American Land Use Planning and Development Regulation System?," outlines the legal foundation of MDBPP in the context of the American Land Use Planning and Development Regulation System. Prior to the Great Recession, it was assumed that only developers and their financial backers were at risk and as such offered compelling arguments to local governments to have their development proposals approved. However, this argument proved wrong, as it was government at all levels—especially local government—that absorbed direct costs in the form of taxpayer-subsidized bailouts and indirect costs in the form of vacant properties, which created blighted neighborhoods, reduced property values, and eroded local tax bases.

The missing link in most local development decision-making process is a plan that is based on market demand–based analysis. Such a plan can help lead to a determination of the extent to which a proposed development is in accordance with it. If it is not, the development should not be approved or the plan may need to be amended allowing it. In either case, the local government should require an impact assessment, demonstrating a market demand for the development.

This is already required in many states and scores of local governments. In our view simply making market demand analysis a required element of impact assessment can improve local government's ability to determine the efficacy of a proposed development project.

In Chapter 2, "In Accordance with a Plan: The Foundations of Market Demand–Based Planning and Permitting," we remind readers that planning is all about projecting future land use, development, and facility needs, and orchestrating resources to meet those needs consistent with an overall set of goals, objectives, and strategies. This chapter will refresh readers on this all-important aspect of planning. Planning's critical importance is noted as far back as the landmark case *Euclid v. Ambler Realty* in which the Supreme Court took note of local governments' use of a comprehensive development plan—as part of a general zoning scheme—to guide local development. Recognition of planning's central role grew steadily throughout the 20th century highlighted famously by Charles M. Haar's article, noted above and articulated most clearly by the New York Court of Appeals in *Udell v. Haas*. This chapter also reviews key features of statewide land use planning policy in several states that require planning based on projected needs. Those states include California, Florida, Georgia, Hawaii, New Jersey, Oregon, and Washington, among others. Special reference is made to developments of regional impact, since every state that enables them requires a needs-based assessment. A key part of this chapter is drawing the connection between planning and reducing financial hazard risks.

We build on the need for MDBPP in Chapter 3, "The Savings and Loan Crisis as a Taxpayer Tragedy." We begin with a review of President Ronald Reagan's Economic Recovery Tax Act of 1981, which was intended to stimulate real estate investment to bring the economy out of the deepest recession seen since the Great Depression. It included accelerated depreciation, reduced capital gains taxes, and other real estate development incentives.

By the mid-1980s, America was awash with vacant, newly built commercial buildings because investors could actually make money after taxes by losing money on real estate. In 1986, President Reagan and Congress corrected these perverse incentives with the Tax Reform Act of 1986. It included such wholesale changes to real estate investment that the savings-and-loan (S&L) industry collapsed, which helped trigger the recession of 1990–1991. By some estimates, the S&L collapse cost American taxpayers about $300 billion and the nation's economy more than $1 trillion (in 2015 dollars). The distribution of losses resulted in federal tax dollars being transferred *from* states that had discipline in planning and permitting development based on need, especially such "growth management" states as California, Florida, Oregon, and Washington, *to* states without such discipline, especially Arizona and Texas. The lessons that should have been learned to prevent the next overbuilding-related recession are noted.

Alas, in Chapter 4, "The Self-Interests of Financial Organizations Are Incapable of Protecting America's Economy or Moral Hazard Trumps the Invisible Hand," we show that those lessons were not heeded. We recount that at the end of the Clinton administration and throughout the administration of George W. Bush, home mortgage finance rules were relaxed and those that were not changed were not rigorously enforced. This allowed millions of homes to be financed through subprime mortgages (given to people who would not otherwise qualify). It also stimulated construction of millions of new homes in excess of market demand. By the late 2000s, the oversupply of homes depressed housing values, thereby putting millions of homes "underwater" (where mortgage balances exceeded home values). This led in part to lending institutions' collapse—similar to the S&L collapse two decades earlier. It is as though American politicians and policy-makers, and the public who put them into office, learned little from the S&L debacle. Overdevelopment of homes helped trigger the Great Recession of 2007–2009, which was even more severe than the one two decades earlier. Combined with increasing joblessness and declining incomes, foreclosures soared. By the middle 2010s, housing values throughout most of the nation still had not reached levels seen a decade earlier. Effects of the Great Recession may linger well into the next decade, if not longer. Indeed, when considering the cost of living, home values in large parts of the nation may not reach their highs of the 2000s for many decades, if ever. Again, while most states permitted more residential units than were needed, in many states the excess was substantial, including Florida, which by the early 2000s had abandoned its statewide growth-management efforts. This chapter identifies the lessons not learned from the 1980s overpermitting, with a special focus on Florida, which went from right-size permitting in the 1990s to excessive permitting in the 2000s.

A key driver behind the lessons not learned is the powerful role of "moral hazard." This arises when people make decisions for their benefit without suffering the consequences that are borne by others. Any reforms to development permitting will need to reduce if not eliminate moral hazard.

Even with MDBPP, however, there will always be market cycles. This is the focus of Chapter 5, "The Economics and Economic Implications of Excessive Real Estate Development." This chapter starts with a broad overview of the nation's economy since the Great Depression, showing that economic booms and busts are normal. It then suggests that excess development permitting can be viewed as a leading indicator of recessions. It continues by showing that as real estate is one of the nation's largest economic sectors, its performance has a much greater influence over the nation's prosperity or decline than perhaps any other. The chapter next addresses the effects of excess permitting on home owners, focusing on foreclosures during and after the Great Recession. Implications for local government are outlined. We observe that it is local government that decides to issue permits, and if they issue more than the market can absorb, it is local government that incurs the consequences in the form of lower revenues and rising unemployment that hurts everyone. But excessive permitting by a few local governments can adversely impact many others.

CHAPTER 1

What Is Market Demand–Based Planning and Permitting and What Are Its Groundings in the American Land Use Planning and Development Regulation System?[1]

As set forth in the prologue, the concept of market demand–based planning and permitting (MDBPP) is that new real estate development should be approved only if those seeking to develop can establish that there is sufficient market demand for the development they propose. The origins of our concept lie in the Great Recession of 2007–2009 from which the American economy struggled to recover through most of the next decade.

Business cycles are not new to the United States—or to other nations for that matter. Following past recessions, projected incomes and spending returned to anticipated levels in a relatively short time and often eventually rose above those original levels. In evaluating the legitimate role of growth management during economic malaises, it is important to remember that economic recessions and periods of slow performance are normal events.[2]

Since 1945, there have been eleven officially designated recessions or about one recession every six years. Recessions, however, do not follow a fixed pattern. Since 1945, the shortest time between the end

---

[1] Major portions of this chapter are taken, with permission, from Julian C. Juergensmeyer & James C. Nicholas, *Loving Growth Management in the Time of Recession*, 42/43 URB. LAW. 417 (2011).

[2] *See* Chapter 5.

of one recession and the beginning of another was one year—one ending in July 1980 and the next beginning in July 1981. The longest stretch between recessions was nine years, from March 1991 to March 2000. The most recent recession began six years after the end of the previous one, exactly on the average. The 2007–2009 recession was the longest postwar downturn, at eighteen months, but it was not the most severe. The 1981–1982 recession saw the unemployment rate peak at 10.8 percent, as contrasted with 10.6 percent for 2007–2009. Still, these postwar recessions pale when contrasted with the Great Depression, which lasted one hundred seven months (eight years, eleven months) and saw unemployment rise to 25 percent.

Even though recessions are common, there have been only three in the past twenty years, two of which were short and relatively mild. This has resulted in an expectation of continuous prosperity, and many have simply forgotten the reality of recessions. Local governments and planners have also forgotten, in many instances, the need to incorporate recessions into growth-management planning.

Recessions are general contractions of economic activity, but the most commonly noted characteristic of a recession is an increase in the unemployment rate. The pattern of rising and falling unemployment rates is very apparent when plotted with periods of recession. Periods of contraction see rapid rises in unemployment; the subsequent recovery and expansion sees unemployment fall. The rate at which unemployment falls is generally a measure of the strength of the economic recovery. By this measure, the recovery that began in 2010 is weak.

What makes the 2007–2009 recession different is what happened before the onset: Housing was constructed at rates well above what the market demanded. The average absorption of new housing units runs 1.5 million per year. Prior to the 2007 downturn, privately owned housing starts were as high as 2.1 million per year. Between 2004 and 2007, housing starts averaged about 2 million per year. During this period, nearly an extra 2 million dwelling units were built beyond the average 1.5 million per year. The construction of these excess units was financed by irresponsible means and a larger portion than normal were sold to people with no means or intent to pay for the units.[3] The result was the financial catastrophe that we have seen. Many of the 2 million surplus units were never sold and remain in inventory even

---

[3] *See* Chapters 3, 4, and 5.

today. A large number that had been sold were returned to the inventory through abandonment or foreclosure.

One might note the coincidence between housing starts and the business cycle. Recessions typically commence with overbuilding, followed by a decline in housing starts. General economic recovery typically coincides with a recovery of housing starts. The weakness of the post-2010 recovery may be partially due to a continuation of extraordinarily low housing starts through 2015, which in turn was due to the excessive inventory of unsold units. This would suggest that a robust recovery of the economy may be waiting on absorption of the unsold inventory and the return to a normal pace of housing starts.

Despite all of the hardships associated with the 2007–2009 recession, the economy has mostly recovered and the Great Recession will become an increasingly distant though painful memory. But what lessons have been learned? Perhaps the biggest is that overproduction of any good, especially housing, is an economic mistake that affects far more than just the suppliers who are unable to sell their products and the banks that financed them. The resulting home price decreases that resulted from oversupply of housing affect the neighbors of those homes and the local governments that look to property taxes for their revenues. The long-term unemployment of construction and allied workers was devastating to the workers and their families, not to mention the cost to taxpayers of extended unemployment compensation. Perhaps the greatest cost was that to the public of "bailing out" America's financial institutions because, in a famous confession by former Federal Reserve Board Chair Alan Greenspan, paraphrased bluntly by us, the self-interests of financial organizations are incapable of protecting America's economy.[4]

Prior to this recession, the prevailing thought was that the growth management regulatory system should be confined to matters of environmental impact and infrastructure availability, that matters of market were private and only the developers, builders, and financers were at risk. The recession of 2007–2009 demonstrated that this thought is simply wrong. The public sector, at all levels, was left to pick up the pieces and pay the costs of this "excessive exuberance." Following the old adage *He who pays the piper calls the tune*, should not the public, which suffers the pains and pays the costs, have something to say about the pace at which new development occurs?

---

[4] *See* Chapters 3 and 4.

As early in the Growth Management and Smart Growth Era as 1985, the late Fred Bosselman asked, "Will impact analysis become the universal antidote to land use complaints?" Whether it has become an antidote to complaints or not probably depends on one's perspective, but it has certainly become the guiding principle for development permitting decisions in many states. Bosselman defined *impact analysis* as "the process of examining a particular land development proposal and analyzing the impact it will have on a community."[5] He further opined:

(1) Regulation should respond to specific development proposals: the policy that the formulation of land use controls should be delayed until the developer's intentions are known has been reflected in the weakening of legal support for the principle that a developer should be entitled to develop if his proposal is consistent with pre-established regulations adopted pursuant to a comprehensive plan.

(2) Development standards should be predictable: The policy that a greater degree of predictability ought to be found in the local process of responding to development proposals has been reflected in the increasing uneasiness of courts toward local regulations that lack a "scientific" basis.

The original, and still most frequently encountered, applications of impact analysis in the development process relate to the fiscal impact on an area's infrastructure. The permitting authorities measure and calculate the impact that the proposed development will have on public infrastructure that will be needed to support or service the proposed development. For example, traffic attraction and generation that will be created by the new development are calculated and translated into the number of lane miles of new roads that will be needed to accommodate the new traffic without lowering existing levels of service. The same is done for relevant infrastructure such as utilities, schools, parks, public building, public safety facilities, and the like. The fiscal impact of those demands is then examined.

---

[5] JULIAN CONRAD JUERGENSMEYER & THOMAS E. ROBERTS, Land Use Planning & Development Regulation Law, Sect 9:1 at 498 (2012) (unpublished manuscript, *Fred Bosselman, Linkage, Mitigation and Transfer: Will Impact Analysis Become the Universal Antidote in Land Use Complaints?* 1985).

One could argue that the earliest applications of fiscal impact analysis can be found in subdivision regulation's required dedications, since the impact of the platting and subsequent development would necessitate internal improvements such as streets, sidewalks, and drainage easements. However, the infrastructure impact analysis era, according to most commentators, began when capped property taxes combined with decreased or no longer available state and federal infrastructure funding grants left local governments financially desperate to find new sources of revenue for infrastructure. They adopted the concept that development should pay for itself and turned to developer construction and dedication of necessary improvements or developer funding devices such as impact fees and related development charges as conditions imposed as a prerequisite for development approval.

Even though the impact of new development on a community is by no means confined to the physical or "hard" infrastructure items such as roads, parks, schools, and public buildings—or even to infrastructure of any type—local governments were slow to adopt and courts were slow in approving the extension of conditioning approval based on impact analysis beyond "hard" infrastructure. The early extensions of the concept related to what was often called *social* or *soft infrastructure.* Jurisdictions sought to include in the impact analysis such infrastructure items as childcare facilities, public transit, art in public places, and affordable or workforce housing. Requirements that developers construct or fund such "social" infrastructure items were often classified as "mitigation" requirements or fees and in some jurisdictions had relaxed requirements compared to hard impact fees, even though the concept was identical in the sense that impacts of proposed development had to be mitigated or development permission would be withheld.[6]

Environmental impacts of proposed developments were the next to be included in the impact analysis requirement and for which mitigation was required. Open space requirements, protection of prime agricultural land, scenic view, ridgeline protection, and stream bank buffer dedications all fell within the expanded list of the impacts of a proposed development that would be analyzed and turned in to mitigation requirements prerequisite to development approval.

At the same time that the list of impacts to be considered expanded, an accompanying consideration was introduced and combined with

---

[6] *See generally* JULIAN CONRAD JUERGENSMEYER & THOMAS E. ROBERTS, LAND USE PLANNING AND DEVELOPMENT REGULATION LAW § 9. 9 (Thomson West, 3d ed. 2012).

fiscal impact analysis requirements. This new concept is often referred to as the *temporal element*. Land use regulation authorities considered what should be developed and where it should be permitted as well as *when* it should be allowed. The introduction of a timing element was usually tied to when infrastructure would be available— for example, when would the proposed development be adequately served by roads, parks, schools, sewer, and water treatment facilities. The Ramapo Plan of Professor Robert Freilich was the seminal application of factoring temporal considerations in to the development process, and the Ramapo case[7] in which he successfully obtained approval of the introduction of the temporal element is considered by many to be the legal beginning of the growth management/smart growth era.

The current state of our land use regulatory system is therefore based on our hundred-year-old zoning system being used to determine what development shall be allowed and where. Many growth management/smart growth systems add fiscal impact analysis considerations to determine whether various types of physical infrastructure are available or need to be partially or totally constructed or funded by the developer. Overlaid with that is the mitigation concept, which includes social and environmental needs such as affordable housing, child care, and climate change protection facilities. Another overlay is an analysis of *when* development should be allowed because of its various other impacts on the community. In Ramapo, for example, development permission was delayed until the developer could demonstrate that adequate infrastructure was available.

Our proposal for market demand–based planning and permitting builds on the growth management framework though in ways that make explicit consideration of market forces. It would create another overlay or another impact that needs to be evaluated in the development process. As explained earlier, we suggest that the impact of the proposed development on the market for the type of development proposed—for example, single family homes, apartments, senior living facilities, office parks, condominiums, commercial buildings, and so on—be added to the impact analysis that guides the community in whether development would be permitted. To state it another way, development permission should be withheld if those who seek to build cannot establish that there is sufficient market demand for what they propose to build; if they cannot do so, development permission

---

[7] *Golden v. Planning Bd. of Town of Ramapo*, 30 N.Y.2d 359 (1972).

should be withheld until such time as that development demand can be demonstrated.

Those who decry regulations on the private sector may consider this proposal an interference with property rights. On the contrary, it is designed to protect the property values of home owners, or firms that lose market value of their homes and establishments, or who, in some instances, lose their properties to foreclosure or bankruptcy due at least partially to the construction of unmarketable dwelling or business units.[8] Market demand–based planning and permitting will further protect citizens and firms from decreases in the quantity and quality of public services that result from decreases in local government revenue stemming from the prolonged effect of recessions occasioned by the permitting of residential and nonresidential development in excess of demonstrated market needs.[9]

We would suggest that courts have placed too much emphasis on protecting the rights of owners of undeveloped property and too little emphasis on protecting the interests of owners of already developed land. When considering scenarios in which the interests conflict, shouldn't there be an attempt to balance the property interests of individuals seeking to develop their land with those who own already developed land? Is it fair and equitable that our takings jurisprudence is generally confined to protecting the owners of undeveloped or underdeveloped land to the exclusion of the property interests of owners of previously developed parcels?

Local governments also must learn a lesson from this recent economic debacle. Growth projections should be assessed more frequently and more conservatively, and surpluses should be accumulated in operating and capital accounts, even if holding back the construction of infrastructure means delays in approving developments until needed infrastructure projects can be assured of having adequate financing. This is especially true in instances where development charges and fees are bonded, because if impact fee receipts are inadequate, the public will have to make up the differences. Bonding of projected impact fee revenues must take into account possible downturns in the economy, even if the resulting more conservative estimates delay the availability of infrastructure improvements. When bonds are issued, the burden will be placed on someone. Local governments owe it to their residents to place a reasonable share of these

---

[8] *See* Chapter 10.
[9] *See* Chapters 3, 4, and 5.

burdens on the development community. This would be in addition to justifying the proposed development from a marketability standpoint.

To protect property rights, American land use planning and development regulation programs must play a larger role in ameliorating the "normal" business cycles. In the past, growth management programs' lack of emphasis on market factors on the rate or pace of development has caused them to be inadequate in offering a moderating influence on economic downturns fueled or at least prolonged by irresponsible lending and building. We thus view MDBPP as a logical extension of growth management (and smart growth). If local governments add considerations of market demand to planning and development approval processes, they will remain viable during times of recession and possibly play a key role in decreasing the depth and length of economic downturns.

CHAPTER 2

In Accordance with a Plan: The Foundations of Market Demand– Based Planning and Permitting

▌INTRODUCTION

Planning is all about projecting future land use, development, and facility needs and orchestrating resources to meet those needs consistent with an overall set of goals, objectives, and strategies. This chapter establishes the overall framework for planning, beginning with the Standard City Planning Enabling Act of 1928. We review how scholars—notably Charles M. Haar—have interpreted it to mean that all local land-use decisions must be in accordance with a plan. We review the debate by scholars over whether plans should be strictly or loosely interpreted by those implementing them—chiefly planners and land-use decision-making bodies. This will include a general discussion of the role of land-use regulations in implementing plans, including summarizing how selected states guide planning. This chapter concludes with a call for planning and development permitting to meet market demand, consistent with planning goals.

TOWARD THE SCPEA

The role of planning to shape America's cities began formally with the Standard City Planning Enabling Act (SCPEA).[1] This is an overstatement, of course, since planning was already a widely known and applied field. What was different about the SCPEA, however, was it became a statement of the federal interest in sound local land-use planning to be based on guidance enabled by state legislatures. Indeed, every state eventually adopted a version of the SCPEA.

We find it notable that the SCPEA was produced by the U.S. Department of Commerce, under then secretary and later president Herbert Hoover. In this capacity, Hoover had access to some of the best available data at the time. He may have seen something about the economy others did not, and his unique insights helped fashion an approach to addressing the problem: looming excess supply of development before the Great Depression. We pose our interpretation here.

The year after October 29, 1929—when the stock market crashed, setting off the Great Depression—Charles Persons wrote in the *Quarterly Journal of Economics*:[2] "The thesis of this paper is that the existing depression was due essentially to the great wave of credit expansion in the past decade."[3] He then reports explosive growth in mortgage debt, in 2015 dollars, growing from $5.6 billion to $52.4 billion, an increase of more than eightfold. Persons asserts, "The past decade has witnessed a great volume of credit inflation. Our period of prosperity was based on nothing more substantial than debt expansion."[4]

The year *before* 1929, Secretary Hoover issued the SCPEA. In the first sentence of his foreword to the report, Hoover writes, "In several hundred cities and regions planning commissions are working with public officials to obtain more orderly and efficient physical development of their land areas."[5]

While there were many concerns regarding development patterns evident during the early to middle 1920s, we suspect there may have been an underlying concern about burgeoning mortgage obligations

---

[1] ADVISORY COMMISSION ON CITY PLANNING AND ZONING, STANDARD CITY PLANNING ENABLING ACT ("SCPEA"), U.S. Department of Commerce (1928).
[2] CHARLES E. PERSONS, *Credit Expansion, 1920 to 1929, and Its Lessons*, Q. J. ECON 45, 94-130.
[3] *Id.* at 94.
[4] *Id.* at 116.
[5] SCPEA at iii.

fueled by expanding housing supply. Hoover may have sensed this, though future historians will need to confirm our conjecture. The heart of the SCPEA provides the following:

Such plan, with the accompanying maps, plats, charts, and descriptive matter shall show the commission's recommendations of said territory, including, among other things, the general location, character and extent of streets, viaducts, subways, bridges, waterways, water fronts, boulevards, parkways, playgrounds, squares, parks, aviation fields, and other public ways, grounds and open spaces, the general location of public buildings and other public property, and the general location and extent of public utilities and terminals, whether publicly or privately owned or operated, for water, light, sanitation, transportation, communication, power, and other purposes; also the removal, relocation, widening, narrowing, vacating, abandonment, change of use or extension of any of the foregoing ways, grounds, open spaces, buildings, property, utilities, or terminals; as well as a zoning plan for the control of the height, area, bulk, location, and use or buildings and premises.[6,7]

Further, the plan is to be based on[8] "careful and comprehensive surveys and studies of present conditions and future growth of the municipality and with due regard to its relation to neighboring territory."[9]

In reflecting on the role of the comprehensive plan in guiding community development nearly thirty years after the SCPEA was published, Haar wrote:

The (comprehensive plan) symbolizes a change in the organization of the land market. Its primary justification is an assumption that the interdependence of land uses in an industrialized society makes necessary municipal controls over private property. This

---

[6] SCPEA at 14-16.
[7] Footnotes appearing in the original are removed.
[8] See STUART MECK, GROWING SMART LEGISLATIVE GUIDEBOOK: MODEL STATUTES FOR PLANNING AND THE MANAGEMENT OF CHANGE (2002), noting several administrative limitations to the SCPEA, though they do not affect the plan content provisions.
[9] SCPEA at 16-17.

*is the challenge—to create an institutional arrangement which
can give meaning to planning ideas by delimiting them for effective use in the enactment of regulatory ordinances, and which
can supply the courts with a sensible and reasonably precise
basis for evaluation and review.[10]*

Haar's paragraph is prescient because local land-use controls over
private property has evolved since the 1920s by these ways:

- Zoning and the development it allows must be in accordance
  with a comprehensive plan leading to
- Growth management that choreographs the timing and location
  of development as the precursor of
- Smart growth that influences the design of development with a
  logical extension to
- Needs-based planning and permitting to ensure there is a legitimate market demand for the proposed development.

But first we need to resolve two opposing schools of thought on the
role of comprehensive planning in guiding community development.

THE COMPREHENSIVE PLAN AS AN IMPERMANENT CONSTITUTION VERSUS AD HOC BARGAINING TO ADVANCE EFFICIENT LAND-USE MARKETS WITH A BALANCING PERSPECTIVE

Haar makes the case that a comprehensive plan is an "impermanent
constitution."[11] Much as the constitutions of the United States and
each of its states establish rights and procedures and implementing
institutions, a local government prepares a comprehensive plan that
has constitutional qualities as it establishes rights and procedures along
with implementation institutions. By their nature, comprehensive

---

[10] CHARLES H. HAAR, *In Accordance with a Comprehensive Plan*, 68 HARV. L. REV. 1154-1175 (1955).
[11] Charles H. Haar, *The Master Plan: An Impermanent Constitution*, 20 LAW AND CONTEMPORARY PROBLEMS 353-418 (1955), retrieved December 10, 2016 from http://scholarship.law.duke.edu/lcp/vol20/iss3/2.

plans anticipate changes over five to twenty years (rarely longer), so they require periodic remaking to reflect new challenges informed from past plan implementation experience to guide public land-use decision-making over the next planning horizon.[12]

To understand the role of states in guiding local plan making and implementation, Haar produced a content analysis of all states that had adopted the SCPEA by the middle 1950s. He found that:

The larger share of the typical enabling act concerns itself with the making of plans. The uses to society of this mechanism are envisioned as six broad types: (1) a source of information; (2) a program for correction; (3) an estimate of the future; (4) an indicator of goals; (5) a technique for coordination; and (6) a device for stimulating public interest and responsibility.[13]

These are the basic elements of land-use planning today.[14]

The institutions of plan implementation are outlined in the U.S. Department of Commerce's Standard State Zoning Enabling Act (SZEA).[15] The principal purposes of zoning are to (1) protect residential properties from incompatible uses, (2) craft a police-power argument to support zoning, and (3) facilitate a clear delegation of zoning as a police power function to local governments.[16] Those and other arguments helped persuade the U.S. Supreme Court in *Village of Euclid, Ohio v. Ambler Realty Co.*, 272 U.S. 365 (1926) to uphold zoning as a constitutional exercise of the police power. Haar reminds us that:

Section 3 of (the SZEA) provides in part that ordinances shall be drawn "in accordance with a comprehensive plan." These words appear to be a directive to put zoning on a base broader

---

[12] Thomas Jefferson had a different opinion about the "permanence" of constitutions: "Every constitution, then, and every law, naturally expires at the end of nineteen years. If it be enforced longer, it is an act of force, and not of right." Thomas Jefferson to James Madison, 1789. ME 7:459, Papers 15:396.

[13] Haar, *supra* note 11, at 356.

[14] See JULIAN CONRAD JUERGENSMEYER & THOMAS E. ROBERTS, LAND USE PLANNING, AND CONTROL LAW (2013); PHILLIP R. BERKE, DAVID R. GODSCHALK & EDWARD J. KAISER, URBAN LAND USE PLANNING (2006).

[15] ADVISORY COMMITTEE ON ZONING, A STANDARD ZONING ENABLING ACT. U.S. Department of Commerce (1926).

[16] Meck, *supra* note 8, at Chapters 8 and 10.

than and beyond itself, and a warning that an ordinance not "in accordance with a comprehensive plan" is ultra vires the enabling act.[17]

We know this today as the "consistency doctrine" in planning. Zoning and other land-use controls must be consistent with a comprehensive plan.[18] By implication, development permitted on the basis of zoning and other land-use controls must also be consistent with a comprehensive plan.[19]

Haar's content analysis of state comprehensive plan enabling acts revealed a second set of enabling functions relating more directly to local legislative controls of land-use development:

These uses seem to divide into five broad types: (1) a prophesy of public reaction; (2) a tool for the planning commission in making reports; (3) a guide to effectuating procedures and measures; (4) an ordinance regulating the use of land; and (5) a guard against the arbitrary.[20]

These again are in common practice today, mostly codified as procedural requirements of plan-making and implementing ordinances. A key provision is the last one: a "guard against the arbitrary," which we will discuss in more detail later.

Unfortunately, as Hills and Schleicher point out, the political economy of land-use decisions such as zone changes and variances is such that "most courts give the phrase 'in accordance with a comprehensive plan' little meaning, and academics treat planning mandates with a skepticism bordering on contempt."[21]

The reason is a certain allure among locally elected officials to engage in ad hoc bargaining with competing interests to resolve disputes around land-use decisions. For instance, Carol M. Rose[22] argues

---

[17] Haar, *supra* note 10, at 1156.

[18] JOSEPH DiMENTO, THE CONSISTENCY DOCTRINE AND THE LIMITS OF PLANNING (Concord, MA, Oelgeschlager, Gunn & Hain 1980).

[19] Juergensmeyer & Roberts, *supra* note 14.

[20] Haar, *supra* note 11, at 356.

[21] RODERICK M. HILLS JR & DAVID SCHLEICHER, CITY REPLANNING, NYU Marron Inst. of Urban Mgmt., Working Paper No. 12 (2014) at 2.

[22] CAROL M. ROSE, *Planning and Dealing: Piecemeal Land Controls as a Problem of Local Legitimacy*, 71 CAL. L. REV. 837 (1983); CAROL M. ROSE, *New Models for Local Land Use Decisions*, 79 NW. U. L. REV. 1155 (1985).

that making land-use decisions such as zone changes and variances consistent with a comprehensive plan can deprive politicians of the ability to bargain with developers and neighbors. Some economists, notably Robert H. Nelson and William A. Fischel,[23] endorse this view, arguing that parcel-specific negotiated agreements create more efficient outcomes because developers and residents resolve "externality" concerns that address the negative impacts of development on nearby property. We review both ad hoc perspectives.

Our interpretation of Rose's position is that since no one can accurately predict the future, no one, least of all elected officials, wants to create conflict among constituencies in the present. Plan-making thus becomes an exercise of general policy-making without parcel-based property rights allotments. Rose reasons that "local governments have a good reason for keeping their land use plans rather fuzzy; they may not want a fixed plan because they cannot realistically see very far into the future. Neither can anyone else."[24]

Hills and Schleicher offer a succinct summary of Rose's view that ad hoc processes, instead of end-state comprehensive plans, are both necessary and legitimate as a democratic decision-making process:

Local tastes are likely to be idiosyncratic: two projects that look similar to an outsider expert in terms of their effects on a community may seem very different to the local insider. In order to express idiosyncratic taste preferences, local governments needed to make individualized determinations about proposed building projects, rather than ex ante neutral determinations. Power over land use could not be removed from politics and handed to impartial planners because land use decisions are inherently political: they involve conflicts between different types of property rights claims and different values.[25]

---

[23] See Robert H. Nelson, Zoning and Property Rights (1978); William A. Fischel, The Economics of Zoning: A Property Rights Approach to American Land Use Controls (1985); William A. Fischel, The Homevoter Hypothesis: How Home Values Influence Local Government Taxation, School Finance, and Land-Use Policies (2005).

[24] Rose 1985, *supra* note 22, at 1163.

[25] Roderick M. Hills Jr. & David Schleicher, *supra* note 21 (emphasis in original).

Rose then asserts that "if piecemeal changes are treated as medi-ations, their 'dealing' aspects are not an undesirable aberration but natural parts of . . . dispute resolution."[26]

To Rose, since planning did not realistically provide an end-state—the progress toward which politicians could be judged—planning was itself political. Of course, by the 1960s, it was widely known that a key failure of SCPEA was in making plans themselves only advisory and nonbinding on any private or public land use decision.[27] So, if plans were irrelevant, planning as a day-to-day mediation process to resolve current issues was indispensable.[28] Politics is nothing if it is not deal making in the constructive sense of the term to resolve con-flicts between interests.

R. H. Nelson and Fischel echo Rose's concerns by arguing that piecemeal, even parcel-specific negotiated agreements create more efficient temporal outcomes than adhering to a comprehensive plan crafted years ago. One key reason is that developers and residents resolve their disputes essentially one or a few parcels at a time.

They begin by suggesting that a key purpose of zoning is to estab-lish property rights.[29] At the neighborhood scale, these property rights enable property owners to bargain with developers. Neighbors can identify ways in which they may be harmed by new development, the developers can pose payments or other mitigating strategies to compensate for negative externalities imposed on neighbors, and the "deal" is approved by local government. *Transaction costs* (the cost of complying with the agreement) are reduced through this ad hoc rezoning process of bargaining. For their part, local governments need the flexibility to change zoning without having to revisit a compre-hensive plan through a plan amendment process:

If zoning's foundation is planning, then developers will not be able to buy their way out of zoning restrictions through individ-ualized transactions that ignore the larger goals of the compre-hensive plan . . . (S)uch limits on a community's individualized responses to developers' parcel-specific proposals rendered

---

[26] Rose 1983, *supra* note 22, at 891.

[27] See T. J. KENT, THE URBAN GENERAL PLAN (1961).

[28] With all due respect to Dwight D. Eisenhower, who said, "In preparing for battle I have always found that plans are useless, but planning is indispensable." COLUM-BIA WORLD OF QUOTATIONS, Quotation 1861 (Robert Andrews et al. eds).

[29] We are paraphrasing Hills's and Schleicher's summary of R. H. Nelson's and Fischel's works.

*zoning an inflexible straitjacket indifferent to the joint prefer-
ences of potential residents and incumbent neighbors.[30]*

The implication is that neighborhoods and developers bargain
from equal positions. It also implies that supply of new development
should equal demand, though given the complexities of bargaining, it
would not be surprising if supply lagged. The reason is that if demand
exceeded supply substantially, bargaining would lead to more concessions that would lead to more development approvals; if demand
was weak, developers would be less willing to make the concessions
needed to induce neighbors' approval.

On the other hand, John R. Logan and Harvey L. Molotch[31] argue
that members of the "growth machine"—developers, bankers, real
estate brokers, contractors, and unions—have more influence in elect-
ing local officials than unorganized individuals. The result would be
more new development approved than the market needed, at least
until it became obvious that the market was substantially oversupplied, in which case the growth machine itself would throttle back on
new proposals. (We suspect undersupply is also possible.)

A thread common with Rose and Fischel is the dynamic competition between jurisdictions through a process called "Tiebout sort-
ing," named after Charles M. Tiebout[32] and often called *voting with
one's feet*. The idea is that people, including developers, will gravitate
toward those communities whose mix of services, prices (taxes and
fees), and socioeconomic composition are most satisfactory to them.
If one community does not want a particular development, another
might. If many communities want a particular project, they will compete for it. If a community loses its luster by failing to be attractive
to the next wave of opportunities, existing politicians will be replaced
with those who will make the community attractive again. Comprehensive plans written years ago and especially those not updated periodically can get in the way of needed change. Voting with one's feet,
however, also allows for some communities to become exclusive or
able to use their resources to siphon "desirable" development away
from other communities resulting in regionally inefficient outcomes.

---

[30] HILLS & SCHLEICHER, *supra* note 21.
[31] JOHN R. LOGAN & HARVEY L. MOLOTCH, URBAN FORTUNES: THE POLITICAL ECON-
OMY OF PLACE (1987).
[32] CHARLES M. TIEBOUT, *A Pure Theory of Local Expenditures*, J. POLIT. ECON. 64,
416-424 (1956).

Of course, comprehensive plans do not necessarily prevent from happening anyway.

Rose posits four models for land-use decision-making, in descending order of efficiency: legislation, adjudication, market, and negotiation. The least efficient is legislation. Under this model, any land-use decision could be deemed "legislative" but would be clumsy for small-scale decisions. Legislative decisions are very much what was anticipated by the SCPEA and elaborated by Haar. They are long-term, sweeping, and deliberate, sometimes taking years to conclude.

An improvement in Rose's view is the adjudicative model, which sets the boundaries for "quasi-judicial" decisions. To describe how this works, Rose relies heavily on *Fasano*,[33] a case arising from Oregon, which arguably has one of the nation's most rigorous statewide land-use planning programs:

> *For the reviewing court, this model entails a change in the questions to ask about the legitimacy of a local council's decision to grant or deny the developer a permit to construct the corner gas station. Instead of a vague query as to the "reasonableness" of the decision, the reviewing court can direct its questions to the correctness of the council's "adjudicative" processes. Did the council have standards (particularly those of the city's general plan) when it made the decision to permit the gas station? Was it actually applying those standards? Did it provide notice and an appropriate hearing to interested parties? Could witnesses be cross-examined? Did the council keep an adequate record of the proceedings and make findings and a decision on the record? Were the decision-makers impartial? In short, the reviewing court can ask whether the decision met the model for a proper adjudication—even though the decision-making body is a group of elected politicians.*[34]

All conditions must be met to make a quasi-judicial decision. We note the very first question raised is whether the decision was essentially consistent with the city's general plan. The others are purely procedural. While Rose points out several reasons why plans offer

---

[33] Fasano v. Bd. of Cty. Comm'rs, 264 Or. 574, 507 P.2d 23 (1973).
[34] ROSE 1985, *supra* note 22, at 1161 (emphasis added and footnote to quote removed).

inconclusive guidance,[35] the presumption is that if the plan meets certain standards, courts would be obliged to assess whether a land-use decision was "in accordance with a comprehensive plan."

Rose suggests that the "market model" leads to more efficient decisions than either the legislative or adjudicative models:

> *Underlying this model is the idea that land use decisions can be made more efficient if they are analogized to private market transactions in which resources travel to their most valued uses through a series of trades.*
>
> *The market model for land use decisions tells us that we can forget about plans and substantive standards and complex adjudicative processes for land use decisions because we do not really need them. A local legislature can figure out what to do by looking to the willingness of interested parties to pay for what they want. If the neighbors want to keep the Victorian mansion from being razed and replaced with a gas station, they can do so, and the city need not issue the demolition permit; the neighbors or the city, however, will have to pay the owner to keep the structure as it is.[36]*

There is much to commend the market model if it institutionalizes pricing mechanisms to improve efficiency in land-use decisions, such as transfer of development rights, development impact fees, certain user fees, and so forth. But the model presumes that the market can "price" everything, which it cannot—not even historic preservation. The market is not capable of putting a price on such public goods as clean air, safe streets, or community character through historic preservation[37] or such "merit" goods as working landscapes (farms and forests) and other open spaces.[38]

A market with proxy prices may exist when some people can move away from polluted areas to less polluted ones (where homes have higher value away from pollution), but that assumes there are options and that everyone is equally mobile, which is not the case.

---

[35] *Id.* at 1162-63.
[36] *Id.* at 1164-65 (footnote to quote removed).
[37] See ANNE STEINEMANN, MICROECONOMICS FOR PUBLIC DECISIONS (2011).
[38] See RICHARD A. MUSGRAVE & PEGGY B. MUSGRAVE, PUBLIC FINANCE IN THEORY AND PRACTICE (1973).

The market model is also inherently designed to be exclusionary: The very ability of the market to use covenants and property owner associations to "price" itself out of affordability to lower income, usually minority, groups is well known.[39] If all markets met such conditions as perfect information, abundant supply, homogeneity of tastes and preferences, constant and predictable returns, complete internalization of externalities and related factors, intervention by government into land-use decisions (or anything else) would not be needed; it is because the market is imperfect that imperfect institutions such as government are sometimes needed to manage processes to improve social welfare.[40]

Negotiation is Rose's fourth model, and at the lowest geographic level of decision-making, such as the parcel or neighborhood, it may lead to the most efficient outcomes, similar to the views of R. H. Nelson and Fischel. Rose writes:

> *Generally speaking . . . [negotiation means]. . . that the decision-making process should be opened up rather than narrowed; that the process should be fairly loose about such matters as who can talk, what sorts of issues they can raise, and what sorts of solutions they can suggest; and that it should include a whole range of possible tradeoffs instead of a flat "yes or no" decision. The idea here is to come to a resolution that satisfies or at least mollifies everyone, and not to arrive at the win-or-lose solutions typical of judicial decisions. The goal is to assure the interested parties' future ability to get along, and not their present victory or defeat.[41]*

In our view, it is because of rigorous procedures required of plans in several states noted later—perhaps too rigorous for Rose, R. H. Nelson, and Fischel—we are confident that decisions made based on the legislation and adjudication models will not be arbitrary, and if they are, courts will likely rule accordingly. We worry that decisions based on the market and negotiation models invite arbitrariness. This

---

[39] See EVAN MCKENZIE, PRIVATOPIA: HOMEOWNER ASSOCIATIONS AND THE RISE OF RESIDENTIAL PRIVATE GOVERNMENT (1994).

[40] See DOUGLASS B. LEE, JR., *Land use planning as a response to market failure*. In THE LAND USE POLICY DEBATE IN THE UNITED STATES (Judith I. De Neufville, ed., 1981).

[41] Rose 1985, *supra* note 22, at 1168.

is the danger Haar posed as being preventable when land-use decisions are made "in accordance with a comprehensive plan":

A basic legal consequence of the master plan follows from its "comprehensiveness." This can be broken down into two aspects: by its requirement of information gathering and analysis, controls are based on facts, not haphazard surmises hence their moral and consequent legal basis; by its comprehensiveness, diminished are the problems of discrimination, granting of special privileges, and the denial of equal protection of the laws. Hence, the two most frequent sorts of attack upon government regulation become less available to the private landowner. If the local community has gone to the point of preparing a master plan, his chances of success in attacking an ordinance, based on the plan, are considerably diminished.[42]

The Rose–R. H. Nelson-Fischel perspective is rooted in "Coase's theorem"—after Ronald H. Coase.[43] In the context of rezoning as a kind of land-use decision, it goes something like the following.

Suppose Arthur C. Nelson and James C. Nicholas own equivalent ten-acre parcels of land adjacent to each other on a dirt road. Both grow strawberries. Nelson decides to subdivide. The subdivision will require a zone change that is not consistent with the comprehensive plan for the area. State law does not require consistency between plans and zoning codes. Nelson files the zone change request, but at the hearing Nicholas objects because of road traffic and because Nelson's buyers may wander onto Nicholas's berry patch to help themselves before it can be harvested. Nelson says Nicholas could build a fence at his own expense and that the new traffic is negligible because the dirt road can handle it. The county commission[44] rejects the rezoning.

Nelson goes back to Nicholas and offers to build a fence at Nelson's expense. The *negative externalities* imposed by Nelson's buyers helping themselves to Nicholas's berries would be mitigated by it. Because Nelson still makes money, the *transaction costs* (building the fence)

---

42 Haar, *supra* note 11, at 365-366.
43 RONALD H. COASE, *The Problem of Social Cost*, J.L. & ECON. 3, 1-44 (1960).
44 Although the planning commission is usually the first stop, we are going straight to the county commission in this example since that is the final local decision-making body for legislative acts such as zone changes in our simple example.

are affordable. Nicholas agrees and would not object to keeping the road unpaved. Nelson refiles, offering to build the fence but not pave the road. Nicholas supports it and the commission approves the rezoning with the fence as a condition. According to Coase, this is an *efficient* outcome accomplished through *bargaining*. The deal is approved. Commission members get good press because conflict is averted and they get reelected. Rose would contend this is what give-and-take representative democracy is all about. This is a simple case of Coase's theorem at work.

Sometime later, Julian Conrad Juergensmeyer and John Travis Marshall become owners of two equivalent ten-acre parcels across from Nelson and Nicholas. Juergensmeyer and Marshall also want to subdivide. At the rezoning hearing, neither Nelson nor Nicholas objects. The county commission decides, however, that the road needs to be paved at Juergensmeyer's and Marshall's expense. Being influential attorneys in the county, Juergensmeyer and Marshall point out that Nelson did not have to pave his share of the road and that the new development would generate new taxes to the county. Moreover, their developments would pay road impact fees. Although this road segment was not on the road impact fee improvement plan, the commissioners direct staff to do so and then approve the rezoning. Again, this would seem an efficient piecemeal Coasian solution to conflict.

Juergensmeyer, Marshall, and Nelson all subdivide but Nicholas does not; he has never asked for and did not receive a zone change, preferring to grow strawberries. The fence is built and the road is paved, though at substantial cost to the county because of such issues as grading, drainage, and the need for a bridge to replace a culvert under the narrow dirt road. The road improvements are financed through bonds issued and secured by the full faith and credit of the county. In theory, road impact fees assessed on new development would cover some of these costs but only if development occurs.

Because Juergensmeyer, Marshall, and Nelson all subdivided at the same time, they flooded the market with lots. As supply vastly exceeded demand, lot prices fell to levels below costs. Since they could not pay their land development loans, they are foreclosed. The lenders do not know what to do with the lots in an oversupplied market, so they sell them at auction to a syndicate headed by Dwight Merriam. It pays pennies on the dollar and can afford to wait many years until there is sufficient market demand. Since road impact fees were not paid, the county had to divert general fund revenues to help cover debt service, which it did by laying off several first responders.

But Nicholas continues to raise strawberries, as strawberry fields can sometimes be forever. From a broad societal perspective, this is not an efficient outcome.

To make Coase's theorem work, all parties must have the same information and must also share all information they acquire. In our case, none of the parties produced market analysis to determine if there was a demand for all thirty acres of subdivided lots. Conceivably one or more of the developers did have that information but did not share it. The commissioners decided to trust the statements of the developers rather than pay for their own market analysis. If all parties relied on the same information, the ultimate outcome would be inefficient. If one or more parties withheld information, Coasian conditions would be violated.

The keen observations of Rose, R. H. Nelson, and Fischel notwithstanding, we worry that American governance as it pertains to land-use decision-making has devolved to the level of implicit corruption[45] described by James A. Kushner:

Land use planning and regulation in American municipal governments often appears structured to permit the maximum amount of corruption possible. Developers and other contractors are typically expected to pay exactions or make political campaign contributions to politicians who possess the apparent power of blocking or facilitating development and public contracts. In Los Angeles, it appears that there is an understanding among members of the city council that they will typically defer to the council representative from the district where the development is proposed on zoning matters, such as proposals for zoning amendments, variances, subdivisions, or site plans. This allows legislators to have free reign over whether the project is approved and thus facilitates corrupt exactions as a price of development. In Philadelphia, at least before that city's recent overhaul of its zoning code, zoning and other regulatory measures prevented developers from enjoying any development of right, whereby a developer would be informed from codes that a certain type and intensity of development was permitted. Instead, the codes were

---

[45] Of course, there are numerous examples of explicit corruption evidenced by scores of politicians who have been convicted—many going to jail—for manipulating land-use decision-making processes, including council members, commissioners, mayors, governors, and a vice president of the United States.

so prolix that every development project required the equivalent of a variance, and thus the system encouraged political exploitation of developers. Typically, and in every jurisdiction, all but the smallest of projects requires some form of discretionary approval in the form of subdivision, site plan, variance, plan or zoning amendment, thus facilitating political exploitation.[46]

If conventional comprehensive plans have such little currency in most courts and if the default is piecemeal, ad hoc decisions that can lead to arbitrary outcomes, if not corruption, what can be done to prevent the oversupply of development and protect existing property rights against diminution of value because of oversupply?

∎ THIS IS NOT MR. HOOVER'S COMPREHENSIVE PLAN

Rose's conclusion is our point of departure:

No one seriously quarrels with the "legislative" designation of major decisions concerning controversial, large-scale projects, even when such decisions are made by local boards. But the one-lot decisions are simply a different kind of beast. They bring out all the chumminess, informality, and dealmaking qualities of local government. Local government need not be bad government, but, as small-scale land decisions show, local government simply does not operate the way a big legislature does. Local government requires its own models for small-scale land use decisions. The new models for local land use, more than anything else, represent an effort to come to grips not only with land use but also with local decisionmaking generally. They are cause for cheer in that they illustrate how other lines of thought—administrative law, economics, alternative dispute resolution—can enrich the way we think about local government and local decisionmaking processes.[47]

---

[46] JAMES A. KUSHNER, *Comparative Urban Governance: Why the United States Is Incapable of Reform*, FORDHAM URB. L.J. 61, 20-28 (footnotes appearing in the original are removed).

[47] Rose 1985, supra note 22, at 1170-71 (footnotes removed).

Given apparent judicial contempt for comprehensive plans across the nation, we understand and even appreciate the view of our colleagues, who explain, however apologetically, how the status quo works. There is a better way and it is through the "new" comprehensive plan.

To be sure, there key conceptual flaws with Hoover's SCPEA and its relationship with the SZEA:

- No requirement to plan, so if there was zoning, it need not be in accordance with a plan that does not exist;
- Little specificity in plans to guide development over a manageable period of time to a measurable outcome; instead, plans were viewed as end-state urban form outcomes.
- Failure to understand that as a non-elected body, the planning commission cannot override decisions of elected officials. This is important because the SCPEA viewed planning to be too important to be drafted by elected officials, yet without their allocation of resources, plans could be not be implemented.
- Almost by design, "planning" devolved to incremental zoning decisions because that was the purview of a planning staff accountable to elected officials.

The attacks on comprehensive planning leveled by Rose, R. H. Nelson, and Fischel are based on practice in most states well into the 1980s and that continue today in most. But scholars note that planning institutions in several states have evolved considerably. Without being exhaustive, they include Fred Bosselman's and David Callies' "quiet revolution of land use control" states along with Dennis E. Gale's[48] review of eight state growth-management statutes, Arthur C. Nelson and James B. Duncan's[49] outline of growth-management principles and practice, and John M. DeGrove's[50] assessment of the interplay between planning and policy in selected states. We also consider the role of regions and local governments in reshaping this part of comprehensive

[48] FRED P. BOSSELMAN & DAVID L. CALLIES, The Quiet Revolution in Land Use Control (1971); DENNIS E. GALE, Eight State-Sponsored Growth Management Programs: A Comparative Analysis, J. AM. PLANN. ASSOC. 58(4), 425-439 (1992).
[49] ARTHUR C. NELSON & JAMES B. DUNCAN, GROWTH MANAGEMENT PRINCIPLES AND PRACTICE (1995).
[50] JOHN M. DEGROVE, PLANNING POLICY AND POLITICS: SMART GROWTH AND THE STATES (2005).

planning such as Arthur C. Nelson and Casey J. Dawkin's[51] history, models, and techniques for regional and metropolitan growth management; Robert H. Freilich et al.'s[52] historical perspectives on effective regional and local comprehensive planning innovations to manage urban growth patterns; and Julian Conrad Juergensmeyer and Thomas E. Roberts's[53] comprehensive review of land-use and development control. These works collectively paint a different picture.

We will start with a summary of the extent to which most states have moved away from the strict application of the SCPEA, illustrated in Figure 2.1. As we review changes briefly, we recommend Edward J. Sullivan and Matthew J. Michel[54] for details. Columns in Figure 2.1 show the states that have substantially retained the SCPEA structure. In many states, zoning and planning are viewed by the courts as being essentially one and the same, or "unitary"— for instance, being in accordance with a comprehensive plan is achieved automatically by being in accordance with a zoning code. This applies to ten states. Another eleven states, however, have acted to create a special "planning factor" for courts to consider when reviewing land-use decisions; in these states, zoning codes must be "in accordance with a comprehensive plan." But none of these states require planning. Fifteen states have moved substantially away from the SCPEA structure, though seven still conflate zoning with planning. Two more states mandate planning among all local governments, but clear planning guidance is not provided. Twelve states have moved completely away from the SCPEA, though one still conflates planning and zoning. Our focus is on the structure of planning in those eleven states.

In four states ("planning mandate" and "total revision"), planning is mandated with financial or other penalties, including loss of certain home rule authority (e.g., building permit authority in Oregon) if plans are not approved by the state (the "stick" approach). In the

51 ARTHUR C. NELSON & CASEY J. DAWKINS, URBAN CONTAINMENT IN THE UNITED STATES: HISTORY, MODELS, AND TECHNIQUES FOR REGIONAL AND METROPOLITAN GROWTH MANAGEMENT (2004).
52 ROBERT H. FREILICH, ROBERT J. SITKOWSKI, SETH D. MENNILLO, FROM SPRAWL TO SUSTAINABILITY: SMART GROWTH, NEW URBANISM, GREEN DEVELOPMENT, AND RENEWABLE ENERGY (2010).
53 JULIAN CONRAD JUERGENSMEYER & THOMAS E. ROBERTS, LAND USE, PLANNING, AND CONTROL LAW (2013).
54 EDWARD J. SULLIVAN & MATTHEW J. MICHEL, *Ramapo Plus Thirty: The Changing Role of the Plan in Land Use Regulation*, 35 URB. LAW. 75 (2003).

				CA, WI	DE, FL, OR, WA
JUDICIAL INTERPRETATION	Planning Mandate				
	Planning Factor	AK, CO, IA, IL, KS, MT, NC, NE, SD, VA, WY	NV, NY, MN	ID, KY, MA, PA, SC	GA, HI, ME, MD, NJ, RI, VT
	Unitary	AL, IN, LA, MO, ND, NM, OH, OK, TX, WV	AR, CT, MS, MI, UT	AZ, NH	TN
	SPEA	Moderate, significant Changes	Many, significant Changes	Total Revision	
		Enabling Legislation			

Figure 2.1 Legal and Statutory Significance of Comprehensive Plans
Source: Sullivan and Michel (2003)

other seven states ("planning factor" and "total revision"), local governments need not plan, but if they do and their plans are approved by a state agency, they become eligible for important state resources (the "carrot" approach).[55] In all eleven of these states, plans must be comprised of most or all of the following elements.

GOALS

Goals are a key part of planning, recognized in the SCPEA as well. Where traditional planning goals were end-state oriented, however, many goals in most state-mandated planning are combined with specific 5- to 20-year targets within a "planning horizon."

PROJECTIONS, INVENTORIES, ASSESSMENTS, AND ALLOCATIONS

Unlike SCPEA-style comprehensive plans, state-mandated plans usually include statutes and/or administrative rules outlining the technical analysis needed to support planning policies. For instance, suppose a community projects a need for 10,000 more residential units in ten years. Its assessment of facilities indicates water and wastewater systems will need to be expanded, as will parks and recreation and educational facilities. But its road system already serves vacant and

---

[55] Maine's state role in local plan review has since been repealed. *See generally,* Me Stat. tit. 30-A § 4301–4457 (2016), *available at* http://legislature.maine.gov/legis/statutes/30-A/title30-Ach187sec0.html.

underdeveloped areas, so conceivably all new residential and related development could occur without expanding the road system. Maybe some of this land has constraints such as wetlands or steep slopes or there is active farming that ought to be preserved. Land for new development would need to be identified that meets projected development needs while satisfying other needs. Arthur C. Nelson[56] provides a step-by-step process of converting projections into land-use and facility needs, assessing current conditions, identifying net new needs, and allocating those needs across the community. For brevity, we have collapsed many steps into just this broad category.

All states mandating plans give guidance about the process of projecting development needs and allocation resources to accommodate them. Florida's land-use planning requirements are instructive and include the following:[57]

All elements of the comprehensive plan and plan amendments shall be based upon relevant and appropriate data and an analysis by the local government that may include, but is not be limited to, surveys, studies, community goals and vision, and other data available at the time the comprehensive plan or plan amendment is adopted. To be based on data means to react to it in an appropriate way and to the extent necessary indicated by the data available on that particular subject at the time the plan or plan amendment at issue is adopted.

A future land-use plan element designating proposed future general distribution, location, and extent of the uses of land for residential, commercial, industrial, agricultural, recreational, conservational, and educational purposes, as well as for public facilities and other purposes. The approximate acreage and the general range of density or intensity of use shall be provided for the gross land area included in each existing land use category. The element shall establish the long-term end toward which land-use programs and activities are ultimately directed.

Each future land-use category must be defined in terms of uses included, and must include standards to be followed in the

[56] Arthur C. Nelson, Planner's Estimating Guide: Projecting Land-Use and Facility Needs (2004).
[57] This is an adaptation of Fla. Stat. Ann. § 163.01–163.819 (2016), guiding comprehensive planning in that state. We have edited it for flow.

control and distribution of population densities and building and structure intensities. The proposed distribution, location, and extent of the various categories of land use shall be shown on a land-use map or map series, which shall be supplemented by goals, policies, and measurable objectives.

The future land-use plan and plan amendments shall be based upon surveys, studies, and data regarding the area, as applicable, including the:

- amount of land required to accommodate anticipated growth.
- projected permanent and seasonal population of the area.
- character of undeveloped land.
- availability of water supplies, public facilities, and services.
- need for redevelopment, including the renewal of blighted areas and the elimination of nonconforming uses that are inconsistent with the character of the community.
- compatibility of uses on lands adjacent to an airport.
- discouragement of urban sprawl.
- need for job creation, capital investment, and economic development that will strengthen and diversify the community's economy.

The future land-use plan element shall include criteria to be used to:

- encourage the location of schools proximate to urban residential areas to the extent possible.
- coordinate future land uses with the topography and soil conditions, and the availability of facilities and services.
- ensure the protection of natural and historic resources.
- provide for the compatibility of adjacent land uses.

The amount of land designated for future land uses should allow the operation of real estate markets to provide adequate choices for permanent and seasonal residents and businesses and may not be limited solely by the projected population.

To some this may seem daunting, but for a state that spends more than a quarter trillion dollars every decade on new and replaced development, the few millions of dollars spent on land-use and infrastructure planning and implementation to maximize development benefits to its citizens seems trivial.

CONSISTENCY

Local plans must be consistent with regional plans and state goals. This is called *vertical consistency*.[58] In areas with regional plans, this also means cooperative planning among local governments within the same region, in which local plans must be have *lateral consistency* between them so that what one community does is not harmful to another. Among local governments, plan elements must be *internally consistent*, meaning, for example, that one element cannot provide for 10,000 new homes while another element provides for twice or half that.

CAPITAL FACILITY PLANNING AND FINANCIAL FEASIBILITY

Some state-mandated plans require local governments to not only accommodate projected development needs but also choreograph capital facilities to meet the needs of new development in a financially feasible capital improvements plan.

STATE-REGIONAL-LOCAL COORDINATION

In states where plans are both mandated and subject to review by state agencies, there is often tension between state and local officials. These tensions led substantially to the dismantling of state-level review in Florida with disastrous results that we will show in Chapter 4. Nonetheless, the balancing of state, regional, and local interests is needed to ensure that local and regional plans address the widest range of issues possible.[59] We might call it a codependent relationship where both levels of government depend on each other to advance society—it might also be called *federalism*.

PERIODIC REVIEW AND PLAN UPDATES

While updated plans are implied in the SCPEA, they are mandated in the modern planning scheme. All these states require a periodic review or full revisions of a plan that compare projected needs to actual outcomes with corrective actions to guide the plan to its regularly scheduled full update.

---

[58] Nelson & Dawkins, *supra* note 52. For consistency in general, see DANIEL MANDELKER, *The Role of the Local Comprehensive Plan in Land Use Regulation*, 76 MICHIGAN LAW REVIEW 899 (1976).

[59] See RAYMOND J. BURBY & PETER J. MAY, MAKING GOVERNMENTS PLAN: STATE EXPERIMENTS IN MANAGING LAND USE (1997).

IMPLEMENTATION

The litmus test in the success of any government policy is efficiency in implementation. In planning, such implementing devices as zoning, subdivision, and other land-use control ordinances must be consistent with the comprehensive plan. Land-use and development permitting consistent with implementing devices would be considered consistent with the comprehensive plan. Zone changes resulting in different classes of land uses or magnitudes of development inconsistent with the zoning code may need a plan amendment as well as a zone change. If the planning regime is too detailed, perhaps by specifying uses and development parameters for each parcel, the process of amending the plan and rezoning parcels can be inefficient in ways warned by Rose, R. H. Nelson, and Fischel.

But if the administrative structure by design is efficient, then small area or even-parcel specific decisions may also be efficient. For instance, if a community projects a need for 10,000 new residential units over the next ten years, its plan needs to allocate sufficient land to meet this need. The plan is implemented through ordinances that must be unequivocal in allowing such development. Such predictability is a hallmark of efficient decision-making. Oregon is considered a leader in creating predictability in land-use and development decision-making. Key elements of its system include:[60]

Clear policy direction: Oregon requires every city and county to have a comprehensive plan and the implementing measures necessary to make that plan work.

Protection from conflicts: One of the main reasons for land-use planning is to reduce the number and extent of conflicts between land uses. In Oregon, all privately owned land in the state has been zoned, a main purpose of which is to prevent incompatible land uses.

Coordination: Coordination has two meanings. First, it means ensuring that what one community does is compatible with another's. Second, it means having local, state, and federal agencies together make decisions consistent with the state-approved

---

[60] These are an adaptation of Oregon's land-use planning administrative structure provided by the governor's office. OREGON DEPARTMENT OF LAND CONSERVATION AND DEVELOPMENT, PREDICTABILITY IN PLANNING, www.oregon.gov/LCD/docs/publications/predict.pdf.

local plan. Such coordination enhances predictability by ensuring that one local government's land use decision will not be thwarted by the actions of other local, regional, state, or federal government or agency.

One level of review: One of the most important features of Oregon's planning program is its single tier of planning and permitting administration at the local level. The state-approved local land-use plan becomes the controlling document for all land-use decisions, and land-use permits are administered by local officials.

Clear and objective approval standards: Oregon requires clear and objective review standards in the review of development applications. Under Oregon law, development officials cannot use vague standards such as "compatibility with the neighborhood" to deny an application for a needed housing type in an appropriate zone. Clear and objective standards protect developers and permit applicants from arbitrary and inconsistent decisions, thereby enhancing predictability.

Centralized appeals: In 1979 the Oregon legislature created a special land-use court, the Land Use Board of Appeals (LUBA). The result has been a dramatic decrease in the time needed to resolve appeals and an increase in the consistency of decisions.[61]

The "Raise It or Waive It" standard: After LUBA had been in operation for a few years, there was concern that some were ambushing developers by raising a host of new issues in the appeal before LUBA. Legislation in 1989 says that to have standing in an appeal before LUBA, petitioners must first participate at the local level and raise all issues there. Petitioners may not raise issues at LUBA that were not raised during the local review. LUBA's review is therefore "of the record" before it only. Accordingly, all the evidence supporting the local government decision must have been presented to and deliberated by the local governing body, and thus LUBA would not engage in a *de novo* proceeding where new evidence would be presented.

Statutory deadlines: Oregon law specifies that local governments must render decisions on land-use permits within 120 days for cities and 150 days for counties of receiving a complete application for such a permit. Any local appeals—for example, for

---

[61] Nelson & Duncan, *supra* note 50.

planning commission to city council—are included in that time limit. There are similar time limits on LUBA's decisions.

While the foregoing are elements common to selected post-SCPEA states we note above, several regions and local governments also employ them. These are reviewed by Arthur C. Nelson and Casey J. Dawkins, as well as Robert H. Freilich et al.[62]

THE WAGES OF EXCESSIVE DEVELOPMENT

Only a few years after Haar's 1955 articles, Marion Clawson,[63] an imminent land economist, wrote the following:

> *If planning . . . were firm—enforceable and enforced—then the area available at any one time for each kind of use would bear some relationship to the need for land for this use. That is, area classified for different purposes could be consciously manipulated or determined in relation to market need. Sufficient area for each purpose, including enough area to provide some competition among sellers and some choice among buyers, should be zoned or classified for development, but no more. (Emphasis in original.)*

Accordingly, in our view, success in comprehensive planning is achieved when plans project future development needs; allocate land, capital facilities, and other resources to meet those needs; accommodate development that meets those needs through efficient application of implementing devices; and periodically update plans to account for new or unforeseen needs. The outcome of such plans and the analysis that goes into them improves the likelihood that sufficient development is permitted based on market needs—no more and no less.

Let us be more blunt: Not making plans based on market demand-based assessments and then permitting excessive development that is

---

[62] See ARTHUR C. NELSON & CASEY J. DAWKINS, *Urban Containment in the United States: History, Models, and Techniques for Regional and Metropolitan Growth Management* (2004) and ROBERT H. FREILICH, ROBERT J. SITKOWSKI & SETH D. MENNILLO, *From Sprawl to Sustainability: Smart Growth, New Urbanism, Green Development, and Renewable Energy* (2nd ed. 2010).

[63] MARION CLAWSON, *Urban Sprawl and Land Speculation in Suburban Land.* LAND ECON. 38, 99–111 (1962).

not in accordance with the plan can wreak havoc on local governments and society at large. The larger impacts, notably of the savings-and-loan crisis of the 1980s and the Great Recession twenty years later, will be reviewed in Chapters 3 and 4. Here we focus on the local impacts.

In 1986, before the savings and loan debacle we recount in Chapter 3, David A. Dowall wrote, "By the time you read this piece it will be commonly accepted that the nation's office markets are financial basket cases. It seems that we again have wildly overbuilt real estate, this time in office buildings."[64] He goes on to explain the sins of excessive office development, but his observations can apply to all forms of excess development:

First, empty buildings blight surrounding uses, undercut viable markets, and, if serious enough, create economically devastating overcorrections in the local construction industry. Accordingly, given patterns of overbuilding, planners should no longer believe that the developer knows the market best. One developer recently told me it was a developer's "God-given" right to keep building as long as someone financed his projects—even if he and others overbuilt. Planners could provide some correction to the market by gauging the market feasibility of projects or requiring that developers provide evidence of market demand.

Second, overbuilding exaggerates the demand for scarce public facilities. In the worst instance, the local government might build infrastructure for a project for which there is no short-term market. Even in the best case, where the developer agrees to pay for the infrastructure through exactions and dedications, the premature construction of a project and the infrastructure may lead other infrastructure providers to expand at the wrong time.

Third, in overbuilt markets, it is difficult for local governments to levy exactions and dedications and to impose appropriate development controls, since any project ultimately becomes less profitable. Thus if planners are charged with generating fee revenues, they should monitor market conditions to avoid overbuilding.

---

[64] David E. Dowall, *Planners and Office Overbuilding*, J. Am. Plann. Assoc. 52(2), 131-32.

Fourth, empty buildings may bankrupt developers and force them to breach contracts with local governments to provide downstream fees, exactions, or financial support for ongoing programs such as traffic management.

Fifth, for planners who are attempting to structure public-private partnerships with developers, caution is the rule of the day when considering project proposals if the developer defaults, the public could end up having to carry the entire project in an overbuilt market. [65]

Dowall concluded in 1986 as we do more than 30 years later:

Perhaps now, as it becomes clear that developers and lenders are abdicating their responsibility to exercise stewardship over the real estate market, planners should incorporate project market and financial feasibility into their normal process of evaluating development proposals. [66]

Failure to create and implement market demand–based planning and permitting systems led in large part to the savings-and-loan crisis and the Great Recession, as we show next in Chapters 3 and 4.

---

[65] *Id.* at 132.
[66] *Id.* at 132.

CHAPTER 3

The Savings and Loan Crisis as a Taxpayer Tragedy

▌PRELUDE TO ACT 1

From the presidency of Ronald Reagan through that of George W. Bush, the behavior of America's real estate investment institutions led to what may be best described as a tragedy comprised of two acts: The savings and loan (S&L) crisis and the Great Recession. In this chapter, we review the S&L crisis of the 1980s, which cost America's economy more than $1 trillion. The chapter outlines the inability of federal institutions to protect state and local governments from the costs imposed on them and their citizens by excessive risk-taking among real estate developers and their financial backers, eventually bailed out by taxpayers. The S&L crisis generated important lessons that could have prevented future real estate-driven taxpayer tragedies—if only they were heeded. Chapter 4 presents Act 2, the Great Recession, lamenting that lessons from Act 1 were apparently not learned. This led to the loss of trillions of dollars and unfathomable pain and suffering for millions of Americans. Chapter 4 explains both Acts as a failure of American financial institutions—both public and private—to guard against "moral hazard." The curtain for Act 1 now rises.

ACT 1: THE SAVINGS AND LOAN CRISIS

The real estate development market is composed of developers who acquire land and build products to meet market needs and make a profit. Developers are "community builders"[1] because they shape entire urban areas for generations to come but they do not act alone; developers often join forces with allied interests to become what Logan and Molotch[2] call the "growth machine." It survives only so long as perceived public benefits exceed costs. In many rapidly growing communities, the public has become increasingly dissatisfied with the environmental, fiscal, and social costs imposed on them by the growth machine.[3]

Consider overbuilding of the built environment. As the term implies, overbuilding means that local markets become saturated with more product than is warranted by market demand. Results can include higher vacancy rates, lower sales prices and rents, and, for some investors and their financial underwriters, lost equity and even bankruptcy. In a market not distorted by public policy that rewards speculation, this may be desirable. But what if public policy induces speculation, which leads to overbuilding, which then undermines financial institutions? And what if the public policy response is a taxpayer-financed bailout? Is this a socially desirable outcome? We think not. Yet this is exactly what happened during the late 1980s and early 1990s as taxpayers bailed out the S&L industry when it financed more real estate development than the market could absorb.

We begin this act with a review of how the S&L collapse came about. We then observe that those states with growth-management regimes that matched market-demand needs as a condition of development permitting required far less federal taxpayer money to bail out S&Ls than states that had no such checks and balances. We will further show that taxpayers in states acting responsibly in preventing

[1] See MARC A. WEISS, THE RISE OF THE COMMUNITY BUILDERS: THE AMERICAN REAL ESTATE INDUSTRY AND URBAN LAND PLANNING (1987).
[2] JOHN R. LOGAN & HARVEY L. MOLOTCH, URBAN FORTUNES: THE POLITICAL ECONOMY OF PLACE (University of California Press 1987).
[3] See generally ROBERT H. FREILICH, ROBERT J. SITKOWSKI & SETH D. MENNILLO, FROM SPRAWL TO SUSTAINABILITY: SMART GROWTH, NEW URBANISM, GREEN DEVELOPMENT, AND RENEWABLE ENERGY (American Bar Association, 2d ed. 2011).

large-scale overbuilding subsidized those states that allowed excessive permitting. We go on to evaluate the variation in S&L bailouts based on types of growth-management regimes employed by different states. We conclude this chapter with lessons that were apparently not learned, as just two decades later America overbuilt its real estate once again, helping trigger the Great Recession—the subject of Act 2, presented in Chapter 4.

∎ THE SAVINGS-AND-LOAN CRISIS

The S&L industry had its start in the early 1800s when banks did not provide loans for residential purchases.[4] To solve this problem, prospective home buyers would form a group who would pool their savings to make loans to some members to buy homes. Loan repayment proceeds would be recycled to help others finance their homes.[5] By 1980, there were about 4,000 of these "thrifts," as they were informally called, which together held about $600 billion in assets, two-thirds of which were mortgages being equivalent to about half of the nation's residential mortgages.

About the same time, interest rates rose dramatically, making the S&Ls uncompetitive in the lending market. A key reason was that interest rates S&Ls could pay depositors were less than banks could offer because of federal regulatory limitations. Then, as interest rates increased, S&Ls holding hundreds of billions of dollars in fixed-rate mortgages lost value because when purchasing mortgage paper, the market pays less for mortgage-backed securities fixed at low rates of return than mortgages with higher returns or those that can be adjusted as the market changes—called adjustable rate mortgages (ARMs). S&Ls were losing money and many were closing. The solution by Congress was to deregulate the S&L industry, assuming new revenues would allow them to grow out of their financial condition. This was done through the Depository Institutions Deregulation and

---

[4] KENNETH J. ROBINSON, *Savings and Loan Crisis: 1980–1989*, FED. RESERVE HISTORY (Nov. 22, 2013), www.federalreservehistory.org/Events/DetailView/42.

[5] The 1946 movie *It's a Wonderful Life* featured Jimmy Stewart as George Bailey, the owner of the Bailey Building and Loan, which is another name for a savings and loan. See https://en.wikipedia.org/wiki/It's_a_Wonderful_Life.

Monetary Control Act of 1980, signed into law under then-president Jimmy Carter.

This was not enough. By 1983, the thrift's collective insolvency reached $25 billion, but the industry's insurance agency, the Federal Savings and Loan Insurance Corporation (FSLIC), had only $6 billion available. Congress's solution was to allow federally chartered S&Ls to make new kinds of loans, such as commercial loans, in addition to issuing residential mortgages. Many states extended similar powers to state-chartered S&Ls. To attract depositors, the FSLIC increased deposit insurance from $40,000 to $100,000.

But something else was happening. By the end of the 1970s, inflation in the United States was running in the double digits. In 1979, President Jimmy Carter appointed Paul Volcker as chair of the Federal Reserve Board. In this capacity, Volcker used monetary policy to raise interest rates (with long-term mortgage rates hitting more than 20 percent) to slow inflation. This in turn led to the Recession of 1980–1981, the most severe since the Great Depression.

To bring the U.S. out of recession, newly elected president Ronald Reagan advanced the Economic Recovery Tax Act (ERTA) of 1981. A key purpose of ERTA was to stimulate real estate development. It did so in part by accelerating depreciation so that many new commercial buildings could be depreciated mostly over five to ten years, instead of the thirty-one years for residential and thirty-eight years for non-residential property, as was the case prior to the Act. It also reduced capital gains taxes from 28 percent to 20 percent.[6]

Prior to ERTA, the S&L industry was principally engaged in residential and smaller personal loans (such as for automobiles) but not commercial real estate. When interest rates increased under Volcker, many S&Ls could not attract capital to remain solvent. To assist the industry, Congress allowed S&Ls to offer a larger range of mortgage products—such as adjustable rate mortgages—and to expand their portfolios to include commercial and other nonresidential purposes. Oversight rules were also relaxed.[7]

---

[6] For a synopsis of the Economic Recovery Tax Act of 1981, *see Economic Recovery Tax Act of 1981*, WIKIPEDIA, https://en.wikipedia.org/w/index.php?title=Economic_Recovery_Tax_Act_of_1981&oldid=747766661 (last visited Nov. 22, 2016).

[7] For a synopsis of the history of the savings-and-loan industry, including its substantial collapse from the late 1980s into the middle 1990s, *see Savings and Loan Crisis*, WIKIPEDIA, https://en.wikipedia.org/w/index.php?title=Savings_and_loan_crisis&oldid=750887442 (last visited Nov. 22, 2016).

One result of ERTA of 1981, combined with S&L deregulation, was the proliferation of loans made for commercial real estate development, especially offices. Indeed, investors could make money after taxes from vacant buildings. To correct for this, several changes to real estate investment laws were made after 1981, especially the Tax Reform Act of 1986, which restored depreciation to about their pre-ERTA levels[8] and limited deductibility of investment losses by "passive" investors (those not actively engaged in real estate investment or management) against taxable income. Ultimately, the S&L house of cards collapsed as real estate investments that were profitable mainly because of tax laws became unprofitable after 1986.

Between 1986 and 1989, the FSLIC effectively closed nearly 300 S&Ls while its successor, the Resolution Trust Corporation (RTC), closed another nearly 750 S&Ls, the total representing about a third of all S&Ls existing in 1986. For its part, the RTC was charged with liquidating most real estate assets of S&Ls declared insolvent by the Office of Thrift Supervision (OTS). Both the RTC and the OTS were formed by Congress in response to the S&L crisis. The RTC also took over the regulatory functions of the former Federal Home Loan Bank Board, which previously provided S&L oversight.[9]

In all, about half the S&Ls existing in 1986 no longer operate. More than 1,600 were closed or bailed out. Data from the U.S. General Accountability Office indicates that the crisis cost American taxpayers more than $300 billion (in 2015 dollars) and robbed the economy of more than $1 trillion (in 2015 dollars) in economic activity.[10] Would the legal and planning tools that represent the core recommendation of our book—market demand–based planning and permitting—have made a difference? The next sections answer this question showing that states that require market demand–based planning and permitting incurred fewer S&L bailout losses but subsidized those that did not.

---

[8] The key depreciation periods are now twenty-seven and a half years for residential property and thirty-nine years for nonresidential property. See INTERNAL REVENUE SERVICE, Publication 946 (2015), How to Depreciate Property.

[9] For a review, see TIMOTHY CURRY & LYNN SHIBUT, The Cost of the Savings and Loan Crisis: Truth and Consequences, FDIC BANKING REV. 26 (2000).

[10] See ARTHUR C. NELSON. Reducing Financial Risk Through Needs Certification. J. URBAN PLAN. D. 126(1), 39–54 (2000). Note that only some of the taxpayer costs were absorbed by the RTC.

GROWTH MANAGEMENT STATES SUBSIDIZED NON-GROWTH-MANAGEMENT STATES: A DESCRIPTIVE ASSESSMENT

The Congressional Budget Office (CBO)[11] cites overbuilding as a significant cause of the S&L collapse, subsequent bailout, and ultimate cost to the economy. The CBO points out that the one-two tax punch of the 1981 ERTA (which induced real estate development) and the Tax Reform Act of 1986 (which undid many of the 1981 policies retroactively) caused many S&Ls to fail.[12] But this raises the question: Was overdevelopment of real estate tax driven or demand driven? If development occurred commensurate with demand, the bailout should never have happened, or at least to the extent it did. In our view, overbuilding was probably driven in part by tax policies combined with lax efforts to match development supply with market demand–based analysis.

We are attracted to David E. Dowall's argument for planning to achieve such a balance.[13] In essentially predicting the S&L crisis, he wrote:

Real estate is notorious for boom-and-bust cycles: construction surges when office vacancies fall and declines when they increase. But things have changed. . . . The current boom continues in the face of clear overbuilding and rising vacancy rates. Why?

. . . Many real estate analysts have been arguing that the deregulation and changing priorities of the financial institutions and the specter of tax reform have spurred the office overbuilding boom. . . .

What is clear . . . is that the normal checks and balances associated with the financing of real estate are gone. No longer are banks and savings and loan institutions carefully assessing market conditions for projects.[14]

---

[11] CONGRESSIONAL BUDGET OFFICE, THE ECONOMICS EFFECTS OF THE SAVINGS & LOAN CRISIS (1992).

[12] *Supra* note 11, at 10.

[13] See DAVID E. DOWALL, *Planners and Office Overbuilding*, J. AM. PLANN. ASSOC. 52(2), 131–32.

[14] *Id.* at 131.

This is consistent with themes presented in Chapter 2, that the role of the public sector is to craft plans based on market demand–based analysis and then approve only the development that is in accordance with a plan. But do such plans work? That is, in the face of a common national phenomenon—deregulation of the S&L industry allowing it to make commercial investments—are variations in the amount of S&L bail-out costs related to differences in market demand–based planning and permitting (MDBPP)? Here we present descriptive evidence suggesting that states that require MDBPP among their local governments— what we call *growth management states*—do a better job matching supply with demand than non-growth-management states. We will also show that growth-management states' prudence effectively subsidized non-growth-management states' excessive permitting.[15]

Using literature as a guide, we identify ten growth-management states with such requirements in place since at least the middle 1980s: California, Florida, Hawaii, Maine, Maryland, New Jersey, Oregon, Rhode Island, Vermont, and Washington.[16] Table 3.1 shows the RTC costs for all states that grew during 1980–1990 (thus excluding Iowa,

---

[15] Much of the foregoing analysis is adapted and updated from Arthur C. Nelson, *Growth Management and the Savings-and-Loan Bailout*, Urb. Lawyer 27(1), 71–85 (1995). We are indebted to *The Urban Lawyer* for permission to do so.

[16] *See e.g.,* John M. DeGrove, Land, Growth & Politics (1984); John M. DeGrove, The New Frontier for Land Policy: Planning and Growth Management in the States (1992); John M. DeGrove, Planning Policy and Politics: Smart Growth and the States (2005); Dennis E. Gale, *Eight State-Sponsored Growth Management Programs: A Comparative Analysis*, 58 J. Am. Plan. Ass'n 425 (1992). While some commentators have more "Growth Management," Minnesota was excluded since much of the state is not under any coherent growth-management scheme (American Planning Association, Growth Smart Legislative Guidebook, 2002). Georgia was excluded since at the time it did not have enforceable growth-management systems (Arthur C. Nelson, *The Design and Administration of Urban Growth Boundaries*, Real Estate Finance 8(4), 11–22 [1990]). Connecticut, Massachusetts, New Hampshire, and New York were excluded because significant growth management in those states was limited to small areas established by separate statutory arrangements (American Planning Association, Growth Smart Legislative Guidebook, [2002]). Colorado was excluded because its legislature abandoned growth-management laws in the 1970s, and the only growth management of any consequence occurred in isolated ski resorts and not in major urban areas. John M. DeGrove, Land, Growth & Politics (1984). The list includes several states with recently implemented statewide planning policies even though the S&L bailout costs are substantially attributable to decisions made in the early 1980s. However, major urban areas and certain previously adopted statewide policies put those states on the clear path toward growth management a decade or more before statewide laws were passed.

Table 3.1 RTC Taxpayer Costs by State with Positive Growth, 1980–1990

State	Growth Management State?	Growth Management Taxpayer RTC Cost 1/27/93 ($Millions)[a]	Growth Management Population Change 1980–1990	Non-Growth-Management Taxpayer RTC Cost 1/27/93 ($Millions)[a]	Non-Growth-Management Population Change 1980–1990
Alabama	N			$625	147,000
Alaska	N			$355	148,000
Arizona	N			$10,512	947,000
Arkansas	N			$3,701	64,000
California	Y	$18,742	6,092,000		
Colorado	N			$3,160	404,000
Connecticut	N			$254	180,000
Delaware	N			$0	72,000
Florida	Y	$10,867	3,192,000		
Georgia	N			$1,014	1,015,000
Hawaii	Y	$0	144,000		
Illinois	N			$2,366	4,000
Indiana	N			$85	54,000
Kansas	N			$2,603	114,000
Kentucky	N			$85	25,000
Louisiana	N			$3,938	14,000
Maine	Y	$17	103,000		
Maryland	Y	$1,301	564,000		
Massachusetts	N			$1,944	279,000
Michigan	N			$85	33,000
Minnesota	N			$1,825	299,000
Mississippi	N			$1,065	53,000

State					
Missouri	N			$2,687	200,000
Montana	N			$0	12,000
Nebraska	N			$913	9,000
Nevada	N			$34	401,000
New Hampshire	Y	$51	365,000		
New Jersey	N			$34	189,000
New Mexico	N			$3,532	212,000
New York	N			$5,205	432,000
North Carolina	N			$68	747,000
Ohio	N			$1,065	49,000
Oklahoma	N			$1,403	120,000
Oregon	Y	$321	209,000		
Rhode Island	Y	$17	56,000		
South Carolina	N			$237	365,000
South Dakota	N			$85	5,000
Tennessee	N			$575	286,000
Texas	N			$43,703	2,757,000
Utah	N			$1,048	262,000
Vermont	Y	$0	51,000		
Virginia	N			$3,988	841,000
Washington	Y	$625	735,000		
Wisconsin	N			$152	186,000
U.S. Total		$31,941	11,511,000	$103,834	11,006,000
Per capita		$2,775		$9,434	
Per household[b]		$7,381		$25,095	

[a] Facsimile transmission received by Nelson (1995a) from Resolution Trust Corporation, January 27, 1993. States with less than $10 million in bailout costs reported as $0. Figures estimated in 2015 dollars.

[b] Based on 2.66 persons per household in 1985 from State and Metropolitan Area Data Book 1991, U.S. Bureau of the Census.

Source: Adapted from Nelson (1995a).

North Dakota, West Virginia, Wyoming, and the District of Columbia). The ten growth-management states collectively grew by more than 11.5 million people, while the remaining thirty-six states grew by slightly more than 11 million. Despite more growth, the growth-management states accounted for about $32 billion[17] in bailout costs while the remaining thirty-six states accounted for more than $100 billion. The bailout costs average $2,775 per new resident among the growth-management states but $9,434 per new resident among non-growth-management states.

Table 3.2 highlights some interesting comparisons between selected state pairs in terms of residential growth that occurred in the period between 1980 and 1990. RTC bailout costs per new resident is the key metric because, assuming loans are made predominantly to meet the needs of growth, states with more discipline in matching supply with demand will incur lower bailout costs relative to growth than those without such discipline.

Arizona (a non-growth-management state) and Florida (a growth-management state at the time) grew by comparable rates (25.8 percent and 24.7 percent, respectively), and each incurred comparable bailout costs. But the bailout costs per new resident in Arizona

Table 3.2 Selected Comparisons of RTC Costs by State Pairs Based on Growth Rate, Land Area and Population Size, and Growth Amount

State	Taxpayer RTC Cost 1/27/93 ($Millions)	Population 1990	Population Change 1980–1990	RTC Cost per Capita Growth 1980–1990
Similar Growth Rates and RTC Costs				
Arizona	$10,512	3,665,000	947,000	$11,100
Florida	$10,867	12,938,000	3,192,000	$3,404
Large Land Area and Population Base				
Texas	$43,703	16,987,000	2,757,000	$15,852
California	$18,742	29,760,000	6,092,000	$3,077
Similar Growth Amount				
New Mexico	$3,532	1,515,000	212,000	$16,661
Oregon	$321	2,842,000	209,000	$1,536

Source: Adapted from Nelson (1995a).

[17] All monetary figures are estimated in 2015 dollars based on the consumer price index calculator. CPI INFLATION CALCULATOR, http://data.bls.gov/cgi-bin/cpicalc.pl (last visited Nov. 22, 2016).

exceeded $11,000 while the costs in Florida were about $3,400. Texas (a non-growth-management state) and California (a growth-management state) are the two largest states in terms of land area within the contiguous forty-eight states and had reasonably comparable growth rates (16.2 percent and 20.5 percent, respectively). The bailout costs per new resident in Texas were nearly $16,000 while the costs in California were about $3,000. New Mexico (a non-growth-management state) and Oregon (a growth-management state) have comparable land area and experienced nearly identical increases in population. The bailout costs per new resident in New Mexico were nearly $17,000 while those costs in Oregon were about $1,500.

Tables 3.1 and 3.2 indicate that growth-management states performed better than non-growth-management states with respect to RTC bailout costs. Table 3.3 goes further by reporting Census projections of state population growth between 1980 and 1990. Rapidly growing states would be expected to permit more development than slower growing ones. But states that permit more development than is projected, whether fast or slow growing, would seem to increase the risk of market-based financial failure (such as loan defaults) and associated taxpayer bailout costs. For instance, Table 3.3 shows that Texas's 1990 population was just about what was projected, a situation similar to the two growth-management states of Florida and Washington. New Mexico nearly matched its projected growth, yet Oregon, because of its timber economy shakeout, was nearly 15 percent lower than projected. Using underachieved population projections as an excuse for the magnitude of the bailout costs is not borne out, because while Florida and Washington should have had the same magnitude of losses per capita as Texas, New Mexico should have had the same magnitude of losses per capita as Oregon, and Oregon should have shown much higher per capita bailout costs. Instead, the growth-management states incurred modest bailout costs while non-growth-management states incurred far greater ones.

The bottom line is reported in Table 3.4. Growth-management states paid more than $5,000 per new resident (and more than $13,000 per new household) for the bailout, while non-growth-management states received more than $2,500 per new resident (and nearly $6,000 per new household). In other words, growth-management states subsidized non-growth-management states. We know from economic theory that subsidized behavior leads to more consumption. Growth-management states were thus penalized economically for doing a

Table 3.3 Projected and Actual Population Change, 1980–1990

State	Census's 1983 Projected Population for 1990[a]	Census's Actual Population for 1990[b]	Difference	Percent Difference
Alabama	4,214,000	4,041,000	(173,000)	–4.11%
Alaska	522,000	550,000	28,000	5.36%
Arizona	3,994,000	3,665,000	(329,000)	–8.24%
Arkansas	2,580,000	2,351,000	(229,000)	–8.88%
California	27,526,000	29,760,000	2,234,000	8.12%
Colorado	3,755,000	3,294,000	(461,000)	–12.28%
Connecticut	3,136,000	3,287,000	151,000	4.82%
Delaware	630,000	666,000	36,000	5.71%
District of Columbia	502,000	607,000	105,000	20.92%
Florida	13,316,000	12,938,000	(378,000)	–2.84%
Georgia	6,175,000	6,478,000	303,000	4.91%
Hawaii	1,138,000	1,108,000	(30,000)	–2.64%
Idaho	1,214,000	1,007,000	(207,000)	–17.05%
Illinois	11,502,000	11,431,000	(71,000)	–0.62%
Indiana	5,679,000	5,544,000	(135,000)	–2.38%
Iowa	2,983,000	2,777,000	(206,000)	–6.91%
Kansas	2,463,000	2,478,000	15,000	0.61%
Kentucky	4,074,000	3,685,000	(389,000)	–9.55%
Louisiana	4,747,000	4,220,000	(527,000)	–11.10%
Maine	1,229,000	1,228,000	(1,000)	–0.08%
Maryland	4,491,000	4,781,000	290,000	6.46%
Massachusetts	5,704,000	6,016,000	312,000	5.47%
Michigan	9,394,000	9,295,000	(99,000)	–1.05%
Minnesota	4,353,000	4,375,000	22,000	0.51%
Mississippi	2,761,000	2,573,000	(188,000)	–6.81%
Missouri	5,077,000	5,117,000	40,000	0.79%
Montana	888,000	799,000	(89,000)	–10.02%
Nebraska	1,640,000	1,578,000	(62,000)	–3.78%
Nevada	1,275,000	1,202,000	(73,000)	–5.73%
New Hampshire	1,139,000	1,109,000	(30,000)	–2.63%
New Jersey	7,513,000	7,730,000	217,000	2.89%
New Mexico	1,536,000	1,515,000	(21,000)	–1.37%
New York	16,457,000	17,990,000	1,533,000	9.32%
North Carolina	6,473,000	6,629,000	156,000	2.41%
North Dakota	678,000	639,000	(39,000)	–5.75%

State	Census's 1983 Projected Population for 1990[a]	Census's Actual Population for 1990[b]	Difference	Percent Difference
Ohio	10,763,000	10,847,000	84,000	0.78%
Oklahoma	3,503,000	3,146,000	(357,000)	−10.19%
Oregon	3,319,000	2,842,000	(477,000)	−14.37%
Pennsylvania	11,720,000	11,882,000	162,000	1.38%
Rhode Island	951,000	1,003,000	52,000	5.47%
South Carolina	3,560,000	3,487,000	(73,000)	−2.05%
South Dakota	698,000	696,000	(2,000)	−0.29%
Tennessee	5,073,000	4,877,000	(196,000)	−3.86%
Texas	17,498,000	16,987,000	(511,000)	−2.92%
Utah	2,040,000	1,723,000	(317,000)	−15.54%
Vermont	575,000	563,000	(12,000)	−2.09%
Virginia	5,961,000	6,187,000	226,000	3.79%
Washington	5,012,000	4,867,000	(145,000)	−2.89%
West Virginia	2,037,000	1,793,000	(244,000)	−11.98%
Wisconsin	5,033,000	4,892,000	(141,000)	−2.80%
Wyoming	701,000	454,000	(247,000)	−35.24%
U.S. TOTAL	249,203,000	248,709,000	(494,000)	−0.20%

[a] U.S. Bureau of the Census, Current Population Reports, series P-25, No. 937.
[b] U.S. Bureau of the Census, 1980 Census of Population, U.S. Summary and 1990 Census of Population, U.S. Summary.

better job matching supply with demand while non-growth-management states were rewarded economically for their excessive permitting behavior relative to projected demand.

∎ LESSONS (THAT SHOULD HAVE BEEN) LEARNED

As the curtain falls on Act 1, we offer two lessons (that should have been learned) from the S&L collapse. The first are federal regulatory lessons which are detailed by William K. Black (2005). They focus on improving fraud management, conflicts of interest, ethics, the need for tightened criminal oversight, and the political pressure regulators receive from politicians who win elections based at least in part on campaign contributions from the real estate lending

Table 3.4 RTC Bailout Subsidy from Growth-Management to Non-Growth-Management States

State	Total Gain (Losses) ($Millions)	State Growth-Management Gain (Losses) ($Millions)	State Non-Growth-Management Gain (Losses) ($Millions)
Alabama	−897	$0	($1,516)
Alaska	776	$0	$1,311
Arizona	7,854	$0	$13,273
Arkansas	9,653	$0	$16,314
California	(11,815)	($19,967)	$0
Colorado	2,421	$0	$4,091
Connecticut	(4,066)	$0	($6,872)
Delaware	−590	$0	($997)
Florida	(3,571)	($6,035)	$0
Georgia	(3,200)	$0	($5,408)
Hawaii	−879	($1,486)	$0
Idaho	−480	$0	($811)
Illinois	(7,967)	$0	($13,464)
Indiana	(3,642)	$0	($6,155)
Kansas	2,783	$0	$4,703
Kentucky	(2,038)	$0	($3,444)
Louisiana	(4,233)	$0	($7,154)
Maine	−785	($1,327)	$0
Maryland	(2,419)	($4,088)	$0
Massachusetts	(6,172)	$0	($10,431)
Michigan	(7,315)	$0	($12,362)
Minnesota	(3,334)	$0	($5,634)
Mississippi	−684	$0	($1,156)
Missouri	−77	$0	($130)
Montana	−418	$0	($706)
Nebraska	(1,286)	$0	($2,173)
Nevada	(1,158)	$0	($1,957)
New Hampshire	(1,117)	$0	($1,888)
New Jersey	(8,302)	($14,030)	$0
New Mexico	6,589	$0	$11,135
New York	(17,486)	$0	($29,551)
North Carolina	(3,964)	$0	($6,699)
Ohio	(7,267)	$0	($12,281)
Oklahoma	(1,076)	$0	($1,818)
Oregon	(1,890)	($3,194)	$0
Pennsylvania	(3,790)	$0	($6,405)
Rhode Island	−827	($1,398)	$0

State	Total Gain (Losses) ($Millions)	State Growth-Management Gain (Losses) ($Millions)	State Non-Growth-Management Gain (Losses) ($Millions)
South Carolina	(1,737)	$0	($2,936)
South Dakota	–372	$0	($629)
Tennessee	(2,653)	$0	($4,484)
Texas	81,113	$0	$137,081
Utah	632	$0	$1,068
Vermont	–377	($637)	$0
Virginia	(5,166)	$0	($8,731)
Washington	(3,898)	($6,588)	$0
Wisconsin	(2,896)	$0	($4,894)
Population Change		11,511,000	11,006,000
Total Gains (Losses)		($58,749)	$28,291
Subsidy (Loss) Per Capita		($5,104)	$2,570
Subsidy (Loss) Per Household		($13,576)	$6,837

Source: Adapted from Dr. Edward W. Hill, Cleveland State University, as reported in the Atlanta Journal Constitution, June 26, 1990, p. B-7. Household figure based on 2.66 persons per household in 1985 from State and Metropolitan Area Data Book 1991, U.S. Bureau of the Census. Figures are in 2015 dollars.

industry. But this begs the question—did fraud and political pressure by themselves lead to over-permitting? We think not.

The S&L bailout was the largest taxpayer-subsidized disaster in American history, that is until the Great Recession. Its magnitude swamps the largest losses ever incurred by taxpayers in response to natural disasters. For example, Hurricane Andrew cost $45 billion and the Northridge earthquake $30 billion (in 2015 dollars). But since losses from financial institutions are different from those of natural disasters, reducing risk from each requires different solutions. Reducing risk from natural hazards requires locating development away from hazardous landscapes or using construction techniques that can withstand natural events, or both. In the case of market demand–based development, the objective is to steer permitting to meet market demands but no more in order to reduce risk from losses associated with overpermitting. Though the contexts are different, the conceptual management approaches are similar. As our analysis suggests, reducing financial risk may be accomplished through MDBPP, which does a better job of matching development to market need than the status quo. This is the second lesson.

The problem is that there is no financial incentive for states to unilaterally engage in planning interventions to reduce the risk of loss incurred by financial institutions, while speculators have great incentive in the opposite direction since they often do not bear the brunt of losses associated with overbuilding. The federal government could require planning intervention measures designed to protect portfolio values from overbuilding, but this seems unlikely. Perhaps more likely would be financial institutions themselves recognizing that their losses may vary by planning intervention regimes, and in order to control for losses, premiums, interest rates, or other pricing mechanisms may be tailored to reflect the nature of financial risk within each state. This could also be accomplished through the courts by stockholders and bondholders who recognize that financial institutions have a fiduciary responsibility to protect the value of securities through the use of pricing mechanisms. If pricing mechanisms are differentiated by states based on planning intervention regimes, states may employ such regimes to regain competitiveness. While sensible, we conclude that industry-driven reforms are unlikely.

In the meantime, with few incentives to protect portfolio values of institutions and every incentive to overbuild, the creed of "beggar thy neighbor" among states and communities will surely continue. This is illustrated in Act 2, for which curtain is about to rise.

CHAPTER 4

The Self-Interests of Financial Organizations Are Incapable of Protecting America's Economy or Moral Hazard Trumps the Invisible Hand

▌PRELUDE TO ACT 2

We worry about former Federal Reserve Board chairman Alan Greenspan's apparent confession that (paraphrasing with our blunt interpretation) the self-interests of financial organizations are incapable of protecting America's economy. As the curtain rises on Act 2, we review the key events leading to the Great Recession. We then turn our attention to the failure of local development permitting systems to protect against limitations of financial institutions and the agencies that regulate them. Next, we present data and analysis showing that states with post-SCPEA planning regimes were more responsible on managing permitting than other states. We continue by highlighting two outliers—how Texas went from being the nation's poster child for excesses that contributed to the savings-and-loan (S&L) collapse and how Florida's state-local framework changed from being a model for permitting development commensurate with market demand to becoming the poster child for excessive development permitting before the Great Recession. We conclude that "moral hazard"—in which financial institutions assume their bad behavior will be bailed out by American taxpayers—trumps Adam Smith's "invisible hand" and with it Greenspan's faith in those institutions.

ACT 2: THE GREAT RECESSION

The Great Recession officially started in December 2007 and ended in June of 2009, making it the worst economic downturn since the Great Depression. Nearly 9 million jobs were lost as the unemployment rate rose from 4.7 percent in October 2007 to a peak of 10 percent in October of 2009. By the end of 2016, it returned to 4.7 percent.[1] On the surface, unemployment appears to have dropped to roughly pre-recession levels. However, the Bureau of Labor Statistics has another more thoughtful measure, called U-6, which is "total unemployed, plus all marginally attached workers, plus total employed part time for economic reasons, as a percent of the civilian labor force plus all marginally attached workers."[2] Using this measure, unemployment was 8.3 percent in 2007, rose to 16.7 percent in 2010, and fell to about 10.0 percent in 2016, still higher than pre-recession levels. Needless to say, the recovery was long and weak.

What happened?

First, there is considerable consensus that the Great Recession was caused by the bursting of the U.S. "housing bubble." Between 2000 and 2007, the United States added about 2.4 million more homes than the market demanded.[3] This is illustrated in Figure 4.1.

Second, easy money flooded the market. This helped induce up to 3 million more households to buy homes than may have qualified under conventional underwriting standards.[4]

With more homes than the market needed and too many people suddenly owning homes they could not afford, foreclosures soared. While the number of foreclosure filings averaged about 600,000

---

[1] *See* Bureau of Labor Statistics, U.S. Dep't of Labor, Labor Force Statistics from the Current Population Survey (2017).

[2] Bureau of Labor Statistics, U.S. Dep't of Labor, Alternative Measures of Labor Underutilization for States, Third Quarter of 2014 through Second Quarter of 2015 Averages (2015).

[3] There are no definitive estimates of the oversupply of homes. Our estimate is based on the annual change in households (the Census generally defines a household as one or more people occupying the same residential unit) plus a 5 percent vacancy factor. See Arthur C. Nelson, Planner's Estimating Guide (2004).

[4] The homeownership rate grew from 66.2 percent in 2000 to 69.2 percent at the end of 2004. Had the ownership rate remained at the 2000 level, there would have been 3 million fewer homeowners. For elaboration, see Arthur C. Nelson, Reshaping Metropolitan America (2013).

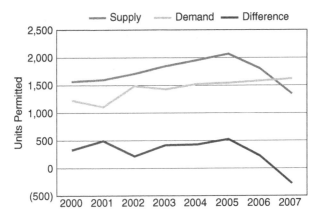

Figure 4.1 Residential units permitted ("supply") compared to new households added plus 10 percent ("demand") and the "difference."

annually between 2000 and 2004, they averaged more than 3.5 million annually between 2008 and 2011—a nearly six-fold increase. Foreclosures remained over 1 million annually into the middle 2010s. In all, foreclosure filings topped 9 million between 2006 and 2012.[5]

Why did it happen? There are several "official" reasons, but there was also unprecedented foreign capital flowing into the U.S. during the early to middle 2000s. We summarize this phenomenon first.[6] We then review many of the other reasons.

UNPRECEDENTED CAPITAL

In *Niagara of Capital*, Anthony Downs traces how America became the world's safe haven for capital.[7] Combined with a weak stock market, trillions of dollars in foreign and domestic funds flooded into America's real estate. In *Real Estate and the Financial Crisis*, Downs further showed that as the supply of capital pushed interest

---

[5] *Home Foreclosure Statistics*, STATISTIC BRAIN (Oct. 30, 2016), www.statisticbrain. com/home-foreclosure-statistics/.

[6] *Great Recession in the United States*, WIKIPEDIA, https://en.wikipedia.org/w/index. php?title=Great_Recession_in_the_United_States&oldid=750749137 (last visited Nov. 21, 2016); *Financial Crisis of 2007–2008*, WIKIPEDIA, https://en.wikipedia. org/w/index.php?title=Financial_crisis_of_2007%E2%80%932008&oldid= 749973129 (last visited Nov. 17, 2016).

[7] ANTHONY DOWNS, NIAGARA OF CAPITAL: HOW GLOBAL CAPITAL HAS TRANSFORMED HOUSING AND REAL ESTATE MARKETS (2007).

rates down, the demand for owner-occupied homes was increased—artificially—while the value of those homes increased in the short term because lower interest rates are capitalized into higher property values, that is until the market corrects itself.[8]

SUBPRIME LENDING

Another reason is that subprime lending is designed to induce people to buy homes they otherwise could not afford. For instance, mortgage underwriting conditions in the middle 2010s required a buyer to have a credit score of 640 or more, ideally a down payment of up to 20 percent, and demonstrated ability to pay off the mortgage. Borrowers meeting these standards are called "prime" credit risks. Former Federal Reserve Board chairman Ben Bernanke was famously denied refinancing because after stepping down from his job he could not demonstrate the ability to pay off the mortgage.[9]

Subprime lending refers to loans made to people who have one or more of the following credit deficiencies:

- Limited debt experience such as no prior loans
- Credit score of less than 640 and sometimes no credit score
- No assets that can be used as security
- Excessive debt
- History of late or sometimes missed payments
- Past failures to pay debts
- Legal judgments

While state and federally regulated banks could not normally issue subprime mortgages, virtually all other lenders could. For instance, one of us (Nelson) had a cat named "Valentine" that received pre-approval in 2005 from one of those lenders for a half-million-dollar mortgage at better terms than Nelson and his wife had on their Alexandria, Virginia, home.

---

[8] ANTHONY DOWNS, REAL ESTATE AND THE FINANCIAL CRISIS (2009).

[9] ELIZABETH CAMPBELL & LORRAINE WOELLERT, *You Know It's a Tough Market When Bernanke Can't Refinance*, BLOOMBERG (Oct. 3, 2014), www.bloomberg.com/news/articles/2014-10-02/you-know-it-s-a-tough-market-when-ben-bernanke-can-t-refinance.

ADJUSTABLE RATE MORTGAGES

Another reason was the rise of adjustable rate mortgages (ARMs). These typically have mortgage payments starting several points below the prevailing market—such as 3.5 percent instead of 5.5 percent—but the rates are adjusted periodically (typically every six months or one year) until they cap at, say for this example, 7.5 percent or two percentage points above the prevailing rate. This enabled many buyers to qualify for a loan they could not otherwise afford based on conventional underwriting requirements.[10] However, if buyers could just afford a home at the lower rate, they may be unable to finance it as the rate rises. After all, once the loan reaches its cap—in this case 7.5 percent—payments will have more than doubled but incomes have not. When the housing boom busted, many millions of homes these buyers purchased lost value so their mortgages exceeded the value of their homes—a situation called *being underwater.*

LOOSE MORTGAGE UNDERWRITING

Prior to the early 2000s, people seeking mortgages usually did so in person, with the lender's staff verifying all the mortgage application information. But mortgage underwriting standards declined during the 2000s (remember Valentine?) through such features as borrowing incentives and automated loan approvals. But as standards declined, defaults rose to unprecedented levels.

Loose mortgage underwriting was often fueled by fraud. As early as 2004, the Federal Bureau of Investigation warned of the potential for an "epidemic" in mortgage fraud that could lead to "a problem that could have as much impact as the S&L crisis."[11]

---

[10] Standard underwriting practices would qualify home buyers only if the combination of principle, interest, taxes, and insurance did not exceed about 30 percent of their income. By cutting mortgage payments about half for the first year, many buyers met the 30 percent requirement in only the first year. *See* MARY SCHWARTZ & ELLEN WILSON, *Who Can Afford to Live in a Home? A Look at Data from the 2006 American Community Survey Census Bureau* (2008), www.census.gov/housing/census/publications/who-can-afford.pdf.

[11] RICHARD B. SCHMITT, *FBI Foresaw Mortgage Sector Mess*, CHI. TRIB. (Aug. 26, 2008), http://articles.chicagotribune.com/2008-08-26/business/0808250439_1_mortgage-fraud-fbi-official-financial-crimes-section.

Low Down Payments and Negative Equity

While a 20 percent down payment has been the standard in the United States for securing mortgages—though lower down payments have been possible through mortgage insurance that adds to the mortgage costs—the housing bubble saw new meaning of the concept. Through aggressive ARM practices, combined with no mortgage insurance requirements, down payments as low as zero became common. And sometimes the borrower could get money back at settlement if the home appraised for more than the mortgage even with zero down payment, a concept called *negative equity*.

Corrupt Appraisals

As the housing bubble grew, many lenders pushed their appraisers to inflate the value of homes so as to increase the number of mortgages that could be underwritten.[12] In some cases, appraisers would value homes substantially higher than the mortgage, which meant in the case of zero or very low down payments the borrower would actually receive money at closing, even though their homes were really worth less.

Predatory Lending

Subprime lending and ARMs helped fuel "predatory lending."[13] This is the practice of deceiving borrowers in various ways. As one example, borrowers were told they were getting a very low interest rate —as low as 1 percent—but the real rate was many times higher, resulting in negative amortization where the mortgage balance actually increases after every payment.

Bundling Bad Mortgages with Good Ones

Mortgage-backed securities (MBS) and collateralized debt obligations (CDO) are key ways in which money for mortgages is raised. Very generally, thousands of mortgages are bundled into master MBS and CDO instruments that are sold to investors. Once they are sold,

---

[12] Joe Eaton, *The Appraisal Bubble*, The Center for Pub. Integrity (Apr. 14, 2009), www.publicintegrity.org/2009/04/14/2895/appraisal-bubble (providing lucid accounts of corrupt appraisal practices).

[13] For details on the practice, *see* Freddie Mac, Combating Predatory Lending (2016).

new money becomes available to make new mortgages. The investors receive the cash flow from mortgages based on mortgage terms. When those bundles are acquired and sold by the Federal National Mortgage Association (Fannie Mae) and the Federal Home Loan Mortgage Corporation (Freddie Mac), the returns to investors are guaranteed by the full faith and credit of the United States because they are government-sponsored enterprises. The problem is, because the bundles include thousands of mortgages, it is practically impossible to distinguish underperforming mortgages from performing ones. American taxpayers were essentially left to secure these guaranteed returns to investors for questionable, if not fraudulent, mortgages. On the private sector side, the failure to deliver promised returns sank finance firms such as the multi-billion-dollar investment firm Lehman Brothers.[14]

THE FAILURE OF REGULATION

Finally, the regulations that are supposed to protect the economy and society from calamitous economic events were not enforced rigorously. In 2011, the U.S. Financial Crisis Inquiry Commission concluded that "the crisis was avoidable" (p. 414):

. . . Widespread failures in financial regulation and supervision proved devastating to the stability of the nation's financial markets. (p. xviii)

. . . Dramatic failures of corporate governance and risk management at many systemically important financial institutions were a key cause of this crisis. (p. xviii)

---

[14] We recommend readers to review the demise of Lehman Brothers offered by the Yale program on financial stability. ROSALIND Z. WIGGINS, ET AL, THE LEHMAN BROTHERS BANKRUPTCY A: OVERVIEW (Yale Program on Financial Stability Case Study 2014-3A-V1, 2014). Its review recounts that on "September 15, 2008, Lehman Brothers Holdings, Inc., the fourth-largest U.S. investment bank, sought Chapter 11 protection, initiating the largest bankruptcy proceeding in U.S. history. *Id.* The demise of the 164-year old firm was a seminal event in the global financial crisis. *Id.* Under the direction of its long-time Chief Executive Officer Richard Fuld, Lehman had been very successful pursuing a high-leverage, high-risk business model that required it to daily raise billions of dollars to fund its operations. Beginning in 2006, Lehman began to invest aggressively in *real-estate-related assets and soon had significant exposures to housing and subprime mortgages,* just as these markets began to sour." *Id.* (Emphasis added.)

. . . A combination of excessive borrowing, risky investments, and lack of transparency put the financial system on a collision course with crisis. (p. xix)

. . . The government was ill prepared for the crisis, and its inconsistent response added to the uncertainty and panic in the financial markets. (p. xxi)

. . . a systemic breakdown in accountability and ethics (p. xxii)

If the federal government is not capable of preventing such calamities as the S&L collapse and the Great Recession, who is? We posit that the planning and development permitting system administered by state and local governments may be. Our evidence is reported next.

PATTERNS OF HOUSING INVENTORY CHANGE AND FORECLOSURES

In this section, we report and explain patterns of excess housing inventory change leading to the Great Recession and foreclosures relating to it.

EXCESS HOUSING AND FORECLOSURES

For the most part, residential lending practices of the 2000s led to the overconstruction of homes, especially for owner occupancy. Normally, residential development is driven by market demand so when fewer homes are permitted than needed to meet market demand, developers complain. But few seem to complain when more development is permitted than the market needs. This occurred during the 1980s in the context of commercial development fueled by S&L loans. It happened again in the 2000s with respect to the residential market. In the face of excess supply, developers continued proposing projects while planners continued approving them. Developers, lenders, planners, and local governing bodies may have been blinded by the Niagara of capital that fueled demand for millions of new owner-occupied homes than needed. No one seemed to question whether those new home owners could really afford their mortgages; few if any knew that the housing boom of the 2000s was largely artificially created. When questioned about whether the market could sustain more owner-occupied homes, many developers responded that they were the ones willing to bear the risk, which often proved sufficient to local decision-makers. Of course, developers merely delivered products financial institutions would underwrite regardless of what the market could really support. And for the most part it was financial institutions that assumed much of the loan risk.

HOW DO WE KNOW THERE WERE MORE HOMES BUILT THAN NEEDED?

Here we estimate the oversupply of homes built in the 2000s. Table 4.1 summarizes the extent to which the housing inventory expanded during the 2000s beyond market demand. The columns labeled "Housing Units 2000," "Housing Units 2010," and "Net Change 2000–2010" report total housing units in 2000 and 2010 and net change in units, respectively, including all occupied, vacant, seasonal, and other units. The column labeled "Household Growth 2000s" indicates household growth and implicitly the rate of change in housing units needed to meet demand, which is reported in the "Housing Units Needed 2010" column.[15] The "Excess Units 2000–2010" column shows the difference between net increase in the inventory needed to meet market demand and the actual change in inventory. From this, we calculate the "Excess Units as Share of Net Change." The last column reports "Foreclosures 2008–2011."

Using this method, we find that the nation as a whole overbuilt about 3.6 million residential units during the 2000s,[16] of which 80 percent or more were intended for owner occupancy.[17] Nationally, we find that the housing inventory increased about 23 percent more than needed based on market demand. Very few states added

---

[15] This assumes the number of housing units in 2000 was normal. We suspect it was, considering it was not a recession year, unemployment was low, and median household income was actually higher in real terms in 2000 than 2010. For the calculation methodology, see ARTHUR C. NELSON, PLANNER'S ESTIMATING GUIDE (2004).

[16] Estimates suggest an oversupply of up to 3.5 million units through 2007. ANDREW HAUGHWOUT, ET AL., THE SUPPLY SIDE OF THE HOUSING BOOM AND BUST OF THE 2000S (Federal Reserve Bank of New York Staff Report No. 556, 2012). Our estimate includes units permitted through 2009.

[17] Census permitting data show 75 percent of all units permitted during 2000 through 2009 were single-family residential units. Of the remaining quarter comprising attached residential some of them were for owner occupants such as townhomes and condominiums. Some reports estimate that more than 80 percent of all new homes constructed between 1989 and 2009 were for owner occupants. ARTHUR C. NELSON, RESHAPING METROPOLITAN AMERICA: DEVELOPMENT TRENDS AND OPPORTUNITIES TO 2030 (2nd ed. 2013).

Table 4.1 Excess Units Built 2000–2010 and Foreclosures 2008–2011

State	Housing Units 2000	Housing Units 2010	Net Change	Household Growth 2000s	Housing Units Needed 2010	Excess Units 2000–2010	Excess Units as Share of Net Change	Foreclosures 2008–2011
United States	115,905	131,705	15,800	10%	128,125	3,580	23%	5,053
Alabama	1,964	2,172	208	8%	2,125	47	22%	35
Alaska	261	307	46	17%	305	2	5%	3
Arizona	2,189	2,845	655	25%	2,730	114	17%	249
Arkansas	1,173	1,316	143	10%	1,288	28	20%	25
California	12,215	13,680	1,466	9%	13,356	324	22%	768
Colorado	1,808	2,213	405	19%	2,145	68	17%	85
Connecticut	1,386	1,488	102	5%	1,458	30	30%	21
Delaware	343	406	63	14%	392	14	22%	20
District of Columbia	275	297	22	8%	296	0	1%	2
Florida	7,303	8,990	1,687	17%	8,531	459	27%	881
Georgia	3,282	4,089	807	19%	3,903	185	23%	176
Hawaii	461	520	59	13%	520	(1)	–1%	9
Idaho	528	668	140	23%	649	19	14%	9
Illinois	4,886	5,297	411	5%	5,140	157	38%	267
Indiana	2,532	2,796	263	7%	2,707	89	34%	159
Iowa	1,233	1,336	104	6%	1,309	27	26%	20
Kansas	1,131	1,233	102	7%	1,211	22	21%	34
Kentucky	1,751	1,927	176	8%	1,890	37	21%	34
Louisiana	1,847	1,965	118	4%	1,929	36	30%	60
Maine	652	722	70	7%	699	23	33%	8
Maryland	2,145	2,379	234	9%	2,334	45	19%	76
Massachusetts	2,622	2,808	186	4%	2,728	80	43%	107
Michigan	4,234	4,532	298	2%	4,317	215	72%	272

Minnesota	2,066	2,347	281	10%	2,270	78	28%	66
Mississippi	1,162	1,275	113	6%	1,237	38	34%	7
Missouri	2,442	2,713	271	8%	2,638	74	27%	69
Montana	413	483	70	14%	470	13	18%	4
Nebraska	723	797	74	8%	782	15	20%	8
Nevada	827	1,174	346	33%	1,100	74	21%	163
New Hampshire	547	615	68	9%	596	19	28%	13
New Jersey	3,310	3,554	243	5%	3,467	87	36%	78
New Mexico	781	901	121	17%	910	(8)	-7%	17
New York	7,679	8,108	429	4%	7,955	154	36%	61
North Carolina	3,524	4,328	804	19%	4,203	125	15%	64
North Dakota	290	317	28	9%	317	0	2%	2
Ohio	4,783	5,128	344	3%	4,942	185	54%	331
Oklahoma	1,514	1,664	150	9%	1,647	17	11%	35
Oregon	1,453	1,676	223	14%	1,650	26	12%	36
Pennsylvania	5,250	5,567	318	5%	5,513	54	17%	135
Rhode Island	440	463	24	1%	444	19	81%	12
South Carolina	1,754	2,138	384	17%	2,055	82	21%	60
South Dakota	323	363	40	11%	359	5	11%	3
Tennessee	2,439	2,812	373	11%	2,717	95	26%	84
Texas	8,158	9,977	1,820	21%	9,844	134	7%	212
Utah	769	980	211	25%	959	20	10%	37
Vermont	294	323	28	6%	313	10	35%	0
Virginia	2,904	3,365	461	13%	3,285	80	17%	80
Washington	2,451	2,886	435	15%	2,821	64	15%	59
West Virginia	845	882	37	4%	875	7	18%	3
Wisconsin	2,321	2,624	303	9%	2,532	93	31%	93
Wyoming	224	262	38	17%	262	(0)	-0%	2

inventory commensurate with demand: only the District of Columbia, Hawaii, North Dakota, and Wyoming. On the other hand, Rhode Island (81 percent), Michigan (72 percent), and Ohio (54 percent) led states with oversupply of homes relative to demand.

Is there a pattern of excess inventories and foreclosures with respect to states that mandate market demand–based planning and permitting? We believe so, as shown next.

THE ROLE OF MARKET DEMAND–BASED PLANNING AND PERMITTING IN PREVENTING OVERSUPPLY

Using several sources as a guide, we classify states based on whether their statute-based planning regimes mandated projections of development need and then planning for that need, and whether there was state-local collaboration in monitoring the relationship between demand and supply through residential permitting.[18] Dennis Gale[19] provides a useful set of criteria for our purposes:

• Mandates or encourages preparation of local comprehensive plans and, in some states, county or regional plans

• Mandates or encourages plan submittal to state and/or substate body for review and comment, approval, or negotiation

• Maintains a system of incentives and/or disincentives to encourage compliance or cooperation

• Mandates or encourages limits on the number and/or character of plan amendments

Considering Gale's eight state growth-management systems, in the middle 1990s the following eleven states had moderate to strong

---

[18] These sources include JOHN M. DEGROVE, LAND, GROWTH AND POLITICS (1984), PLANNING AND GROWTH MANAGEMENT IN THE STATES: THE NEW FRONTIER FOR LAND POLICY (1992), and PLANNING, POLICY AND POLITICS: SMART GROWTH AND THE STATES (2005); DeGrove (1984, 1992, 2005), Gale (1992), and Nelson and Dawkins (2004), and ARTHUR C. NELSON AND CASEY J. DAWKINS, URBAN CONTAINMENT IN THE UNITED STATES: HISTORY, MODELS, AND TECHNIQUES FOR REGIONAL AND METROPOLITAN GROWTH MANAGEMENT (2004).

[19] GALE, DENNIS E., *Eight State-Sponsored Growth Management Programs: A Comparative Analysis*, JOURNAL OF THE AMERICAN PLANNING ASSOCIATION, 58:4, 425–439 (1992).

state oversight in designing plans to meet market needs: Colorado (DeGrove 1984),[20] Florida, Georgia, Hawaii (Callies 1985),[21] Maine, New Jersey, Oregon, Rhode Island, Vermont, and Washington. However, Colorado and Maine no longer have state planning offices, and Rhode Island's office does not provide rigorous review of local plans. Closer scrutiny of Georgia reveals that it provides only weak review of local plans with no meaningful enforcement for failure to comply (Weitz 1999).[22] Though it was during the 1990s (see Chapter 3), Florida was not a demand–based planning and permitting state during much of the 2000s, especially during the latter half leading into the Great Recession. We discuss Florida in particular below.

We theorize that states with market demand–based planning and permitting management will see fewer foreclosures compared to other states controlling for growth rates and regional location. We use statistical regression analysis to test the hypothesis using the number of foreclosures in a state as the dependent variable. The general model is:

$$\text{Foreclosures} = f \, (\text{growth, socioeconomic conditions,} \\ \text{region, MDBPP})$$

In this model, the number of foreclosures in a state between 2008 and 2011 (logged because the distribution is not normal) is dependent on the following:

- The number of households existing in 2000 (logged): a positive association is expected because the larger the household base the higher the volume of foreclosures.
- The number of units existing in 2010 in excess of demand (logged) as we reported in Table 4.1: a positive association is expected, as the more excess units relative to demand, the higher the volume of foreclosures.
- The percent of the population that was white non-Hispanic in 2000: the higher the percentage, the higher the number of foreclosures, as whites purchase homes at a higher rate than the rest of the population as a whole.

---

[20] JOHN M., DEGROVE, LAND, GROWTH AND POLITICS (1984).
[21] DAVID L. CALLIES, REGULATING PARADISE: LAND USE CONTROLS IN HAWAII (1985).
[22] JERRY WEITZ, SPRAWL BUSTING: STATE PROGRAMS TO GUIDE GROWTH (1999).

- The unemployment rate in 2000 as an indicator of economic stability: the higher the unemployment rate, the lower the number of foreclosures because lagging economics also have lagging development.
- The location of the state within the Northeast, Midwest, and South census regions: foreclosures in those regions will be lower than in the West (excluded as the referent region against which the others are compared because the West had the highest number of foreclosures after controlling for other factors).
- Whether the state mandated market demand–based planning and permitting (MDBPP) during the 2000s.

Results are reported in Table 4.2. All variables are significant at better than the 0.05 level of probability. There is no problematic collinearity between the variables. The overall model explains 85 percent

Table 4.2 Regression Analysis of the Association between Demand–Based Planning and Permitting and Foreclosures during the Period 2008–2011

Variable	Coefficient	t score	Significance
Constant	−2.35	−3.07	0.00
Growth Variables			
Households in 2000 logged	1.15	8.04	0.00
Units built in excess of demand logged, 2000–2010	0.14	2.66	0.01
Socioeconomic Variables			
Population percent white non-Hispanic, 2000	0.01	3.42	0.00
Unemployment rate, 2000	−0.12	−2.91	0.01
Regional Variables (West States Excluded)			
Northeast states	−0.36	−2.92	0.01
Midwest states	−0.30	−2.26	0.03
South states	−0.43	−3.68	0.00
Policy Variable			
Market demand–based planning mandate	−0.32	−2.37	0.02
Model Performance			
Number of cases (all states plus DC)	51		
Adjusted R^2	0.85		
F-ratio	36.81		
F-significance	0.00		

of the variation in foreclosures. While we do not establish cause-and-effect, the model performance and relationships between foreclosures and factors are consistent with theoretical expectations. Interpretations of individual relationships follow.

The model shows a very high level of elasticity between the number of households at the beginning of the study period, 2000, and foreclosures between 2008 and 2011—that is, for every 1.0 percent increase in the baseline number of households, there was an 1.15 percent increase in foreclosures, all other factors considered. This seems reasonable because a large base would be expected to be associated with high foreclosure levels.

A key relationship of interest to us is the association between units built in excess of demand between 2000 and 2010 and the number of foreclosures between 2008 and 2011. Here there is a relatively inelastic but significant relationship where a 1.0 percent change in excess supply is associated with a 0.14 percent increase in foreclosures, all other factors considered.

The model also indicates that a 1.0 percent increase in the white non-Hispanic population is associated with a 1.0 percent increase in foreclosures. Also, a 1.0 percent increase in the unemployment rate in 2000 is associated with a 0.12 percent decrease in foreclosures. Looking at the regional control variables, we see that compared to states in the West, states in the Northeast, Midwest, and South had 36 percent, 30 percent, and 43 percent fewer foreclosures, respectively.

Lastly, we find that market demand–based planning states had 32 percent fewer foreclosures than other states, all factors considered. We thus show the expected associations between excess development and foreclosures, and that market demand–based planning states moderate foreclosures. We next compare states' growth projections to actual outcomes to determine the extent to which states' projections were accurate, a key indicator of the kind of good planning that is associated with MDBPP.

COMPARING STATE PROJECTIONS TO GROWTH AND FORECLOSURE OUTCOMES

Planning relies on projections of population, employment, and associated development needs. Without them, communities would not know how many schools to build, how to size water and wastewater treatment facilities, and how to allocate land for development, among many other needs. The Census Bureau periodically makes population projections for individual states and the nation as a whole, looking several decades into the future. States also make their own projections, often disaggregating them to counties, substate regions, and occasionally larger cities. Ideally, state projections would guide planning to meet but not exceed projected needs, and permitting would be based on those projections. This is the very essence of MDBPP. In Table 4.3, we report states' individual population projections from 2000 to 2010 and the census projections for states from 2005 to 2010 compared to the actual 2010 population. The sum of individual state projections is used to estimate their collective projection for the nation's 2010 population. We offer these findings:

- The Census Bureau's 2010 population projections for the nation as a whole and for most states were more accurate than for individual states.

- Arizona, California, Illinois, Michigan, Nevada, and Ohio— among the nation's top foreclosure states during the period from 2008 to 2011—projected substantially more population growth than the Census. Different states employ different demographic projection techniques as well as make different assumptions. In these cases, past trends were likely extrapolated, and more optimistic assumptions were made about growth than may have been prudent. In all cases, actual population at mid-decade— 2005—indicated projections were too optimistic for 2010.

- Projections by Florida for its 2010 population were very close to the Census projection as well as the actual population enumerated in 2010. Yet, its local governments produced nearly 500,000 more homes than needed. It would seem that despite market demand–based planning in that state, market demand–based permitting did not guide development decisions. That is why we do not consider Florida's planning system as consistent with principles of market demand–based planning and permitting.

Table 4.4 reports the ten states with the highest rates of foreclosures as a percent of homeowners. Nevada and Arizona were in the top three, and they ranked first and second in growth during the 2000s. But they also vastly overprojected their growth relative to Census projections and actual results. In making projections, there is always the danger of the self-fulfilling prophesy that what one projects is what one receives. Perhaps, the development communities in those states built vastly more homes than were needed in part because of over-optimistic state projections. Comparing those states' individual projections with those of the Census shows that individual state projections need to be reconciled with other states and the nation.

Attention is drawn to Ohio, Michigan, Indiana, and Illinois, which ranked 5th through 8th in foreclosure rates, yet also ranked between 32nd and 46th in growth. Those states' own projections acknowledged low growth rates, yet residential units permitted vastly exceeded demand. For instance, Ohio added about 160,000 households, but its local governments permitted about 340,000 new residential units, or more than two homes per new household.[23] Rapid growth, and even misleading projections about growth (e.g., Arizona and Nevada), certainly has a role in oversupplying the residential market, but we find excessive development occurred in even the slowest-growing states.

What about states with market demand–based planning and permitting systems? Results for them are reported in Table 4.5. As a whole, they performed much better than the nation and the states listed in Table 4.4. For instance, all those states had foreclosure rates considerably less than for the nation as a whole. We discuss these relationships next.

These findings lead to three recommendations:

Market Demand–Based Planning Recommendation 1: The federal government needs to issue periodic population and other demographic projections for the states. This practice would be useful for a variety of federal resource allocation programs. If states generate their own projections, there needs to be reconciliation between federal and state projections. These projections should be in 10 year increments to at least 30 years into the future and updated every five years.

Market Demand–Based Planning Recommendation 2: State population and other demographic projections need to be disaggregated to at least each county. These allocations would be made

---

[23] We find it ironic that as a rule of thumb one new home is needed for about every 2.5 new residents, but in Ohio, 2.1 new homes were built for every new resident. For elaboration on calculation of housing demand based on population, see ARTHUR C. NELSON, PLANNER'S ESTIMATING GUIDE (2004).

Table 4.3 Variation of Actual 2010 Population to Census and State 2010 Projections

State	Census Projection Variance	Census Projection/ Actual Ratio	State Projection Variance	State/Actual Ratio	Difference of State and Census Projection Variances
United States	187	0.1%	2,955	0.5%	2,767
Alabama	(183)	-3.8%	59	1.2%	242
Alaska	(16)	-2.3%	(12)	-1.6%	4
Arizona	245	3.8%	608	9.5%	362
Arkansas	(41)	-1.4%	19	0.7%	60
California	813	2.2%	1,882	5.1%	1,069
Colorado	(198)	-3.9%	143	2.8%	340
Connecticut	3	0.1%	(181)	-5.1%	(184)
Delaware	(14)	-1.5%	(1)	-0.1%	13
District of Columbia	(75)	-12.4%	(7)	-1.2%	67
Florida	450	2.4%	80	0.4%	(370)
Georgia	(99)	-1%	177	1.8%	276
Hawaii	(20)	-1.4%	(61)	-4.5%	(41)
Idaho	(50)	-3.2%	(70)	-4.5%	(20)
Illinois	86	0.7%	438	3.4%	352
Indiana	(92)	-1.4%	(60)	-0.9%	32
Iowa	(36)	-1.2%	(18)	-0.6%	19
Kansas	(48)	-1.7%	(51)	-1.8%	(3)
Kentucky	(74)	-1.7%	(0)	-0.0%	74
Louisiana	79	1.7%	(164)	-3.6%	(243)
Maine	29	2.2%	35	2.6%	6
Maryland	131	2.3%	6	0.1%	(126)
Massachusetts	102	1.6%	9	0.1%	(92)
Michigan	545	5.5%	238	2.4%	(307)
Minnesota	117	2.2%	149	2.8%	32

Mississippi	4	0.1%	8	0.3%	4
Missouri	(67)	-1.1%	(10)	-0.2%	57
Montana	(21)	-2.1%	(3)	-0.4%	17
Nebraska	(57)	-3.1%	(9)	-0.5%	48
Nevada	(10)	-0.4%	263	9.7%	273
New Hampshire	69	5.2%	49	3.7%	(20)
New Jersey	226	2.6%	(5)	-0.1%	(231)
New Mexico	(79)	-3.8%	103	5%	182
New York	66	0.3%	240	1.2%	174
North Carolina	(190)	-2%	36	0.4%	226
North Dakota	(36)	-5.3%	(27)	-4.1%	9
Ohio	40	0.3%	130	1.1%	91
Oklahoma	(160)	-4.3%	(44)	-1.2%	115
Oregon	(40)	-1%	13	0.3%	53
Pennsylvania	(118)	-0.9%	(295)	-2.3%	(177)
Rhode Island	64	6.1%	22	2.1%	(42)
South Carolina	(179)	-3.9%	(76)	-1.6%	102
South Dakota	(28)	-3.4%	2	0.3%	30
Tennessee	(115)	-1.8%	(117)	-1.8%	(1)
Texas	(497)	-2%	(815)	-3.2%	(318)
Utah	(169)	-6.1%	164	5.9%	333
Vermont	27	4.3%	0	0.0%	(27)
Virginia	9	0.1%	9	0.1%	0
Washington	(183)	-2.7%	68	1%	250
West Virginia	(24)	-1.3%	(30)	-1.6%	(6)
Wisconsin	40	0.7%	85	1.5%	45
Wyoming	(44)	-7.8%	(24)	-4.2%	20

Sources: State 2010 population projections from individual states dating from the late 1990s to early 2000s. Census projections from U.S. Census Bureau (2005).

Table 4.4 Top Ten States for Foreclosures as a Percent of Homeowners

State	Population Growth	Growth Rank	Growth Rate	New Units Needed	Excess Units Permitted	Homeowner Foreclosure Rate
United States	28,061		9.9%	12,220	3,580	6.7%
Top Ten Foreclosure States Ranked from Highest to Lowest						
Nevada	946	1	46.9%	272	74	27.5%
Florida	2,834	8	17.7%	1,228	459	17.6%
Arizona	1,833	2	35.5%	541	114	15.8%
California	5,137	11	15.1%	1,141	324	10.9%
Ohio	303	43	2.7%	159	185	10.6%
Michigan	166	46	1.7%	83	215	9.7%
Indiana	333	35	5.5%	174	89	9.1%
Illinois	831	32	6.7%	254	157	8.2%
Delaware	110	13	14%	49	14	7.9%
Georgia	1,635	4	19.9%	622	185	7.5%

Table 4.5 Foreclosure Rates among Market Demand–Based Planning States

State	Population Growth	Growth Rank	Growth Rate	New Units Needed	Excess Units Permitted	Homeowner Foreclosure Rate
United States	28,061		9.9%	12,220	3,580	6.7%
Market Demand–Based Planning States						
Hawaii	88	29	7.3%	60	(1)	3.4%
Maryland	469	24	8.8%	188	45	5.2%
New Jersey	356	38	4.2%	157	87	3.7%
Oregon	413	16	12%	197	26	3.8%
Vermont	16	44	2.6%	18	10	0.2%
Washington	881	12	14.9%	370	64	3.5%

by states and reported to the Census Bureau to be included in a national database of projections. They would be for time frames consistent with Recommendation 1.

Market Demand–Based Planning Recommendation 3: These county-based projections need to include basic projections of housing needs, such as the categories of housing units permitted (or units permitted and completed) already used by the Census: one unit, two units, three and four units, and five units or more. As permitting data are already reported to the Census in these categories, periodic comparisons between projected housing needs and actual units permitted or completed can be made efficiently.

The bottom line is this: If states and the federal government agreed on a single set of population projections, there would be a smaller variance between actual and projected demographic figures between periods. In retrospect, a protocol to reconcile federal and state projections followed by intrastate allocations may have led to an even closer match between projected and actual outcomes between 2000 and 2010.[24] A common set of projections, updated regularly, provides real estate decision-makers with information about overall development needs and, through Census permit reporting, allows those decision-makers to track permitting with respect to meeting market needs.

We turn next to case studies of two states whose residential development performance during the 2000s before the Great Recession were vastly different: Florida and Texas.

∎ PERFORMANCE OF FLORIDA AND TEXAS: ∎ A STUDY IN CONTRASTS

Because of their large amounts of growth leading to vastly different permitting outcomes, we assess the performance of two states: Florida and Texas. The performance of these two states stands out in very different ways and for very different reasons. Each offer lessons about market demand–based planning and permitting.

FLORIDA

Faced with rapid growth rates and ecologically sensitive landscapes, Florida has had a long history of attempting to manage growth.

---

[24] There is an argument that population and other kinds of projections are self-fulfilling prophesies—that if one could concoct higher or lower future figures than models predict, then the outcome would be higher or lower growth. On the contrary, development trends are actually quite difficult to shift unless cataclysmic events occur such as large-scale natural disasters, war, epidemics, and so on. Our view is that rigorous projections are a starting point for understanding challenges. A collaborative process can refine the allocations but are unlikely to change their order of magnitude. For elaboration on the role of projections in land-use planning, see Arthur C. Nelson, PLANNER'S ESTIMATING GUIDE (2004).

Stroud (2012)[25] provides a comprehensive review. For our purposes, the key legislation that requires local governments to project future development needs and then allocate sufficient land to meet but not exceed those needs is the Local Government Comprehensive Planning and Land Development Regulation Act of 1985.[26] It is commonly known as the Growth Management Act (GMA). In 1985 the legislature also adopted a new state comprehensive plan.[27] Until 2011, the GMA and the state comprehensive plan were implemented through Florida Administrative Code, Rule 9J-5.

In Chapter 2, we outlined the land-use planning requirements of the GMA. In review, development needs are to be projected over a planning horizon, and land is to be allocated to meet those needs. Rule 9J-5 also provided for periodic review through an "evaluation and appraisal report," essentially monitoring progress toward meeting development needs as well as identifying emerging issues. Until 2011, the Department of Community Affairs (DCA) was charged with administering the GMA, especially through Rule 9J-5. Though some would view the planning process in Florida to be complicated, in fact all cities and counties had DCA-approved plans by the middle 1990s.

How effective was the GMA in matching development supply with demand? While this is perhaps a difficult question to answer conclusively, we use statewide vacancy rates as an indicator. In 1990, when the GMA had not been fully implemented, Florida's residential vacancy rate was 15.3 percent. In 2000, after a full decade of GMA implementation, Florida's residential vacancy rate had fallen to 12.8 percent. We note that both are prerecession years. Though circumstantial, it would seem that the GMA may be associated with improving the balance between supply and demand. But in 2010, a year after the Great Recession, the vacancy rate was 17.5 percent.

There is a nuanced reason for vacancy rates declining through the 1990s but rising substantially in the late 2000s: Florida's development

---

[25] NANCY STROUD, *A History and New Turns in Florida's Growth Management Reform*, 45 J. MARSHALL L. REV. 397 (2012).

[26] FLA. STAT. §§ 163.3161–3215 (1986).

[27] FLA. STAT. § 187 (1986). The plan contains goals and policies for the state in the areas of education, children, families, the elderly, housing, health, public safety, water resources, coastal and marine resources, natural systems and recreational lands, air quality, energy, hazardous and nonhazardous materials and waste, mining, property rights, land use, public facilities, cultural and historical resources, transportation, governmental efficiency, the economy, agriculture, tourism, and employment. *Id.*

of regional impact (DRI) process. As part of the GMA, large-scale developments and especially those having multicounty impacts were subject to a separate review process. More so than local plans, DRI proposals needed market demand–based analysis to justify their approval. DRIs were also long-term in nature to meet near- and long-term market needs. Approved DRIs could be amended as market conditions changed. Our view based on professional practice in Florida during the 1990s is that the market demand–based planning component instilled discipline among both developers and local governments to prevent overpermitting relative to demand. But from the late 1990s to the early 2010s, the DRI process was steadily weakened.[28] By the middle 2000s, more development capacity was approved in new DRIs than the market seemed able to absorb.[29]

Changes in the DRI process merely reflected a larger, sustained shift in the level of state review of local plans that often included adding more development capacity than market demand–based assessments indicated were needed. During a succession of Republican governors (i.e., Jeb Bush, Charlie Crist, and Rick Scott), support for the DCA's plan review function was cut, and eventually in 2011 it was substantially removed. For their part, local governments allocated much more land for development than projections warranted, despite state review. Data collected by the Southwest Florida Regional Planning Council showed that the cumulative development capacity of all land-use plans in the state exceeded 90 million people.[30] Despite this, local governments increased capacity even more. In the middle 2000s, a movement called *hometown democracy* was launched that would have put all plan amendments to a local vote. Though the ballot measure failed by a two-to-one margin, Tom Pelham[31] observes:

The prospect of having to get referendum approval of plan amendments triggered a statewide stampede by developers and landowners to obtain plan amendments before the 2010 election.

---

[28] See Tim Chapin, Harrison Higgins & Evan Rosenberg, Comparison of Florida's Approaches to Large-Scale Planning (2007).

[29] Tom Pelham, *Florida's Retreat from Planning and Growth Management*. Practicing Planner, Vol. 9 (online) (2011a).

[30] Our calculations exceeded 110 million at the maximum and 70 million at the moderate level. Southwest Florida Regional Planning Council, Maps & Data (2010). The midpoint of 90 million can be also used for assessment.

[31] Tom Pelham, Florida Comprehensive Planning System Encounters Stormy Weather. Chicago, Am. Bar Assoc. (2011b).

Local governments accommodated them by transmitting tens of thousands of plan amendments to the already-understaffed DCA in the four years leading up to the election. During this period, DCA approved over 2,500 large scale local plan map amendments covering about 2 million acres of land. These map amendments . . . increased potential residential development capacity by about 1 million residential units and potential nonresidential development capacity by 2.7 billion square feet. This potential development capacity was added to local plans that already had large allocations of unused development capacity and that had, by some counts, produced more than 1 million vacant residential units. (p. 1)

By 2011, the DCA's plan review function had been limited in its legal authority, stripped of staff resources, and placed in an economic development agency. Nancy Stroud observes:

Beginning in 2009 and through 2011, the Florida legislature substantially revised the growth management system to significantly reduce the state and regional management components of the system, and to release local communities from mandates intended to ensure that growth pays for itself and to discourage urban sprawl. Although initially justified as a response to the economic downturn of the time, this counter-revolution has ideological foundations that may be the harbinger of future changes for growth management in other states as well. (p. 397)

In an apparent mischaracterization of Florida's GMA, Wendell Cox[32] opines that:

Florida's restrictive land-use policies helped inflate its property bubble to massive size, making its bursting all the more economically painful. Such growth policies—better known as "smart growth" or "urban containment"—limit urban expansion, prohibiting new housing except in small sections of already dense metropolitan areas.

---

[32] WENDELL COX, *Florida Sheds Its "Smart Growth" Dunce Hat: Land-Use Laws Meant to Limit Urban Sprawl Instead Prompted One of the Nation's Biggest Housing Bubbles*, WALL ST. J. (October 18, 2013), www.wsj.com/articles/SB10001 4240527023048646504579143371449924220.

But Bob Graham,[33] former Florida governor and U.S. senator, replies:

> *Mr. Cox makes the argument that Florida's economy crashed in 2007 due to an undersupply of housing because Florida's growth management laws artificially restricted supply. But in reality our bubble—like those in the Sunbelt states of Arizona, California and Nevada—burst due to rampant speculation and oversupply—the same reasons for Florida's crashes in the 1920s and 1970s, before Florida's growth laws were even enacted.*
>
> *Florida's traditional rate of demand for new housing was 150,000 units per year. But in the years leading up to 2007, developers were constructing more than 200,000 units per year. On top of this, between 2007 and 2010, 660,000 more residences of all types were approved in Florida as well as more than 6 billion square feet of commercial and institutional space, most of which has not been built.*
>
> *As a member of the national committee looking into the collapse of the housing bubble, I can say that it did not find a nexus with smart growth programs. The real culprits were inadequate regulation of financing practices, including sub-prime lending, weakened credit requirements, and loan securitization. Builders in Florida and elsewhere in the nation could not secure financing to build new projects, and our state's growth laws had nothing to do with that.*

The overproduction of housing—not its underproduction as claimed by Cox—led to Florida permitting nearly 600,000 more residential units than the market needed, resulting in a vacancy rate of 17.4 percent in 2010—a 36 percent increase from 2000. The oversupply simply caught up to Florida's economy. Lacking assertive state review to prevent the overallocation of land for development, this is the very outcome one would expect from a "growth machine" that manipulates local development overpermitting, as theorized by Logan and Molotch, reviewed in Chapter 2.

In review, Florida has been a national leader in development extremes, noted by former Governor and Senator Graham. One aim of its GMA is to moderate the cycles of overproduction through a

---

[33] BOB GRAHAM, Communication provided to the authors via e-mail on October 29, 2013.

state-local process that attempts to match land-use and development decisions with market needs. During the 1990s, Florida's approach seemed to work. Court cases and changes in political leadership however, led to the unraveling of the state-local relationship, ceding much of the development approval process to local officials only. Consistent with the "growth machine" hypothesis, Florida overbuilt its housing stock to such an extent that it led the nation.

Though we have offered evidence that planning and permitting based on market needs can be effective in reducing oversupply, there is another approach that is used only in Texas—regulatory constraints on homeownership.

TEXAS

We showed in Chapter 3 that Texas led the nation in Resolution Trust Corporation payouts. We surmised that states doing a better job matching supply with demand through market demand–based planning and permitting ended up subsidizing states that did not. This is a phenomenon called *moral hazard*, where costly behavior is rewarded and prudent behavior is punished. (We address moral hazard in the next section.) Yet Texas did not overdevelop residential supply during the 2000s. One reason may be its fossil fuel–driven economy, leading to one of the highest economic growth rates in the nation. But there is another.

In 2003, Texas voters adopted amendments to the state constitution. Key changes include these:

Sec. 50. HOMESTEAD; PROTECTION FROM FORCED SALE; MORTGAGES, TRUST DEEDS, AND LIENS.

(a) The homestead of a family, or of a single adult person, shall be, and is hereby protected from forced sale, for the payment of all debts except for:

(6) . . . an extension of credit that:

(B) . . . is of a principal amount that when added to the aggregate total of the outstanding principal balances of all other indebtedness secured by valid encumbrances of record against the homestead does not exceed 80 percent of the fair market value of the homestead on the date the extension of credit is made.

While this provision did not prevent home purchases from sub-prime and other nonconventional financing options in the 2000s, it did limit home equity loans such that the total of all debt secured by the home could not exceed 80 percent of the fair market value of the home when the home equity loan closed. This limit on home equity loans likely reduced the number of foreclosures in Texas associated with the Great Recession.[34]

The examples of Florida and Texas offer important insights for market demand–based planning. While Florida ostensibly requires all local governments with planning authority to project and plan for future needs, there was in fact little state oversight to ensure this in the latter 2000s. Moreover, during the 2000s, with decreasing state oversight, excess permitting expanded, making Florida the nation's leader in building more homes than needed. Texas, on the other hand, used financial regulatory mechanisms to reduce potential foreclosures. Texas may have learned its lesson when it allowed more nonresidential development than the market needed during the 1980s, which resulted in the nation's largest S&L-related losses.

We hazard to explain the events leading to the Great Recession as a consequence of "moral hazard," which we discuss next.

▌A THING CALLED MORAL HAZARD

Moral hazard describes behavior where decision makers do not bear the full cost of their actions and are thus more likely to take such them.[35]

As we showed in Act 1, the S&L debacle of the 1980s, which cost the American economy more than $1 Trillion (in 2015 dollars), was due in large part to the overbuilding of commercial real estate. As lessons from the crisis were not applied to the residential market, overdevelopment of residential real estate played a substantial role in triggering the Great Recession—which cost the American economy

---

[34] We are grateful to Shannon Phillips Jr., Deputy General Counsel of the Independent Bankers Association of Texas, for this insight in correspondence received February 1, 2016.

[35] GLOSSARY OF STATISTICAL TERMS, ORG. FOR ECON. CO-OPERATION AND DEV. (Sept. 25, 2001), http://stats.oecd.org/glossary/detail.asp?ID=1689.

at least $6 trillion[36] and likely more as we will show in the Epilogue. While both were driven by different policy-related dynamics, they had one thing in common: the inability of the market to discipline itself, combined with regulatory institutions that encouraged and perhaps induced moral hazard. In the aftermath of the Great Recession, Alan Greenspan, then chairman of the Federal Reserve Board who set the philosophical tone for U.S. monetary policy during his term from 1987 to 2006, conceded the following:

> *I made a mistake in presuming that the self-interests of organizations, specifically banks and others, were such as that they were best capable of protecting their own shareholders and their equity in the firms.*[37]

In effect, Greenspan confessed that federal policy alone could not protect against moral hazard, believing the market would regulate itself against this.

In its findings, the National Commission on the Causes of the Financial and Economic Crisis in the United States offered several conclusions relative to the Great Recession, all of which contributed to moral hazard:

- There was an explosion in risky subprime lending and securitization, an unsustainable rise in housing prices, widespread reports of egregious and predatory lending practices, dramatic increases in household mortgage debt and exponential growth in financial firms' trading activities, unregulated derivatives, and short-term "repo" lending markets, among many other red flags. Yet there was pervasive permissiveness; little meaningful action was taken to quell the threats in a timely manner.[38]

- The sentries were not at their posts, in no small part due to the widely accepted faith in the self-correcting nature of the markets

---

[36] For a review of how estimate is derived, *see* EDUARDO PORTER, *Recession's True Cost Is Still Being Tallied*, N.Y. TIMES, Jan. 21, 2014, www.nytimes.com/2014/01/22/business/economy/the-cost-of-the-financial-crisis-is-still-being-tallied.html?_r=0.

[37] BRIAN KNOWLTON & MICHAEL M. GRYNBAUM, *Greenspan "Shocked" That Free Markets Are Flawed*, N.Y. TIMES, Oct. 23, 2008, www.nytimes.com/2008/10/23/business/worldbusiness/23iht-gspan.4.17206624.html.

[38] FIN. CRISIS INQUIRY COMMISSION. THE FINANCIAL CRISIS INQUIRY REPORT. Washington, D.C.: Government Printing Office, 2011, at xvii.

and the ability of financial institutions to effectively police themselves. More than thirty years of deregulation and reliance on self-regulation by financial institutions, championed by former Federal Reserve chairman Alan Greenspan and others and supported by successive administrations and Congresses and actively pushed by the powerful financial industry at every turn, had stripped away key safeguards, which could have helped avoid catastrophe.[39]

- There was a view that instincts for self-preservation inside major financial firms would shield them from fatal risk-taking without the need for a steady regulatory hand, which, the firms argued, would stifle innovation. Too many of these institutions acted recklessly, taking on too much risk with too little capital and with too much dependence on short-term funding. In many respects, this reflected a fundamental change in these institutions, particularly the large investment banks and bank holding companies, which focused their activities increasingly on risky trading activities that produced hefty profits. They took on enormous exposures in acquiring and supporting subprime lenders and creating, packaging, repackaging, and selling trillions of dollars in mortgage-related securities, including synthetic financial products.[40]

- Lenders made loans that they knew borrowers could not afford and that could cause massive losses to investors in mortgage securities. As early as September 2004, Countrywide[41] executives recognized that many of the loans they were originating could result in "catastrophic consequences." Less than a year later, they noted that certain high-risk loans they were making could result not only in foreclosures but also entering potential financial catastrophe for the firm. But they did not stop. And the report documents that major financial institutions ineffectively sampled loans they were purchasing to package and sell to investors. They knew a significant percentage of the sampled loans did not meet their own underwriting standards or those of the originators. Nonetheless, they sold those securities to

---

[39] *Id.* at xviii.
[40] *Id.* at xviii–xix.
[41] In 2006, Countrywide made 20 percent of all mortgages in the United States. *Bank of America Home Loans*, WIKIPEDIA, https://en.wikipedia.org/wiki/Bank_of_America_Home_Loans (last visited Nov. 22, 2016).

investors. The Commission's review of many prospectuses provided to investors found that this critical information was not disclosed.[42]

It would seem that much of the S&L crisis and the Great Recession can be attributed to moral hazard. The rest of this section explores the moral hazard concept, how it relates to the free market, its role in triggering the Great Recession, and how it trumps Adam Smith's "invisible hand."

▌WHAT IS MORAL HAZARD?

For our purposes, Kevin Dowd captures the essence of moral hazard:

A moral hazard is where one party is responsible for the interests of another, but has an incentive to put his or her own interests first: the standard example is a worker with an incentive to shirk on the job. Financial examples include the following:

- *I might sell you a financial product (e.g., a mortgage) knowing that it is not in your interests to buy it.*
- *I might pay myself excessive bonuses out of funds that I am managing on your behalf; or*
- *I might take risks that you then have to bear.*

Moral hazards such as these are a pervasive and inevitable feature of the financial system and of the economy more generally. Dealing with them—by which I mean, keeping them under reasonable control—is one of the principal tasks of institutional design. In fact, it is no exaggeration to say that the fundamental institutional structure of the economy—the types of contracts we use, and the ways that firms and markets are organized—has developed to be the way it is in no small part in response to these pervasive moral hazards.[43]

---

[42] *Supra* note 4, at xxii.
[43] KEVIN DOWD, *Moral Hazard and the Financial Crisis*, CATO JOURNAL, 29(1), 141–166.

▋MORAL HAZARD AND THE FREE MARKET

Moral hazard should not arise in a purely free market. Key conditions necessary for a free market include these five elements that we will apply in the context of moral hazard later:[44]

1. All participants in an economy have full access to sufficient information needed to make their decision.
2. There are no transaction costs.
3. Buyers and sellers always make rational decisions.
4. There are no barriers to buyers and sellers entering or exiting the market.
5. Buyers and sellers fully internalize the private and social benefits and costs of their production and consumption.

In theory, if all these and other conditions exist, there should be no need for government intervention to improve economic exchange. If not all conditions exist, there is the potential for "market failure" and thus the free market is thwarted from achieving its promise. In fact, since it is difficult to achieve all of these conditions for any particular good or service, there is likely always some form of market failure. The question then becomes one of deciding whether or not the intervention itself would lead to outcomes that are better or worse than the market failure itself. But it is when intervention aims to protect against losses that taxpayers may underwrite them. We explore this next in the context of the Great Recession.

---

[44] Douglas B. Lee, Jr., *Land Use Planning as a Response to Market Failure*, in The Land Use Policy Debate in the U.S. 149 (1981). Observing that free markets exist and there is no need for an agent such as government to interfere with the market if all of these conditions are met: (1) there are many buyers and sellers; (2) reasonably accurate information exists at no cost; (3) there are homogeneous products in each market; (4) there is ease of entry and exit for both the buyer and the seller; (5) people who are unwilling or even unable to pay for a good or service can be excluded from using it; (6) inputs and outputs are easily divisible into the amounts required; (7) there are no transaction costs; (8) buyers and sellers fully internalize the consequences of their production and consumption; and (9) there are constant, predictable returns to scale in the long run.

THE ROLE OF MORAL HAZARD IN TRIGGERING THE GREAT RECESSION

In the United States, regulating the financial industry is seen as a necessary market intervention. Edward Murphy offers a succinct rationale:

> *Financial regulatory policies are of interest to Congress because firms, consumers, and governments fund many of their activities through banks and securities markets. Furthermore, financial instability can damage the broader economy. Financial regulation is intended to protect borrowers and investors that participate in financial markets and mitigate financial instability. . . . Some agencies regulate particular types of institutions for risky behavior or conflicts of interest, some agencies promulgate rules for certain financial transactions no matter what kind of institution engages in them, and other agencies enforce existing rules for some institutions, but not for others. These regulatory activities are not necessarily mutually exclusive.*[45]

But this can lead to unintended consequences, such as moral hazard. Indeed, there may be no better example of how financial institutions were fueled by moral hazard than subprime loans. We review how these loans led to moral hazard and helped trigger the Great Recession which then required more than $1 trillion of taxpayer bailouts.

In a market without subprime loans, suppose a bank had only $2 million to loan and ten people secured mortgages averaging $200,000. The bank runs out of money and can make no more loans. But if there is a secondary market to buy the mortgage paper, the bank can sell the loans as a package called a mortgage-backed security (MBS) comprised of those ten loans. In exchange for buying the MBS, the buyers (investors) receive the mortgage payments. The bank effectively recycles its mortgages and gets another $2 million to make new loans.[46] The investors all assume that the borrowers meet high standards of creditworthiness and will honor their mortgage payments, which is

---

[45] EDWARD V. MURPHY, CONG. RESEARCH SERV., R43087, WHO REGULATES WHOM AND HOW? AN OVERVIEW OF U.S. FINANCIAL REGULATORY POLICY FOR BANKING AND SECURITIES MARKETS (2015). See first summary page.

[46] We are being very simplistic with this process. For a full discussion as it pertains to government-sponsored enterprises, *see* CONG. BUDGET OFF., FANNIE MAE, FREDDIE MAC, AND THE FEDERAL ROLE IN THE SECONDARY MORTGAGE MARKET (2010).

why they are willing to buy the MBS package in the first place. It is assumed that buyers of the MBS would conduct due diligence to assure themselves of the quality of each individual mortgage. Before the 2000s, this was standard procedure.

This changed dramatically in the 2000s. Through the globalization of markets, combined with a stagnant stock market and low (though guaranteed) returns from government instruments, trillions of dollars flowed into the American real estate market—from $36 trillion to $80 trillion by one estimate.[47] Real estate investors increasingly bought shares in MBS pools comprised of tens of billions of dollars, backed by tens to hundreds of thousands of mortgages. It was impossible for investors to inspect the quality of each mortgage. Knowing this, MBS bundlers were willing to fold lower-quality mortgages into packages, implicitly warranting that all the mortgages were of comparable quality. Originators of subprime mortgages sold their securities to these bundlers. Neither the originators nor the bundlers analyzed the risk of mortgages to default, nor did they incur the risk. This is one part of the moral hazard.

In the context of free markets, moral hazard illustrates market failure in at least five ways:

1. The buyers of MBS bundles had neither the wherewithal nor the resources to adequately inspect the pool of mortgages within them. Though the bundlers appeared to have known about the quality of their packages overall, it also appears they did not disclose the information.[48] Federal National Mortgage Association (Fannie Mae) and Freddie Mac, two of the nation's leading government-sponsored enterprises, became especially vulnerable.[49]

    Moreover, it appears that the financial industry did not have adequate models to track changes in the market in response to changes in investors' tolerance for risk. Ingo Fender and Martin Scheicher estimated that the market underpriced the risk associated with subprime loans, noting that "declining risk appetite

---

[47] For a narrative on these dynamics, *see The Giant Pool of Money* (THIS AMERICAN LIFE May 9, 2008), www.thisamericanlife.org/radio-archives/episode/355/the-giant-pool-of-money.

[48] NATIONAL COMMISSION ON THE CAUSES OF THE FINANCIAL AND ECONOMIC CRISIS IN THE UNITED STATES. *The Financial Crisis Inquiry Report.* Washington, DC: United States Government Printing Office (2011).

[49] *Supra* note 11.

and heightened concerns about market illiquidity have provided a sizeable contribution to the observed collapse in (MBS)
prices."[50]

These are examples of the failure of the sufficient information condition.

2. The problem is that the sheer cost to inspect each of the mortgages in an MBS package essentially prohibits due diligence.
This is a violation of the transaction cost condition.

3. Because of aggressive marketing and often deceitful practices,[51]
buyers of homes with subprime mortgages and buyers of MBS
bundles could not make rational decisions. This is a failure of
the rational decision condition.

4. Barriers to entry and exit are substantial in the finance industry.
As Gardner observes:

> *Securitization is a complex series of financial transactions
> designed to maximize the cash flow and cash out options
> for loan originators. The securitization and sale of assets
> is what gets the "off the balance sheet" boost in reported
> income for the originator. The originators secure immediate
> liquidity from assets that, in some circumstances, could not
> be readily traded in the capital markets. On paper, it sounds
> simple, in the real world it involves the creation of numer-
> ous Special Purpose Vehicle Corporations (SPVC) designed
> to create the legal impression of an actual BPF sales trans-
> action. However, the residuals, credit enhancements, and
> other derivative rights retained by the originators in the
> transferred assets create a Pandora's Box of problems.[52]*

The processes and costs to engage in MBS markets can be
considerable. The reason is that considerable barriers exist to
enter and exit the market; a violation of the market barrier condition. It is Gardner's last point that leads us to the next.

---

[50] INGO FENDER AND MARTIN SCHEICHER, *The ABX: How Does the Markets Price
Subprime Mortgage Risk?* BIS QUARTERLY REVIEW, September, 67–81 (2008).

[51] JOSEPH WILLIAM SINGER, *Foreclosure and the Failures of Formality, or Subprime
Mortgage Conundrums and How to Fix Them*, 46 CONN. L. REV. 497 (2013).

[52] MAX GARDNER, III, *Mortgage Securitization, Servicing, and Consumer Bankruptcy.*
LAW TRENDS & NEWS (September 2005)—ABA General Practice, Solo and Small
Firm Division, www.americanbar.org/content/newsletter/publications/law_trends_
news_practice_area_e_newsletter_home/mortgagesecuritization.html.

5. To save America's economy, Congress created the $700 billion Troubled Asset Relief Program (TARP), which provided funds to nearly 1,000 entities.[53] Another nearly $200 billion was provided to government-sponsored enterprises (GSEs), such as Fannie Mae and Freddie Mac.[54] Though nearly all the funds have been returned, the overall economy lost trillions of dollars—by some estimates an average of at least $20,000 per American. It seems clear that despite all its regulation, the financial industry cost the American economy dearly.[55] This is a violation of the condition requiring agents to internalize their actions. Hutchinson colorfully summarizes the rise of moral hazard leading to the Great Recession:

If the market is thought to price all risks automatically, then even the doziest mortgage broker can originate subprime mortgages for even the least creditworthy borrowers. The fact that

---

[53] U.S. Dep't of the Treasury, TARP Programs (2016).

[54] For an ongoing tally of recipients and the status of repayments, see *Bailout Recipients*, ProPublica (Nov. 7, 2016), https://projects.propublica.org/bailout/list.

[55] The American Enterprise Institute (AEI) lists numerous ways that the federal government caused the Great Recession, including (1) poor bank regulation, in particular adapting the international Basel capital rules in 2001, which outsourced risk assessment by regulators to government-sanctioned rating agencies such as Standard and Poor (which was accused of ratings fraud by the Justice Department and settled for $1.4 billion), Fitch, and Moody's; (2) allowing Fannie Mae and Freddie Mac credit policies to continually reduce down payment and home-buying underwriting requirements to satisfy its "political obsession with taking credit for increased homeownership"; (3) expanding the pool of "subprime and Alt-A mortgage markets by Fannie and Freddie through the abandonment of proven credit standards"; and (4) the Federal Deposit Insurance Corporation (FDIC), Federal Reserve, Treasury Department, and Congress provided bailouts to large financial institutions starting in the 1980s that had become "too big to fail." Mark J. Perry & Robert Dell, *How Government Failure Caused the Great Recession*, American (Dec. 26, 2010), www.aei.org/publication/how-government-failure-caused-the-great-recession/; see also Press Release, U.S. Dep't of Justice, Justice Department and State Partners Secure $1.375 Billion Settlement with S&P for Defrauding Investors in the Lead Up to the Financial Crisis (Feb 3, 2015). AEI suggests that federal policies got the creditor-shareholder relationship backward: Creditors—not shareholders—normally control business risk-taking. They do this by reducing leverage, demanding higher interest rates, declining to finance risky projects, requiring more collateral, imposing restrictive terms and loan covenants, and moving deposits to safer alternatives (in the case of bank depositors, who are creditors of banks). Without excessive government protection of creditors, there is little doubt we would have seen creditors act to reduce risk in the U.S. financial system, particularly with respect to Fannie and Freddie.

the borrowers are incapable of making payments on the mort-
gage will magically be priced into the mortgage by the securi-
tization process, which will bundle the mortgage with other
mortgages originated by a similarly lax process and sell the lot to
an unsuspecting German Landesbank attracted by the high ini-
tial yield. Everybody will make fees on the deal, everybody will
be happy, and the Landesbank and the homeowner will have
nobody legally to blame when the homeowner is unable to make
payments and the Landesbank finds a shortfall in its investment
income. By making the market responsible, modern finance has
removed the responsibility of all the market's participants.[56]

This is the very incarnation of moral hazard. The trouble is that to prevent the market from collapsing into a true depression, substantial financial interventions are needed, as was seen through TARP. In the meantime, the market "corrects" itself by wiping out trillions of dollars in equity, including that of those who acted prudently.

THE INVISIBLE HAND IS NO MATCH FOR MORAL HAZARD

Which brings us to the concept of Adam Smith's "invisible hand" and why it is no match for moral hazard. In *The Wealth of Nations*,[57] Smith advanced the notion that:

By directing that industry in such a manner as its produce may be
of the greatest value, he intends only his own gain, and he is in this,
as in many other cases, led by an invisible hand to promote an end
which was no part of his intention. . . . By pursuing his own inter-
est he frequently promotes that of the society more effectually than
when he really intends to promote it.[58] *(Emphasis added.)*

In other words, economic actors seeking to maximize benefits for oneself thereby, perhaps necessarily, advance the welfare of all of

---

[56] MARTIN HUTCHINSON, SCRAP HEAP FOR FINANCIAL MODELS (2008), www.silver bearcafe.com/private/2.08/scrapheap.html.
[57] The short title for ADAM SMITH, AN INQUIRY INTO THE NATURE AND CAUSES OF THE WEALTH OF NATIONS (1776).
[58] *Id.* at 246.

society. For instance, in the context of real estate, developers aiming to maximize profits compete for consumers to buy their homes. For the same price, consumers are willing to buy homes that are better built, provide more amenities, and respond best to consumer tastes and preferences than alternatives; they might be willing even to pay more. While successful developers earn profits as more of their homes are sold, buyers of those homes enjoy a place to live for a price they can afford. More developers producing more homes that more people like make society better off. This is the essence of the invisible hand applied to the competitive home-building industry. It mostly works.

Ben S. Bernanke, former chair of the Federal Reserve Board, amplifies on the role of the invisible hand in shaping America's economy:

> *Market forces determine most outcomes in our economy, a fact that helps to explain much of our nation's success in creating wealth. Markets aggregate diffuse information more effectively and set prices more efficiently than any central planner possibly could. The result is powerful competitive incentives for businesses to produce, at the least cost, the goods and services that our citizens value most. Writing in the eighteenth century, Adam Smith conceived of the free-market system as an "invisible hand" that harnesses the pursuit of private interest to promote the public good. Smith's conception remains relevant today, notwithstanding the enormous increase in economic complexity since the Industrial Revolution.[59] (Emphasis added.)*

A century and a half after *The Wealth of Nations* was published, however, Paul A. Samuelson, a University of Chicago economist and Nobel Prize winner, noted the limits of the invisible hand:

> *The mystical principle of the "invisible hand": that each individual in pursuing his own selfish good was led, as if by an invisible hand, to achieve the best good of all, so that any interference with free competition by government was almost certain to be injurious. This unguarded conclusion has done almost as much harm as good in the past century and a half. . . .[60]*

---

[59] BEN S. BERNANKE, FINANCIAL REGULATION AND THE INVISIBLE HAND. Speech at the New York University Law School, New York, New York, April 11, 2007, www.federalreserve.gov/newsevents/speech/bernanke20070411a.htm.

[60] PAUL A. SAMUELSON, ECONOMICS (1948) at 41.

Though the S&L crisis occurred more than thirty years later and the Great Recession a half century later, Samuelson's admonition is applicable to both. According to Bernanke, prudent finance policy manages the invisible hand:

> *In many situations, regulation that relies on the invisible hand of market-based incentives can complement direct government regulation. For market-based regulation to work, the incentives of investors and other private actors must align with the objectives of the government regulator. In particular, private investors must be sophisticated enough to understand and monitor the financial condition of the firm and be persuaded that they will experience significant losses in the event of a failure. When these conditions are met, market discipline is a powerful and proven tool for constraining excessive risk-taking.*[61] *(Emphasis added.)*

Bernanke wrote these words in 2007, before the Great Recession. As he alludes, a key role of regulation in the finance sectors is to "constrain excessive risk-taking" by individual decision-makers otherwise driven by the invisible hand. Yet, the S&L crisis and the Great Recession seem to have been driven in large part by Federal financial policies that encouraged excessive risk-taking, and federally sponsored insurance programs covered much of that risk. When losses mounted, exceeding the capacity of insurance programs to meet their obligations, Congress engineered the S&L bailout and later the Federal Reserve Board and Congress engineered Great Recession bailouts. It would seem that when regulation incentivizes excessive risk-taking, moral hazard trumps the invisible hand.

So now we ask: What are the costs that moral hazard imposes on society and how do they differ between market demand–based planning states and others? Overall, we estimate that the equity of owner-occupied homes fell by more than $3 trillion between 2007 and 2010.[62] In Table 4.6 we assess this question in terms of loss of equity in homes from 2007 to 2010 and change in residential vacancy rate, unemployment rate, and median household income from 2000

---

[61] *Id.* Bernanke.
[62] This is based on Census estimates of median value of owner-occupied homes in the Census's American Community Survey for 2007 compared to the decennial 2010 Census.

Table 4.6 Moral Hazard Outcomes for the Nation, Market Demand–
Based Planning and Permitting States, and All Other States

Metric	Nation	MDBPP States	Other States
Change in Median Home Values, 2007–2010			
Percent change	−16.2%	−13.5%	−16.6%
Comparison to market demand planning	*21%*		*24%*
Change in Vacancy Rates, 2000–2010			
Percent change	55.1%	42.4%	56.0%
Comparison to market demand planning	*30%*		*32%*
Change in Unemployment Rates, 2000–2010			
Percent change	66%	57.5%	66.5%
Comparison to market demand planning	*14.8%*		*15.8%*
Change in Constant Median Household Income, 2000–2010			
Percent change	−7.8%	−2.4%	−8.4%
Comparison to market demand planning	*229%*		*254%*

Note that figures in italics is the ratio of national to market demand state outcomes in the left center column and between other states and market demand states in the right center column.
Note: All differences significant < p = 0.05.

to 2010 between market demand–based planning and permitting states and all other states.

In all comparisons, market demand–based planning and permitting states appear to have been more resilient in weathering the Great Recession than all other states. Homeowner equity losses were about a quarter less than for all other states while the increase in vacancy rates was nearly a third lower. The unemployment rate also fell less. A key indicator of overbuilding is the extent to which residential vacancy rates changed. In Table 4.6, we see that market demand–based planning and permitting states saw their collective residential vacancy rates increase by just 2.4 percent while the vacancy rates for all other states increased by 8.4 percent, or roughly 2.5 times more.

Much has been written about the causes, dynamics, and consequences of moral hazard on America's economy. Some argue that moral hazard would not exist if institutions were allowed to fail instead of being "too big to fail." But if state and local governments permitted only that amount of development the market demanded, then overdevelopment would not occur and possibly moral hazard would be a smaller concern. In effect, we might have it backward. Instead of the nation's financial institutions protecting America's economy, maybe we need to look to states and local governments to protect the solvency of America's financial institutions through market demand–based planning and permitting.

CHAPTER 5

The Economics and Economic Implications of Excessive Real Estate Development

▮ INTRODUCTION

We make the case in Chapter 2 that lending, permitting, and development in excess of market-based demand helped trigger the Great Depression of the 1930s. We surmise that two of the past three recessions[1] (1990–1991, 2001, 2008–2009) were induced in large part by excessive permitting, primarily of residential development.[2] Economic booms and busts always occur—they are part of the natural course of economic events. And most depressions and recessions

---

[1] An economic recession is a period of at least two quarters where GDP declines. There is no exact definition of a depression as contrasted with a recession. *See* NAT'L BUREAU OF ECON. RESEARCH, US BUSINESS CYCLE EXPANSIONS AND CONTRACTIONS, www.nber.org/cycles.html. Two recessions have been so severe that they have been labeled as "Great"—the Great Depression of 1929–1933 and the Great Recession of 2008–2009. The distinction between these two declines is based upon the greater severity of the 1930s depression. In 1933, the unemployment rate peaked at 25 percent, as contrasted with 11 percent in 2010. The severity of the Great Recession is thus put into the context of the Great Depression.

[2] The recession of 2001 was created by the "dot-com" bubble, wherein the stock market corrected for excessive speculation in the technology sector. *See Dot-Com Bubble*, WIKIPEDIA, https://en.wikipedia.org/wiki/Dot-com_bubble (last visited Nov. 21, 2016).

were not caused by excessive development but rather by such economic events as high interest rates, tariff wars, falling manufacturing orders, economic downturns after wars, credit constraints, deflation, and even President Nixon's wage-price controls.[3] The difference with the savings-and-loan (S&L) crisis and the Great Recession–induced downturns is that something entirely within the control of local governments—permitting—could have been managed to prevent them both or at least reduce the magnitude of their impact.

This chapter starts with a broad overview of the nation's economy since the Great Depression, showing that economic booms and busts are normal. It proceeds to suggest that excess development permitting—which is measurable during the years in which it occurs—can be viewed as a leading indicator of recessions. The chapter continues showing that as real estate is one of the nation's largest economic sectors, its performance has a much greater influence over the nation's prosperity or decline than perhaps any other sector. The next section addresses the effects of excess permitting on homeowners, focusing on foreclosures during and after the Great Recession. We conclude with implications for local government. After all, it is local government that decides to issue permits, and if they issue more than the market can absorb, it is local government that incurs the consequences in the form of fewer revenues and rising unemployment.

■ THE CYCLE OF BOOMS AND BUSTS

The boom and bust cycle has been with us throughout our economic history, and all indications are that it will continue to be with us. Adjusting for inflation, between 1929 and 2015, the nation's gross domestic product (GDP) grew by an average of 3.24 percent per year while personal consumption grew at an average of 3.15 percent annually. More important, GDP per capita grew at an average rate of 2.08 percent per year, indicating that economic growth outpaced population growth during this period. These trends are shown in Table 5.1 for the total period from 1929 through 2015.

Notice, however, that the long-term includes several periods of economic decline and expansion, from the Great Depression to the Great

---

[3] For an efficient summary of the causes of depressions and recessions, see KIMBERLY AMADEO, *11 Causes of Economic Recession*, THE BALANCE (Nov. 8, 2016), www.thebalance.com/causes-of-economic-recession-3306010.

Table 5.1 U.S. Gross Domestic Product and Consumption per Person, Selected Years 1929–2015 (in 2009 Dollars)

Year	Gross Domestic Product	Personal Consumption	Population	GDP per Capita	Consumption per Capita
1929	*$1,056.60*	*$781.00*	*121,767,000*	*$8,677.23*	*$6,413.89*
1933	778.30	637.60	125,578,763	6,197.70	5,077.29
1939	*1,163.60*	*860.10*	*130,879,718*	*8,890.61*	*6,571.68*
1940	1,266.10	904.70	132,122,446	9,582.78	6,847.44
1945	2,217.80	1,061.50	139,928,165	15,849.56	7,586.04
1947	1,939.40	1,216.40	144,126,071	13,456.27	8,439.83
1950	2,184.00	1,360.50	152,271,417	14,342.81	8,934.70
1970	4,722.00	2,903.00	205,052,177	23,028.29	14,157.37
1981	6,617.70	4,050.80	229,465,714	28,839.60	17,653.18
1982	6,491.30	4,108.40	231,664,458	28,020.27	17,734.27
1990	8,955.00	5,672.60	249,464,396	35,896.91	22,739.12
1991	8,948.40	5,685.60	252,153,092	35,487.96	22,548.21
2000	12,559.70	8,170.70	282,162,411	44,512.31	28,957.44
2001	12,682.20	8,382.60	284,968,955	44,503.80	29,415.84
2007	*14,873.70*	*10,041.60*	*301,231,207*	*49,376.36*	*33,335.19*
2009	14,418.70	9,847.00	306,771,529	47,001.43	32,098.81
2013	*15,583.30*	*10,590.40*	*316,427,395*	*49,247.63*	*33,468.66*
2015	16,414.00	11,262.40	321,418,820	51,067.33	35,039.64

Source: https://www2.census.gov/programs-surveys/popest/tables/1900-1980/national/totals/popclockest.txt; https://www.census.gov/data/tables/2016/demo/popest/nation-total.html
https://bea.gov/national/index.htm#gdp
Note: The bold italic figures show the peak economic years before the Great Depression and Great Recession, and the years at which economic performance per capita returned substantially to pre-downturn levels.

Recession, as seen by differences between selected years. The Great Depression started in late 1929, so the economic figures illustrate the economic peak that occurred earlier that year. The trough occurred in 1933, and by 1939, nearly three years before America entered World War II,[4] per capita GDP and consumption had returned to pre–Great Depression levels. The peak economic year during the war was 1945, and as the war effort ended, the nation entered a postwar recession, reaching its trough in 1947, as seen by a substantial drop in GDP per capita. Yet, consumption per capita actually rose quite substantially. So, though unemployment increased and the economy contracted,

[4] December 8, 1941, nearly the end of 1941.

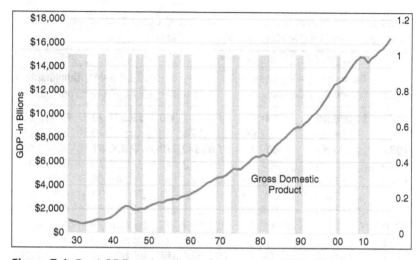

Figure 5.1 Real GDP and periods of recession, 1929–2015

Source: www.census.gov/data/tables/2016/demo/popest/nation-total.html;
http://bea.gov/iTable/iTable.cfm?ReqID=9&step=1#reqid=9&step=3&isuri=1&904=
1929&903=6&906=q&905=1000&910=x&911=0

spending increased largely through the Servicemen's Readjustment Act of 1944,[5] popularly known as the G.I. Bill. It provided such benefits for returning World War II veterans (GIs) as low-interest mortgages; low-interest loans to start businesses; cash payments of tuition and living expenses to cover the costs of attending a university, high school, or vocational training program; and one year of unemployment compensation. There have been numerous recessions since 1947 (Fig. 5.1).

Before the Great Recession, the recession of 1981–1982 is considered by some to be the worst since the Great Depression.[6] It was created by design by the Federal Reserve Board, which raised the rate at which it charges member banks for loans. One effect was pushing mortgage rates to over 20 percent. The overall purpose was to squeeze unsustainable inflation out of the economy.[7] Yet, in Table 5.1, we see negligible changes in GDP and consumption per capita between 1981 and 1982. In response to this recession, Congress passed sweeping changes to finance and tax laws that laid the groundwork for the

---

[5] Pub. Law No. 78–346, 58 Stat. 284m.

[6] RICHARD C. AUXIER, *Reagan's Recession*, PEW RESEARCH CENTER (2010), www.pewresearch.org/2010/12/14/reagans-recession/ (last visited September 21, 2016).

[7] ROBERT B. BARSKY & LUTZ KILIAN, *A MONETARY EXPLANATION OF THE GREAT STAGFLATION OF THE 1970S* (Ford School of Bus. 2010).

S&L crisis later in the 1980s, which is seen in the reduction of both GDP and consumption per capita during the period 1990 and 1991 (see Chapters 3 and 4). The next recession lasted less than one year, in 2001, which saw an even smaller contraction than the recession of the early 1990s yet was also a period of expanding consumption.

The Great Recession started at the very end of 2007 and extended into the middle of 2009.[8] During this period, per capita GDP fell about 5 percent while consumption per capita fell about 4 percent. It was the nation's largest economic contraction since the Great Depression, during which per capita GDP fell 29 percent and per capita consumption fell 21 percent. While the Great Recession may have been less calamitous than the Great Depression, its lingering effects nonetheless lasted longer than any other downturn since.[9]

During this 86-year period, from 1929 through 2015, there have been thirteen economic recessions. Recessions (including the Great Depression) occur on average about every 6.6 years, with the time between recessions tending to be longer in more recent times. Nonetheless, recessions are normal, even if the excess permitting-induced Great Recession is not. As recessions have occurred in the past with some degree of consistency and can be expected in the future, the prudent individual, business, or government should base their plans on a continuation of these historical events. In the context of development permitting, for instance, wise local policy may be to hedge on issuing fewer permits than more. We will offer further thoughts about this later.

EXCESSIVE CONSTRUCTION PERMITTING AS A LEADING INDICATOR OF RECESSIONS

Many recessions are preceded by excessive development permitting that can be a leading indicator of imminent downturn. We will look at two sets of data to show this. The first is of nonresidential development permitted during the 1980s leading to the S&L crisis described in Chapter 3. The second is a longer view of residential permitting over the fifty-year period from 1965 through 2014, focusing on permitting during the 2000s.

---

[8] See JOHN WEINBERG, *The Great Recession and Its Aftermath*, FEDERAL RESERVE HIST. (Dec. 3, 2013), www.federalreservehistory.org/Period/Essay/15.

[9] From Table 4.1, it appears that the Great Depression may have run its course by 1939 or nearly a decade after its start. The Great Recession lasted from late 2007 into the middle of 2009, but its effects lingered into 2013, a period of six years.

Table 5.2 Nonresidential Construction

Period	Average Annual Nonresidential Construction ($millions)	Average Annual Employment (thousands)	Average Annual Nonresidential Construction per Worker	Change in Construction per Worker from 1975–1980 Base
1975–1980 Base	$163,778,914	107,538	$1,522,990	
1981–1985	$221,784,784	117,810	$1,882,570	24%
1986–1990	$243,742,954	132,771	$1,835,819	21%
1991–1995	$190,176,714	141,733	$1,341,794	-12%

Source: Adapted from *Statistical Abstract of the United States*, 1999.
Note: Figures in 2015 dollars.

NONRESIDENTIAL CONSTRUCTION, 1975–1995

The S&L crisis was driven substantially by overpermitting nonresidential development. While national-level permitting and structure records are not available for analysis, aggregate nonresidential construction spending is. Such spending includes new construction, repairs, replacement, and rehabilitation of the nonresidential stock. Spending is divided into five-year periods from 1975 to 1980 through 1991 to 1995, reported in Table 5.2. The period 1981–1985 includes the inflation reduction–induced recession of the early 1980s while the period 1991–1995 includes the S&L crisis–induced recession of the early 1990s. Efforts to stimulate the economy by inducing real estate investment are shown. Construction spending per worker in the first half of the 1980s was 24 percent more than in the last half of the 1970s, while spending for the last half of the 1980s was 21 percent higher. Recall from Chapter 3 that using private inventory records, David Dowell showed that new office space built in the early 1980s could take a decade or more to be absorbed.[10] In effect, excessive nonresidential development during the 1980s allowed Dowell to predict that a recession would occur, and while recessions can be short-lived, effects can linger for years until the excess capacity is eventually absorbed.

---

[10] DAVID E. DOWELL. *Planners and Office Overbuilding.* JOURNAL OF THE AMERICAN PLANNING ASSOCIATION 52(2): 131–132 (1986).

■ RESIDENTIAL CONSTRUCTION, 2000–2015

The Great Recession was driven substantially by overpermitting and construction of residential development. This point was made in Chapter 4 but will be elaborated on here. As in most commodity markets, investors anticipate future demand by making investment decisions. In the face of growing housing demand, developers build homes. But too many developers can build too many homes largely because in the dearth of production information, no one knows what everybody else is doing, and the length of time between conceptualization and completion (see Chapter 6). In the 2000s, in addition to growing housing demand, the market was flooded with money to make frequently questionable home loans. The home ownership rate grew from about 66 percent to more than 69 percent, meaning that nearly all new housing units built were bought as opposed to rented. As housing production exceeded demand, however, the number of vacant units increased, as seen in Table 5.3. Excess supply usually leads to lower prices, so when millions of households could not sell homes even for the price they paid or the amount of their

Table 5.3 Housing Inventory and Vacant Units United States, 2000–2015

Year	Housing Units	Change in Housing Units	Vacant Units	Change in Vacant Units
2000	119,297	13,908		
2001	119,628	331	14,470	562
2002	120,834	1,206	14,332	(138)
2003	121,480	*646*	15,274	*942*
2004	123,318	*1,838*	15,599	*325*
2005	123,925	*607*	15,694	*95*
2006	126,012	*2,087*	16,437	*743*
2007	127,958	*1,946*	17,652	*1,215*
2008	130,113	*2,155*	18,704	*1,052*
2009	130,159	46	18,815	111
2010	130,599	440	18,739	(76)
2011	132,292	1,693	18,758	19
2012	132,778	486	18,266	(492)
2013	132,799	21	18,127	(139)
2014	133,270	471	17,809	(318)
2015	134,700	1,430	17,355	(454)

Source: Current Population Survey, Series H-111, Bureau of the Census, Washington, DC 20233

indebtedness, they faced foreclosure. Indeed, between 2003 and 2008, the number of vacant units increased by about 4.4 million units (see column "Change in Vacant Units" Table 5.3). The reason is that supply increased by 10.5 million units between 2001 and 2008 and the number of households increased by 9.3 million units, but demand (measured as the number of new households) increased by only 5.2 million. The demand was thus 4.1 million less than supply, explaining a large share of the 4.3 million more vacant units. Predictions of an excess housing-related recession were made throughout the early and middle 2000s, but local governments continued to issue more permits.

PREVENTING EXCESSIVE PERMITTING MATTERS BECAUSE REAL ESTATE IS THE LARGEST SINGLE ELEMENT OF THE ECONOMY

In 2015, real estate in the United States was worth about $35 trillion.[11] In contrast, the value of all stocks listed on all the stock exchanges in the United States was $25 trillion.[12] Not only is real estate the largest share of the nation's value, but it also accounts for more than $1 trillion annually to the nation's economy in construction.[13] We estimate that up to 50 million people or about a quarter of all the nation's jobs are directly or indirectly involved in construction, real estate sales and management, finance, law, utilities, and services relating to real estate. We point these facts out because as real estate permitting and development goes, so goes much of the nation's economy. In this section, we will show how vulnerable the nation's economy is to excessive development permitting.

Construction output, both residential and nonresidential, comes to nearly 10 percent of the GDP,[14] but there have been rather wild swings in construction activity. With construction being a significant component of GDP, it would follow that swings in construction activity would

---

[11] FEDERAL RESERVE. FINANCIAL ACCOUNTS OF THE UNITED STATES (Washington, DC: Federal Reserve 2016).

[12] See THE WORLD BANK, MARKET CAPITALIZATION OF LISTED DOMESTIC COMPANIES, http://data.worldbank.org/indicator/CM.MKT.LCAP.CD. Stocks of course include the value of real estate assets (last visited Nov. 21, 2016).

[13] U.S. CENSUS BUREAU, Value of Construction Put in Place at a Glance (2016), www.census.gov/construction/c30/c30index.html.

[14] NAT'L ECONOMIC DATA, U.S. Bureau of Econ. Analysis, http://bea.gov/iTable/iTable.cfm?ReqID=9&step=1#reqid=9&step=1&isuri=1&903=6 (last visited Nov. 21, 2016).

result in swings in aggregate activity. Figure 5.2 plots the quarterly per-cent changes in both construction and GDP and shows that construc-tion is much more volatile than GPD. During the period 2000–2015, while construction accounted for 10 percent of GDP, it also accounted for 30 percent of the change in GDP. Thus, construction or changes in construction are a very significant element in the nation's economic growth or decline. Just as there are economic cycles, there are housing construction cycles, illustrated in Figure 5.3 for the period 1959–2015.

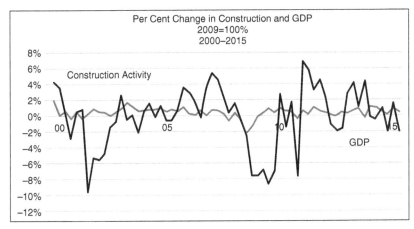

Figure 5.2 Percent change in construction and GPD, 2000–2015

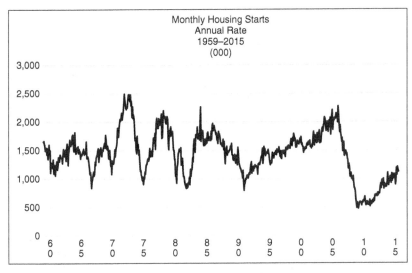

Figure 5.3 Monthly housing starts, 1959–2015

Figure 5.4 Plot of housing starts with total national unemployment

Cycles are a normal part of economic growth and change, but downturns are nonetheless disruptive. A key objective of the Federal Reserve System (Fed) is to dampen the effects of economic downturns, including sometimes committing vast sums of money—more than $1 trillion during the Great Recession—to do so. Its readiness to bail out economic sectors, however, leads to moral hazard, discussed in Chapters 3 and 4. We argue that the Fed should not be the sole source of economic discipline.

What was usual about the Great Recession was the strong correlation between residential permitting and employment, illustrated in Figure 5.4. This is attributable to a decline in housing starts, leading to increased unemployment, which resulted in a reduction in demand for housing, especially new housing.[15]

---

[15] A regression equation found $r^2 = .523$ with the t-ratio of unemployment with respect to housing starts is 16.9, well within a 99 percent level of significance. U.S. CENSUS BUREAU, *New Residential Construction*, www.census.gov/construction/ nrc/ historical data/index.html (last visited Nov. 21, 2016) (housing starts data); U.S. DEPT. OF LABOR, BUREAU OF LABOR STATISTICS, *Labor Force Statistics from the Current Population Survey*, www.bls.gov/cps/tables.htm#charunem (last visited Nov. 21, 2016) (unemployment data).

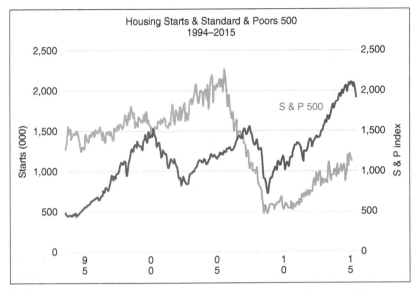

Figure 5.5 House starts plotted with Standard & Poor's 500 Index, 1994–2015

An interesting point is that residential permitting is not correlated with financial or investment activities. Figure 5.5 shows monthly housing starts plotted with the Standard & Poor's 500 Index[16] from 1994 to 2015. During this time, housing starts moved with financial markets but there are significant exceptions. The period 2000–2008 is notable in that as starts declined, markets rose, but as starts increased, the markets declined.[17] An important factor for housing starts is the level of existing inventory, both new construction and existing homes. Housing starts would occur substantially only when new demand for housing absorbs existing excess inventory. Nevertheless, looking to financial markets to gain an understanding of the dynamics of housing does not appear to be productive.

Once a home is built, it goes into the existing stock of housing. If it is unsold, it goes into an inventory of available units, commonly referred to as *inventory*. When inventories are high, new construction will tend to decline, with accompanying declines in economic

---

[16] Historic data for the index were taken from YAHOO FINANCE, http://finance.yahoo. com/q/hp?s=%5EGSPC&a =00&b=3&c=1994&d=01&e=1&f=2016&g=m (last visited Nov. 21, 2016). The data shown is the monthly close of the index.

[17] The regression equation results in r^2 = .01, which indicates virtually no correlation between the S&P 500 Index and housing starts, at least during the period 1995–2015.

activity and employment. There has been a long-term tendency toward increasing numbers of vacant units. This is due in part to the increasing number of vacation or second homes, as they are included in the inventory of vacant homes because they are not occupied year-round. New construction is divided between newly occupied units and additions to vacant inventory (see Table 5.3). Though the two series tend to move together, the correlation is weak.[18] Focusing on the post-2000 period, about half of all new residential units built were vacant on completion (as opposed to being sold before completion) and went into inventory. An increasing inventory of any good, including housing, tends to result in increasing price competition and price reductions.

Housing prices for new and existing homes had been increasing rapidly prior to 2007, and these increases were followed by an equally rapid decline, proving once again that what goes up can also come down. Putting the dynamics of housing supply together with prevailing prices yields a more complete understanding of the housing market. Normal perturbations in year-to-year inventory have no effect on the tendency toward increasing prices of both existing and new homes. However, the sharp increases in construction activity and unsold inventory beginning in 2006 resulted in correspondingly substantial decreases in prices. Between 2003 and 2007, the housing inventory increased by 23 percent, resulting in median price reductions of 12 percent for new homes and 22 percent for existing units. However, this is only very weak statistical correlation between the changes in vacant units and changes in median prices.[19] Nevertheless, there is some inverse relationship between inventories and prices, such that increased housing inventories tend to be associated with decreased prices. These relationships are shown in Figure 5.6.

Though we have established the role of excessive development permitting in triggering the Great Recession as well as the economic and employment fallout, what about the people—especially homeowners—who bore much of the brunt? We address this next.

---

[18] Over the period 1965–2015, the adjusted r^2 is .30, but the t-ratio of new construction and new vacancies is 4.63. So there is some correlation, but the explanatory power is weak.

[19] Adjusted r^2 for changes in median prices for new units was only .145 but the t-ratio was 1.9 and the F statistic is 3.5, indicating that there is some inverse relationship between changes in inventory and median prices for new homes, but explanatory power is weak. There is no apparent correlation between changes in inventory and median prices of existing homes. This indicates that the prices of new homes are more sensitive to levels of inventory than the prices of existing homes.

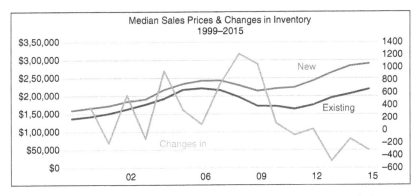

Figure 5.6 Median sales prices of new and existing homes and changes in residential inventories, 1999–2015

▌EXCESSIVE PERMITTING AND FORECLOSURES

Increased unemployment together with declining home prices created a difficult spot for many. Prior to the Great Recession, real estate was "hot." Massive numbers of homes were built and offered for prices that had previously been infeasible. But banks offered mortgages that financed purchases at those prices and it appeared that the sky was the only limit. This period of euphoria, or what Alan Greenspan—then the chairman of the Federal Reserve Board—called "irrational exuberance," came to an end. Declining prices and increasing unemployment were then combined with a collapse of the financial sector of the U.S. economy. Those unsold homes in inventory were joined by short sales and foreclosures to further increase the inventory while financial institutions greatly limited their extension of loans, especially mortgages. Greenspan's "irrational exuberance" began in the 1990s and simply exploded after 2000. The explosion in mortgages was followed by an implosion, where total mortgages outstanding actually decreased. The nadir was reached in 2010, with mortgage activity coming back at a very rapid pace.

These problems combined to create massive and heretofore unheard of rates of foreclosures. While the declining number of housing starts and the growing delinquencies in mortgages have the same basic cause, it follows that they would move together. Declining starts lead to increased unemployment and increased unemployment leads to delinquencies[20] and ultimately foreclosures. These relationships are shown in Figure 5.7.

---

[20] Federal Reserve, *Mortgage Debt Outstanding*, www.federalreserve.gov/econres-data/releases/mortoutstand/current.htm (last visited Dec. 8, 2016).

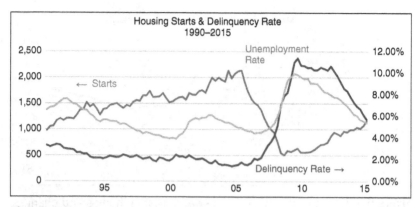

Figure 5.7 Housing starts, delinquency rates, and unemployment, 1990–2015

The chain of causality begins with excess supply of housing, which leads to an increase in unsold inventory and then a decline in housing starts and construction employment. Increased unemployment, and not just construction, results in economic distress of households and increased delinquencies. Adding the unemployment rate to the starts and delinquencies graphic demonstrates this point. Of course, there were many other economic declines and housing did not cause the Great Recession by itself. But the coincidence of declining housing starts, unemployment, and mortgage delinquencies is easily seen.

It would be expected that increasing delinquencies would eventually lead to increased foreclosures, and this is the case. Both the delinquency and foreclosure rates are unprecedented.[21] It is not possible to exactly measure how many foreclosures would have occurred if not for the Great Recession, but the 2000–2005 period does provide some insight. Between 2000 and 2005, the number of foreclosures averaged 602,000 per year. If the 2000–2005 average of 602,000 is accepted as normal annual foreclosures, then 17 million residential foreclosures are attributable to the Great Recession,[22] a phenomenon illustrated in Figure 5.8.

---

[21] These data are not available for the Great Depression of the 1930s, when such rates would have been expected.

[22] A total of 21.3 million foreclosures occurred between 2007 and 2014, as contrasted with an expected 4.2 million. *See* FEDERAL RESERVE BANK OF ST. LOUIS, *Delinquency Rate on Single-Family Residential Mortgages, Booked in Domestic Offices, All Commercial Banks,* https://research.stlouisfed.org/fred2/series/DRSFR-MACBN# (last visited Nov. 21, 2016).

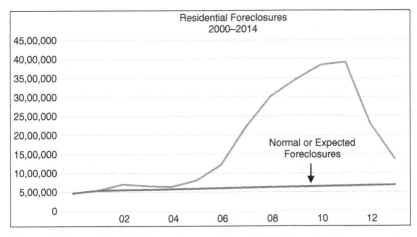

Figure 5.8 Residential foreclosures from 2000 to 2014, comparing actual to expected foreclosures by year

Clearly, the housing market, the stock market, and employment rates were all adversely impacted by excessive residential permitting during the 2000s. How did local government fare? We review this next.

The Great Recession is considered "great" because of the coincidence of many economic calamities. The "irrational exuberance" that was an important cause of the economic cataclysm influenced many of the busts that came together to become the Great Recession. There has been a great deal of discussion in the country about how to avoid a similar economic calamity in the future. Legislation has been passed with the goal of reforming the financial sector and thus to reduce or eliminate the factors that contributed to the Great Recession. Yet, there has been no discussion of how overbuilding contributed to the severity of the downfall. Looking at more recent housing starts data can be a cause of concern. Since the nadir in 2009, construction activity has resumed the rate of growth that was experienced prior to the 2007 bust. Time will tell whether this is the expected recovery or the prelude to another bust.

The Great Recession led to massive unemployment; between 2007 and 2010, 11.7 million people lost their jobs.[23] Three million of these (26 percent) were construction workers and 500,000 were local

---

[23] U.S. DEPT. OF LABOR, BUREAU OF LABOR STATISTICS, *Databases, Tables & Calculators by Subject*, http://data.bls.gov/cgi-bin/dsrv.

government employees. Homeowners saw the value of their properties decline and local governments received fewer property taxes. The major policy question is: "What do we take away from this experience?" Is this something we wish to avoid in the future? If so, then actions need to be taken to prevent the oversupply that was a causal factor. Recent housing starts data raises a question as to whether any lesson has been learned from the Great Recession.

EXCESSIVE PERMITTING AND LOCAL GOVERNMENT FISCAL STRESS

Property taxes are a substantial portion of local government revenues. In 2013, property taxes were 47 percent of all local revenues and 73 percent of all local tax revenues (Table 5.4). While property taxes have been declining as a percentage of all local government revenues, they still remain an important component of local government finance. Property tax receipts are a function of the assessable or taxable value of the properties contained in the tax base.[24] The dynamic of much of the past has been increasing property values, increasing tax bases, increasing property taxes, and increasing taxpayer resistance to property taxes. The so-called taxpayer revolt has forced the shifting of revenue sources away from property taxes, but they remain an important source of revenue.[25] The declines in selling prices of both new and existing homes noted above became incorporated into the taxable values of properties, with the result being a decrease in taxable values and of property tax revenues. Because property taxable assessments are retrospective, commonly it will take two or more years for changes in market values to be reflected in tax bases.

Before the Great Recession, property tax receipts had been growing at 7 to 9 percent per year. After 2008 and the Great Recession, those receipts declined. Adjusting receipts for both inflation and population, real property tax receipts per capita fell by 4 percent, as contrasted with growth of 3 to 4 percent previously. These are national

---

[24] While each state differs in how taxable values are established, all states share the common characteristic of relating that value somehow to market prices.

[25] BENJAMIN HARRIS & BRIAN MOORE, *Residential Property Taxes in the United States*, Brookings (2013), www.brookings.edu/research/residential-property-taxes-in-the-united-states/.

Table 5.4 Local Government Revenues by Source, United States 2012

| | | Percent of | |
	Revenues (000)	Local Revenue	Tax Revenue
All revenue	$1,657,880,868		
General revenue	1,498,797,920		
Local revenue	918,798,330	100.0%	
Taxes	589,963,273	64.2%	100.0%
Property taxes	434,009,448	47.2%	73.6%
Other taxes	282,490,598	30.7%	47.9%
Other local source	46,344,459	5.0%	7.9%

Source: Bureau of the Census, Census of Governments, https://factfinder.census.gov/faces/tableservices/jsf/pages/productview.xhtml?pid=COG_2012_LGF002&prodType=table

Table 5.5 Florida County–Based Total and Property Tax Revenues

Year	Revenue Class	Per Capita	% Change from 2008
2013	All tax revenues	$586	–23%
	Property tax revenues	$429	–29%
2008	All tax revenues	$760	
	Property tax revenues	$602	

Source: Office of Economic and Demographic Research, Florida Legislature, Expenditures and Revenues Reported by County Governments, http://edr.state.fl.us/Content/local-government/data/revenues-expenditures/cntyfiscal.cfm.
Note: Figures are in 2014 dollars.

data. Those states more affected by the Great Recession would have experienced a greater decline (see Chapters 3 and 4). For example, real county property tax revenues in Florida went from $602 per capita in 2008 to $429 in 2013, a decline of 29 percent. Virtually all of the tax revenue decrease is attributable to the decline in property tax revenues. The fallout from the Great Recession has had a substantial impact on all local governments, especially on Florida counties (Table 5.5).

The fallout caused by the Great Recession did not end with unemployment and local government revenue declines. A total of 540,000 local government employees lost their jobs.[26]

---

[26] U.S. Census Bureau, *Government Employment & Payroll*, www.census.gov/govs/apes/ (last visited Dec. 8, 2016).

We surmise that local governments that permit the construction of excess dwellings ultimately bear the costs. Developers or builders certainly will incur losses, with bankruptcy being the likely result and the protections afforded by bankruptcy laws. But it falls to local governments to cope with the consequences of ill-advised development and to do so with declining revenues. The wiser policy is to avoid the situation in the first place.

In Chapter 6, we begin to outline an approach for local government to prevent future excess permitting.

The Role of Institutions in Advancing Market Demand– Based Planning and Permitting, and Its Legal Context

Part 2 asserts that achieving market demand–based planning and permitting (MDBPP) may be much easier than many realize. It starts with Chapter 6, which focuses on the role of market-based information to facilitate efficient market outcomes. We now have the tools to inform all development decision-makers about the supply of development that exists, is under construction, has been permitted, and otherwise is in various stages of planning review. The trouble is that few local governments collect and share that information in a way that is useful to development decision-makers. This chapter is devoted to outlining the elements of such a development information system and how key decision-makers can, should, and even be required to use it.

While some may assume that MDBPP requires special legislation and even major federal action, this may not be the case. Chapter 7 shows that the framework already exists to create local-regional collaborations to craft market demand–based plans and implement them through permitting that is in accordance with those plans. The key is to use existing metropolitan planning organizations (MPOs) and similarly constituted regional agencies to create collaborative market demand–based plans that may already be enabled. Then, using existing technologies summarized in Chapter 6, we recommend that regional agencies use existing powers to generate publicly available analysis showing the progress of each local government in meeting or exceeding market demand–based permitting so that all decision-makers in a region know what all other jurisdictions are doing.

The overall planning framework creating MDBPP can lead to many collateral benefits, only some of which are reviewed in Chapter 8. These include anticipating public facility needs, addressing regional and local affordable housing needs, identifying lands more and less appropriate for development, determining land use configurations that minimize public costs and maximize economic benefits, improving accessibility between land uses, and so forth.

The next two chapters provide the regulatory and legal framework for market demand–based planning and permitting. We are struck by how much has already been done to make this possible, and for the most part the authority seems to already exist to implement many of its key features.

In Chapter 9 we outline key ingredients of a federal and state strategy to use MDBPP to prevent overbuilding in the future. We note that MDBPP is not a novel idea and draw comparisons to the health care industry, where several very conservative states require a Certificate of Need for new or expanded health care facilities. MDBPP is also endemic throughout state public utility statues. The rationale for these MDBPP requirements is to prevent the overbuilding of facilities that may impose excessive costs on taxpayers in the future and to instill discipline in the market for these and related facilities.

This chapter also shows there is ample legal rationale through constitutional, statutory, and case law provisions for MDBPP. We show that several federal environmentally related acts require market demand–based analysis under certain conditions, that federal farm support programs are defended as efforts to more carefully balance demand with supply, and that federal agencies can impose production quotas on various products to ensure an adequate supply relative to demand.

In Chapter 10, we address how government agencies can facilitate MDBPP. In addition to being more diligent in matching planning and permitting with development needs as provided in comprehensive plans, we pose a role for MPOs. Congress has charged them to prepare regional transportation plans for their respective metropolitan areas and to help implement those plans through transportation investments using federal state and local funds. While MPOs would not have the authority to change local development decisions, their transportation plans and funding strategies could be used to facilitate new development at such times and locations to meet market demand in accordance with a plan.

CHAPTER **6**

The Role of Market-Based Information to Ensure Efficient Market Outcomes

▌PERSPECTIVE

People comprise markets that synthesize information to guide their self-maximizing decisions to make and manage investments and to liquidate them. High-quality information can lead to more prudent decisions. Insider information, for instance—where a person knows what is going to be announced before it is—can lead a person to buy or sell assets based on special access to that information. The outcome is profitable to the person possessing insider information but detrimental to others. The result is inefficient allocation of resources because of exclusive access to information. Efficient markets depend on accurate information that is equally available to everyone.

In this chapter we argue that an important role of government is to provide high-quality information about real estate markets—information that is equally accessible to all real estate decision-makers. We start by reviewing key elements of efficient real estate markets. We proceed to outline a structure for real estate information that should be assembled and made available at the regional level. We then review models of such systems used across the country, focusing on how they elevate real estate decisions in ways that facilitate MDBPP—especially preventing overpermitting.

ELEMENTS OF AN EFFICIENT REAL ESTATE MARKET

Efficient real estate development occurs when maximum total benefits exceed maximum total costs. Benefits and costs fall broadly into five categories: private, public, social, equity, and intergenerational. Private costs are mostly the province of real estate developers and users of real property. When private revenues exceed costs, profit is earned and efficiency is achieved from the private perspective. If real estate development generates more fiscal revenue (from taxes, fees, and other sources) than the costs to serve it, efficiency is achieved from the public perspective. One can imagine situations where private efficiency is achieved but public efficiency is not. A solution would be exactions on new development to mitigate adverse impacts provided they result in more benefits than costs for both private and public entities.

Social efficiency is more complex, as it can include such factors as environmental protection, public health, public safety, and the provisions of public goods (e.g., open spaces, historically/culturally/scientifically significant landscapes, scenic views and vistas). Developments that are efficient from both private and public perspectives may be inefficient from social perspectives. Identifying whether and the extent to which social efficiencies are achieved often requires expert analysis as well as negotiation and sometimes litigation.

Efficiency from an equity perspective can be viewed as a Pareto optimum challenge. The Pareto optimum requires that no action be taken unless at least one person is made better off and no one is made worse off. Private decisions are not normally made this way, even though they have Pareto-relevant outcomes. For instance, a development decision can benefit many people (e.g., investors, workers, financiers, Realtors) but arguably harm others (e.g., some neighbors, taxpayers if there are net negative fiscal outcomes, consumers if facilities become congested). So long as one person is worse off, the Pareto optimum is not achieved. This may be impossible to attain. The alternative concept of potential Pareto optimum provides that so long as more people are better off than worse off, the decision is efficient. But equity also requires that gains from the winners be used to offset the losses from the losers—this would be the compensatory Pareto optimum. If that calculus includes social efficiency considerations, the outcome would be efficient because benefits exceed costs and equity is achieved through mitigation, compensation, or other means.

Intergenerational efficiency may be the least well understood. Conceptually, actions by the current generation should not compromise choices of future generations—a foundation of sustainability. But few if any decisions made today do not compromise decisions of future generations.

Private decisions in real estate development can be efficient from the perspective of only those decision-makers but can lead to inefficient public, social, and intergenerational outcomes. Those outcomes can be considered market failures. Douglass B. Lee, Jr., succinctly reviews the nature of market failure and the need for intervention.[1] To reiterate and expand on the points raised in Chapter 4, efficiently functioning markets must meet conditions such as the following, for which we also note limitations:

- There are many *buyers and sellers* for any given property. This ensures choice, which creates competition among sellers. For many kinds of properties, however, there are few buyers and sellers.

- There are no *transaction costs*, such as the cost of title insurance, real estate commissions, closing costs, legal services, and enforcement of contracts. However, in real estate, there are always transaction costs and, often, the more complex the property, the higher the transaction costs.

- Developers can *enter or leave markets* instantly and are not saddled by excess stock when demand softens, such as when unemployment increases or interest rates go up. The reality is that once committed to a transaction, developers cannot easily exit markets but once outside, it is also difficult to enter markets.

- Real estate developers and tenants (including owners) fully *internalize the externalities* they impose on others or society because of the manner in which they use property. Lacking information or institutions that generate such information, developers and tenants do not internalize their externalities, which results in other individuals or society as a whole paying those costs in many ways.

- All decision-makers have *perfect information* about any given property, including the physical property characteristics, social and equity impacts, intergenerational implications, and especially market-demand details. The problem is that information

---

[1] DOUGLASS B. LEE, JR., *Land Use Planning as a Response to Market Failure*, in THE LAND USE POLICY DEBATE IN THE UNITED STATES (Judith I. De Neufville, ed., 1981).

is never perfect. Instead, information is often proprietary so only some decision-makers have access to it—often excluding public officials.

As a result, private real estate development decisions do not meet many of these conditions. But neither does public management of development processes necessarily lead to efficient real estate decisions. What is missing is a land development information system (LDIS) that can be used to improve market dynamics in ways that help overcome market limitations. For instance, the LDIS used by Corvallis, Oregon—a city of about 50,000—has these objectives:[2]

- Achieve diversity in type, scale, and location of professional, industrial, and commercial activities to maintain a low unemployment rate and to promote diversification of the local economy

- Monitor changes in demographic information to ensure that the type, quantity, and location of services, facilities, and housing remain adequate to meet changing needs

- Work with other jurisdictions to ensure that adequate land in the urban area is available to meet housing needs during the planning period and to prevent development patterns that preclude future urbanization

- Continue to identify housing needs and help find ways in which to address them

- Ensure that adequate land is designated and districted to allow for manufactured home parks and subdivisions

- Publish an annual report that includes an assessment of progress in these respects

Several objectives address market concerns. By seeking to achieve diversity in development, an effort is made to expand the supply of buyers and sellers. This is also made directly in terms of meeting housing needs. Notice especially the provision to provide adequate land to meet housing needs (which when read with the first provision implies providing land to meet all projected development needs). As a matter of law, Oregon requires all local governments to zone sufficient land

---

[2] CITY OF CORVALLIS, OREGON, CORVALLIS LAND DEVELOPMENT INFORMATION REPORT (2015), www.corvallisoregon.gov/modules/showdocument.aspx?documentid=9470.

in the present to meet projected future needs.[3] This obviates the need for zone changes that can lead to procedural delays and court challenge. In this way, transaction costs are reduced.[4] Moreover, by zoning land that is sufficient to meet future needs in Oregon usually means that environmental and other concerns have already been addressed, thus avoiding case-by-case rezoning decisions. This process addresses the need to internalize externalities. Finally, by providing sufficient land to meet projected future needs, better (though not perfect) information is provided to the market, enabling more efficient decision-making by all actors in the development decision-making process.

The next section reviews how land development information systems are designed and work in ways that help facilitate MDBPP.

FOUNDATIONS OF A LAND DEVELOPMENT INFORMATION SYSTEM

In Chapter 2 we reviewed the basic elements of planning, namely projections of development needs; inventory and assessment of the capacity to accommodate future development without any change in current plan designations or infrastructure capacity; identification of land needed to be developed or redeveloped to meet future development needs along with the new or expanded facilities needed to serve it; and a development monitoring system to track plan progress. In this section, we outline the LDIS development and monitoring process. Ours is just another name for the genre of geographic information system-based spatially related databases that inform actors in the development decision-making process.[5]

An LDIS is often organized into several parts that address land supply, development capacity, inventory of development from a baseline year (such as when a plan and implementing ordinances were adopted), assessment of remaining capacity, and sometimes a

3 Gerrit J. Knaap & Arthur C. Nelson, The Regulated Landscape (Lincoln Inst. of Land Policy 1992).
4 Arthur C. Nelson & James B. Duncan, Growth Management Principles and Practice (Am. Planning Ass'n 1995).
5 There are perhaps dozens of alternative names used in practice, but they all have common features. Common names include land information system, development monitoring system, development information management system, land supply and capacity monitoring, automated land supply information system, and land monitoring system, among many others.

summary of the extent to which assumptions underlying the current plan and allocation of land remain current. During the planning process, the LDIS can aid in the allocation of land for development using the following highly generalized steps:

- Inventory total land in the planning area and determine that which is already developed and vacant but cannot be developed or redeveloped because of environmental or other constraints;

- Assess the capacity of developed land to absorb projected new development such as through infill and redevelopment during the planning horizon—if less than needed, then add more land to the planning area or increase the development capacity of existing land;

- Provide sufficient infrastructure to meet projected development needs; and

- Through zoning and other land-use regulations, allocate sufficient land to meet projected development needs through the planning horizon.

In allocating land for development through the planning horizon, Knaap and Hopkins (2001) recommend the following additional adjustments:[6]

- *Lead-time inventory*, including land that is needed to accommodate projected growth in the planning area, such as land that may not be available for development until infrastructure capacity is provided or other constraints are removed;

- *Safety-stock inventory*, which is land needed in case growth is faster than projected; and

- *Market-factor inventory*, which is land needed to provide developer options and consumer choice to prevent market monopolies from rising.[7]

Historically, once a plan had been prepared, it was difficult to monitor development and the extent to which it occurs in accordance with

---

[6] GERRIT J. KNAAP & LEWIS D. HOPKINS, *The Inventory Approach to Urban Growth Boundaries*, 67 J. AM. PLAN ASS'N 314 (2001).

[7] *See also* ARTHUR C. NELSON, PLANNER'S ESTIMATING GUIDE: ESTIMATING LAND USE AND FACILITY NEEDS (Am. Planning Ass'n 2004).

a plan. This has changed. There is now the potential to monitor development and infrastructure activities continuously, compare them to planning benchmarks, and identify unforeseen needs or circumstances requiring plan or regulatory adjustments.

A key advance has been in the quality of data and the ability to evaluate those data spatially through LDIS approaches. Foundational thinking about this potential has its roots in David Godschalk et al. (1986).[8] Such a system would be comprised of three sets of spatially interactive data:

• Parcel data records assessor records, including such information as ownership, land use, values, and jurisdictional location;

• Planning data linked to each parcel, such as planning designation, zoning and other land-use controls, and (ideally) environmental constraints such as wetlands, floodplains, slopes, fault lines, liquefaction areas, and so forth; and

• Development project information collected for approved subdivisions, site plan approvals, and other forms of land-use approvals relating to approval conditions, permits issued, and the overall progress of development through a tracking system.

A decade later, however, Anne Moudon and Michael Hubner lamented the paucity of jurisdictions that established monitoring systems to generate routine inventory assessments of its entire land supply or development capacity.[9] Nor had many existing monitoring systems "used it as a tool to measure on a regular basis the effectiveness of policies and regulations and the possible impacts of new regulations, policies, or land development practices."[10] Into the early decades of the 2000s, however, such systems have become commonplace.

Though the pioneering literature on land development information systems was extensive from about the middle 1990s to middle 2000s, there has been a remarkable dearth since then. We surmise that LDISs are becoming increasingly commonplace. The next challenge is to

---

[8] DAVID R. GODSCHALK, SCOTT BOLLENS, JOHN S. HEKMAN & MIKE MILES, LAND SUPPLY MONITORING (Oelgeschlager, Gunn & Hain 1986).

[9] ANNE MOUDON & MICHAEL HUBNER, MONITORING LAND SUPPLY WITH GEOGRAPHIC INFORMATION SYSTEMS: THEORY, PRACTICE AND PARCEL-BASED APPROACHES (Wiley 2000).

[10] ANNE & MICHAEL HUBNER, MONITORING LAND SUPPLY AND CAPACITY WITH PARCEL-BASED GIS (1999) (unpublished manuscript) (on file with University of Washington).

make them more proactive in planning, development, and market-based permitting processes. The example of the Portland Metro Council may be instructive, which we review next.

CASE STUDY: PORTLAND METRO REGIONAL LAND INFORMATION SYSTEM

Oregon may be unique in the nation in requiring all cities and counties to identify market demand–based development needs, especially relating to housing, design plans to meet all those needs, and designate sufficient land through zoning and other development tools to meet those needs over a planning period—typically ten years.[11] Though Oregon's system can be viewed as being too restrictive in using urban growth boundaries (UGBs) to preserve farmland and other important open spaces, thereby restricting supply and raising prices,[12] research shows prices are actually lower than market-based predictions, presumably because demand is met more efficiently in Oregon than elsewhere.[13] Indeed, "it is erroneous to conclude from Portland's experience that UGBs inevitably cause home prices to rise faster."[14] How is this possible? The Portland Metro Council's regional land information system (RLIS)[15] may be one reason.

Because Oregon requires that all urban development needs be identified and met within UGBs, and given that UGBs constrain the supply of land, the Portland Metro Council created the RLIS in the late 1980s to help achieve potentially conflicting objectives. It consists of more than one hundred geographic information system (GIS) data layers that comprise the entire spatial data infrastructure for the metropolitan Portland area. The layers are regularly updated and made available online through a suite of Web services linked to large datasets.

Portland Metro's RLIS serves the needs of multiple users such as planners, utility companies, realtors, and especially the development industry. For example, for any given parcel, area, or entire jurisdiction,

---

11 *Supra* note 3.
12 ANTHONY DOWNS, *Have Housing Prices Risen Faster in Portland Than Elsewhere?* 13 HOUS POLICY DEBATE 7, at 7 (2002).
13 ARTHUR C. NELSON, *Comment on Anthony Downs's "Have Housing Prices Risen Faster in Portland Than Elsewhere?"* 13 HOUS POLICY DEBATE 33 (2002).
14 *Supra* note 12, at 7.
15 For details, see DATA RESOURCE CENTER, METRO, www.oregonmetro.gov/rlis-live.

the RLIS provides information on environmental features, terrain, development restrictions, planning designations, the nature and characteristics of vacant and developed land, census data, public utilities, streets and transit systems, and so forth. The RLIS even includes sketch plans for infill housing on residential parcels. Through the RLIS, it is possible to know the region's capacity for development to meet specific market needs. The RLIS thus helps the region and its local governments plan ahead to meet needs when supply lags behind demand. It can also be used to change land-use designations to prevent oversupplying land relative to emerging market demand–based needs.

THE FUTURE OF LAND DEVELOPMENT INFORMATION SYSTEMS

From a modest number of land development information systems in the early 1980s, LDISs now number well into the thousands. For most jurisdictions, it is now possible to understand the development capacity of jurisdictional land bases. Together with market studies of development need, it is therefore possible to match land supply with development needs.

CHAPTER 7

Local-Regional Collaboration as a New Line of Defense against Cyclical Real Estate Crashes

▌OVERVIEW

Accounts of the Great Recession and its real estate crash fill library shelves. Books and movies, such as Michael Lewis's *The Big Short* and the 2010 documentary film *Inside Job* suggest many of its causes.[1] They highlight the big credit rating agencies' abdication of responsibility in giving investment grade ratings to deeply unstable tranches of mortgage-backed securities. And they document financial institutions' ethically bankrupt practice of making high-interest loans to families that could have qualified for lower mortgage rates. Absent from many of these accounts is the mention of the roles that may have been played by city and county elected officials, real estate developers, local government planning staff, planning and zoning boards, or city and county attorneys among others.

The Great Recession's popular narratives have assigned local governments a comparatively minor part in the recent real estate

---

[1] Several feature films and documentaries detailing the causes of the 2008 real estate crisis are discussed in Tom Huddleston, Jr, *These Seven Movies Tell the Real Story Behind the Financial Crisis*, FORTUNE (Dec. 27, 2015), http://fortune.com/2015/12/27/big-short-wall-street-movies/.

crisis, but it would be a mistake to ignore the role they *could* play in helping to soften the impact of the next real estate downturn.[2] We think some local governments could have been better stewards of neighborhoods. Chapters 3, 4, and 5 explain why it would be foolish to overlook the culpability of certain local governments and metropolitan regions, particularly in higher growth metro areas stretching from Miami to Las Vegas, including parts of the Northwest. In the years leading up to the real estate crash, many jurisdictions in these regions authorized new housing units, office space, or commercial space without any thought about whether market demand existed for those products.[3]

But in searching for a solution to widespread imprudent development approvals, we also realize that it is easy to unfairly characterize city and county development decisions. Local governments' largely enthusiastic approval of sprawling new development was no surprise.[4] They issued development orders in accordance with then-applicable zoning and land-use laws. Their approvals of rezonings or plan amendments reflect a long local government tradition of welcoming new development with the outlook "[i]f you build it; they will come."[5]

Leading up to the Great Recession of 2007–2009, local governments exercised the suite of tried-and-true zoning review powers given to them decades ago. As Chapter 1 explains, the twentieth-century evolution of local government land-use regulation means that cities, towns,

---

[2] Many scholars and practitioners have productively focused on how local and state government can correct the problems that led to the Great Recession and not on fixing blame for the real estate crisis. The Great Recession highlighted critical areas of need for local governments both to re-examine their comprehensive plans and zoning laws and to break new ground in collaborating with private sector stakeholders, state government partners, and neighboring local governments. See JENNIE C. NOLON AND JOHN R. NOLON, *Zoning and Land Use Planning: Land Use for Economic Development in Tough Financial Times*, 40 REAL EST. L. J. 237, 243–44, 255–56, 2014.

[3] See JAN G. LAITOS AND RACHEL MARTIN, *Zombie Subdivisions in the United States and Ghost Developments in Europe: Lessons for Local Governments*, 4 WASH. J. ENVTL L. & POL'Y 314, 321–22 (2015); JIM HOLWAY, DON ELLIOTT & ANNA TRENTADUE, ARRESTED DEVELOPMENTS: COMBATTING ZOMBIE SUBDIVISIONS AND OTHER EXCESS ENTITLEMENTS, 4–8 (2014).

[4] See HENRY R. RICHMOND, *Metropolitan Land-Use Reform: The Promise and Challenge of Majority Consensus* in REFLECTIONS ON REGIONALISM 10 (Bruce Katz, ed. 2000).

[5] HENRY L. DIAMOND & PATRICK F. NOONAN, LAND USE IN AMERICA 7 (1996).

and counties review zoning applications to make sure that proposed development complies with a range of technical restrictions. Cities and counties are required to ensure that new development comports with the property's use restrictions and dimensional zoning standards, such as height, setback, and floor space limitations. In many states, concurrency or adequate public facility requirements must also be satisfied to ensure sufficient infrastructure to support the water, roads, schools, and other amenities that new development will require.

These are the considerations that dominated local deliberations leading up to the Great Recession. The problem is that these time-honored zoning requirements are almost the sole focus of local government land-use restriction. In this chapter, we describe an approach to development review that also requires consideration of market demand, calling for invigorated regional coordination of land-use decisions but necessitating only relatively modest changes to local zoning codes and comprehensive plans.

THE REGIONAL STRUCTURE FOR MARKET DEMAND–BASED PLANNING ALREADY EXISTS

In our view, market demand–based planning and permitting not only obliges but also, through its inherent benefits, incentivizes local governments to cooperate across a metro region to implement a comprehensive and data-driven approach to assess and monitor market demand (as illustrated in Chapter 6 and expanded in this chapter). As detailed below, this approach will require coordinating and refining data collection, deputizing an existing metropolitan agency to analyze regional data and to advise individual local governments regarding anticipated demand, as well as amending existing local development ordinances and comprehensive plans in order to detail the way in which market demand analysis can guide local government development decisions. At the same time, market demand–based planning will give local governments and community stakeholders access to new sources of data that are now generally unavailable to them. An entity whose principal mission is region-wide would be the lead in preparing a regional market demand–based plan. It would also take the lead in developing a land development information system (LDIS), described in Chapter 6, which facilitates the local-regional collaboration in allocating long-term regional demand-based development.

These entities include the following, among others, that are enabled to perform region-scale land-use and development planning:

Metropolitan planning organizations (MPOs). MPOs were initially authorized by the Federal-Aid Highway Act of 1962. MPOs devise plans that guide the expenditure of federal transportation funds. They also coordinate the transportation planning process for their urbanized area. Federal transportation legislation since the 1990s has strengthened the MPO's role in planning and programming federally funded transportation projects by making them responsible for approving the expenditure of federal dollars. As of this writing, there are 420 MPOs. Nearly half of these operate as part of a regional council or council of governments serving the same general geography.[6]

Councils of governments (COGs). COGs can also be called *regional councils, regional planning commissions, regional commissions,* or *planning districts,* among other names. They are multiservice entities that deliver a range of federal, state, and local services in addition to providing planning and technical assistance services. COGs are accountable to the local governments whom they serve as well as to state and federal agencies, depending on specific COG activities. They were initiated by the federal government in the 1960s but have assumed important state roles since. Of the 39,000 local, general-purpose governments in the nation—such as counties, cities, townships, towns, villages, and boroughs—more than 35,000 are served by COGs.[7]

Regional transportation planning organizations (RTPOs). RTPOs serve mostly nonmetropolitan areas, often under contract by state departments of transportation (DOTs). They are also called *rural planning organizations, regional planning affiliations, regional transportation planning agencies,* or *regional planning commissions,* among others. Their principal function is to assist state DOTs with statewide transportation planning requirements. In 2012, federal laws were changed to require RTPOs

---

[6] Language adapted, including portions verbatim, from National Association of Regional Councils, Regional Councils, COGs & MPOs, http://narc.org/about-narc/cogs-mpos/. *See also* Janice C. Griffith, *Regional Governance Reconsidered,* 21 J. L. & POL. 505, 535 (2006) (describing MPOs as one of several existing forms of regional structures).

[7] *Id.*

to develop rural, regional, long-range transportation plans; create short-range transportation improvement programs; conduct public outreach; and coordinate transportation with other relevant planning areas, among other tasks.[8]

We call these as a group regional planning agencies (RPAs).[9] What they have in common is the ability to coordinate local land-use planning to address regional transportation needs.

In most regions, a significant investment of resources will be necessary to implement market demand–based planning. But these resources will be wisely invested if market demand–based planning and permitting is effective in curbing future real estate crises. Resources dedicated to augmenting regional and local data collection capabilities, improving intergovernmental coordination, and enhancing local governments' capacity for reviewing development applications promise to yield long-term returns in the form of steady property tax revenues, smarter investments of limited local government funds, and predictable code enforcement budgets.

There is a wide range of regional approaches to coordinating local development approvals within the context of regional market demand.[10] On one end of the spectrum, local governments could agree to optional compliance with annually generated market-demand estimates. Voluntary regional growth compacts, such as the Mile High Compact that unites metro Denver's local governments, have achieved some success at maintaining regional consensus around basic growth-management principles.[11] At the other end of the spectrum would be a stricter approach that mandates consistency of local government development decisions with periodic demand projections, such as seen with several state approaches outlined in Chapter 2 and those of the Portland Metro Council detailed in Chapter 6.

---

[8] Language adapted, including portions verbatim, from Rural Transportation.org, *About RTPOS*, RURAL TRANSPORTATION.ORG, http://ruraltransportation.org/about-rtpos/.

[9] In many states, this can include, for example, regional water management authorities.

[10] Regional approaches to land-use control are varied and include possibilities ranging from a centralized governmental agency with region-wide authority to make or veto local land-use decisions to a voluntary coalition of local governments and key regional stakeholders. Helpful discussions of these different schemes may be found in Janice C. Griffith, *Regional Governance Reconsidered*, 21 J. L. & POL. 505 (2006) and *Note, Old Regionalism, New Regionalism, and Envision Utah: Making Regionalism Work*, 118 HARV. L. REV. 2291 (2005).

[11] Interview with Daniel Jerrett, PhD, Chief Economist, Denver Regional Council of Governments (DRCOG), in Denver, Colorado (July 15, 2016).

What is needed is a new collaboration between local and regional governments as a new line of defense against cyclical real estate crashes. We do not prescribe a single approach to manage local-regional market demand–based planning activities, but any approach should include three core elements: (1) regional scope with a plan, (2) stakeholder engagement, and (3) implementation of the regional plan informed by market analysis. We elaborate on each of these elements below.

REGIONAL SCOPE WITH A PLAN

Market demand–based planning and permitting requires local governments to recognize that they are not making development decisions in a vacuum. A city or county approves developments that will not only affect its own real estate market but also very likely that of the entire region, though in vastly varying degrees. While one could argue that approving a permit for a small number of single-family residential units in the middle of a very large city will not have any measurable regional effect, the sum of multiple such permit approvals drives a gradual reshaping of a region. Market demand–based permitting acknowledges that all local governments in a region are impacted by the decisions of each. A key role of RPAs is to convene local governments to understand and address long-range development needs, so in this respect we are proposing nothing new. What is different is that local governments would collaborate to allocate development that is projected over a planning horizon. We will not presuppose the criteria used for this process, only that it leads to the allocation of market demand–based development that meets the region's shared development needs in a way that all local governments appreciate.[12]

Market demand–based analysis must be in the context of a regional plan that is comprised of the plans of individual local governments. MPOs already prepare regional transportation plans, and they do so

---

[12] We understand that evaluating demand is a complex task in part because demand analysis is based on different asset classes that are themselves highly segmented by development product and location within the region. But we also know that the capability to collect and analyze data has reached a high level of sophistication at the local and regional levels and that currently the finance, for-profit and nonprofit development, and construction communities already collect and evaluate this data during their due diligence process. Interview with Bill Mealor, Managing Director, Patterson Real Estate Advisory Group, in Atlanta, Georgia (Aug. 4, 2016).

cognizant of local government planning efforts. So we are not really adding anything new to regional planning processes but assembling more and better information about development needs and improved coordination among regional and local governments to allocate projected development. For their part, regional plans need to consider alternative scenarios that meet development needs. Envision Utah, for instance, has assisted numerous regional governments across the nation to understand what is unique about their region, what the core values are of its citizens, as well as projections of market demand–based development, and alternative ways in which to meet development demand that are consistent with core values.[13]

It seems that all RPAs generate population and often employment projections, frequently even for small areas such as transportation analysis zones (TAZs),[14] but very few provide detailed demographic, economic, and development projections. In the absence of detailed real estate market demand–based projections, the ability for regions and their local governments to address development needs is compromised. It need not be so, as demonstrated by the regional planning work that metropolitan regions are already doing and that top regional planning officials consider feasible.[15]

Perhaps the term *market study* has acquired negative connotations. Instead of serving as a rigorous tool for open and honest discussion, market studies are now frequently used by development project proponents as "advocacy tools honed to defend particular policies."[16] For now, we use the term *market demand–based analysis* to guide regional and local allocations of growth. But there is reason for optimism.

---

[13] See ENVISION UTAH, www.envisionutah.org/. *See also Note, Old Regionalism, New Regionalism, and Envision Utah: Making Regionalism Work*, 118 HARV. L. REV. 2291 (2005) (suggesting that Envision Utah provides a template for metropolitan regions grappling with how to establish meaningful regional collaboration for tackling critical regional land use issues).

[14] A TAZ is the unit of geography most commonly used in conventional transportation planning models *Traffic Analysis Zone*, WIKIPEDIA, https://en.wikipedia.org/wiki/Traffic_analysis_zone. While the size of a zone varies, they are typically comprised of fewer than 3,000 people in metropolitan areas.

[15] Interview with Michael Carnathan, Researcher, Atlanta Regional Commission (ARC), in Atlanta, Georgia (Aug. 4, 2016); interview with Daniel Jerrett, PhD, Chief Economist, Denver Regional Council of Governments (DRCOG), in Denver, Colorado (July 15, 2016); interview with Tim Reardon, Data Services Director, Metropolitan Area Planning Council (MAPC), in Boston, Massachusetts (June 17, 2016).

[16] Telephone interview with Ira Goldstein, PhD, President, Policy Solutions, the Reinvestment Fund (Aug. 23, 2016).

Dozens of RPAs generate detailed demographic and economic projections, and many generate affordable housing demand projections for their regions, often disaggregated to local government or smaller units of analysis, such as TAZs. Chapter 6 alluded to how these systems work and provided some examples. We surmise that the necessary digital technology, sophisticated databases, and the computer programs for generating market demand–based analyses already exist and are continually being refined, as we noted in Chapter 6. What might be missing is a universally accepted format for conducting these studies and assessing period performance in meeting market demand–based needs. Thus, we now suggest a possible outline for the market demand–based study.

The cornerstone of market demand–based permitting is a market study that guides the preparation and implementation of comprehensive plans. Many states already require that plans be based on population, housing, and employment projections (see Chapter 2), but we envision more rigorous analysis than is done by most RPAs. Without being prescriptive in detail, such analyses would include the following:

- Population projections by age (to understand age-based needs relating to education, senior services, and related considerations).
- Household projections by age, type (e.g., households with and without children, and single-person households), income, and housing tenure (to understand housing needs).
- Employment projections focusing on those jobs that occupy built space (e.g., offices as opposed to ocean fishing) by general land-use type (e.g., industrial, retail, service, office, education, institutional).
- Projections of change in the built environment such as new and replaced residential units and nonresidential space.
- Assessing projected future market demand–based needs with current supply to estimate the nature of new or infill/redevelopment needed to meet future demand, perhaps down the level of the parcel.

These analyses would be done for the entire region. There would be both a top-down analysis to establish baseline needs for the entire region and a bottom-up analysis to best allocate that demand to individual jurisdictions. These kinds of projections are the very essence of real estate market analysis. Given that governmental units should plan to meet the infrastructure, transportation, land use, and other needs of development, it seems sensible to identify those needs in more detail than is being projected presently by RPAs and the local governments they serve.

Dozens of RPAs already have compiled the core demand and supply data needed to project market demand–based development needs.[17] Using existing modeling software, such as UrbanSim[18] and PECAS (Production, Exchange, and Consumption Allocation System),[19] regions can use much of their own data to not only project future market demand but also to develop alternative growth projections based on alternative planning scenarios.[20] An important advance would be generating development capacity assessments at the parcel level. This would seem to require considerable investment of resources, especially among local governments, in order to adequately consider demand in their decision-making process. Yet, local governments are already collecting most of these data for a variety of purposes anyway.[21] Combined with regional studies on market

---

[17] Interview with Paul Waddell, PhD, Professor of City & Regional Planning, University of California–Berkeley, in Berkeley, California (July 20, 2016); interview with Ezra Rapport, Esq., Executive Director, Association of Bay Area Governments (ABAG), in San Francisco, California (July 19, 2016); interview with Daniel Jerrett, PhD, Chief Economist, Denver Regional Council of Governments (DRCOG), in Denver, Colorado (July 15, 2016); interview with Michael Carnathan, Researcher, Atlanta Regional Commission (ARC), in Atlanta, Georgia (Aug. 4, 2016). Interview with Mary Bo Robinson, Executive Director; Gary Kramer, Planner; and Caitlin Cerame, Planner, West Florida Regional Planning Council, in Pensacola, Florida (July 2, 2015).

[18] UrbanSim can be employed by local and regional governments to carry out a range of growth forecasting activities. See URBANSIM CLOUD PLATFORM, www.urbansim. com/. For example, the Denver metro region uses UrbanSim to perform a regional land-use analysis down to the parcel level for the nine-county region. Interview with Daniel Jerrett, PhD, Chief Economist, Denver Regional Council of Governments (DRCOG), in Denver, Colorado (July 15, 2016).

[19] Information on this system as well as the system's manual can be found at HBA INSPECTO INCORPORATED, www.hbaspecto.com/pecas/.

[20] For instance, Nelson led a team that created an open-source, freely downloadable scenario-planning package for just this purpose. See *Envision Tomorrow Plus*, www.arch.utah.edu/cgi-bin/wordpress-etplus/.

[21] For example, East Baton Rouge Parish has an integrated database that includes zoning designation, tax assessor information, and future land-use designation from the comprehensive plan. This system also includes integrating permit tracking across all departments, and information relating to vacant and abandoned property. Phone interview with Frank Duke, FAICP, Director of Planning, in East Baton Rouge Parish, Louisiana (Aug. 5, 2016).

demand–based needs, technology allows analysts, elected officials, and citizens to see outcomes to different planning scenarios down to the level of the parcel.

Once RPAs project regional market demand–based development needs, allocations are necessary to local governments and submarkets within them. These submarkets often have contrasting levels of market demand.[22] Some submarkets will be built out with very little near-term opportunity for development while others can absorb large amounts of development over the next few years and still others may be candidates for substantial redevelopment in the long-term. The nature and mix of development will also vary considerably between submarkets. But totaled over a market demand–based development time period, the sum of development among all submarkets will need to equal that which is projected for the region. Otherwise, the region's development needs will not be met, which undermines efficient development outcomes. All that is required is a cooperative process to address development needs across the region by all local governments, which we discuss next. These regional market demand–based plans will need to be updated periodically, as we discuss later.

▮ STAKEHOLDER ENGAGEMENT

All permitting authorities within a region and their constituencies will need to accept the allocation of projected development. Local government land-use decisions are sometimes seen as serving the goals of a relative handful of local interests. This concern about the integrity of the land-use approval process is arguably even greater in a market demand–based planning system. Broad community engagement is critical, because the periodic regional market study and associated reports will guide the allocation of development throughout the region.

Though we outlined the key features of market demand–based analysis above, acceptance requires engagement by all stakeholders throughout the analysis and allocation processes.[23] The best way to

---

[22] Interview with Bill Mealor, Managing Director, Patterson Real Estate Advisory Group, in Atlanta, Georgia (Aug. 4, 2016).

[23] Advocates for regional approaches to improved land-use decision-making highlight broad public participation as a key to a successful regional collaboration. *See* Brittan J. Bush, *New Regionalist Perspectives on Land Use and the Environment*, 56 HOWARD L.J. 207, 226–30 (2012).

avoid poor data analysis or misuse of the analysis process is to allow the region's stakeholders to be part of the analysis design and review processes. Many stakeholders will be experts in market analysis, including its limitations. Those stakeholders include a broad range of professional, business, institutional, nonprofit, and civic advocacy groups. The stakeholders for whom the regional market analysis will likely hold greatest interest are developers, bankers, affordable housing advocates, and real estate professionals. They will certainly need to be engaged in the design and interpretation of the periodic analysis. But stakeholders would also include neighborhood organizations, school funding proponents, transit activists, and environmental organizations to name a few.[24]

Market demand–based planning depends on the wisdom of the investment community, perhaps elevating it relative to conventional practice. It is also informed by concerns about affordable housing, protection of unique landscapes and places, and overbuilding. As a consequence of the savings-and-loan (S&L) crisis and the Great Recession, capital markets have become increasingly influential in evaluating market demand, such as issuing loans only when demand reaches a certain threshold. But it was only after the S&L crisis and after the housing bubble's burst that the capital markets begin to keep growth in check in "down cycles" by regulating lending more rigorously— perhaps too rigorously in some respects. Often, the local brokerage community can have important insights on near-term demand in a specific area that is useful when assessing whether a market is undersupplied with a certain product. The bottom line is that the development community writ large will want to share their views on local and regional real estate data and what that data suggests about the their community's development opportunities and constraints.[25]

It should go without saying that the entire process of market demand–based analysis is transparent and that everyone has access to the same information. As we noted in Chapter 6, markets work efficiently when information is plentiful and credible. It is also essential that market demand–based analysis has a solid deliberative and

---

[24] Nonprofit housing advocates stress that "justice requires that the whole community, including the poor and the powerless, be included in market demand analysis." E-mail from Kermit J. Lind, Clinical Professor of Law Emeritus, Cleveland-Marshall College of Law, Cleveland State University to John Travis Marshall (Oct. 11, 2016) (on file with author).

[25] We appreciate an interview on these and related points with Bill Mealor, Managing Director, Patterson Real Estate Advisory Group, in Atlanta, Georgia (Aug. 4, 2016).

democratic foundation; for instance, opportunities to comment on the periodic market demand–based analysis, including public hearings, will help serve these core values. The public feedback will also give the RPA an opportunity to modify the market reports or address criticisms.

IMPLEMENTATION OF THE REGIONAL PLAN INFORMED BY MARKET ANALYSIS

MPO plans are mostly limited to transportation while COG plans—including COGs that serve as MPOs for their regions—prepare more comprehensive regional plans. The scope of regional plans varies across the nation. In most states, there are few if any state guidelines for preparing and implementing regional plans. In some states, such as Georgia, regional plans address selected regional issues such as airshed management, but otherwise those plans are a composite of individual local government plans. In Florida, there are regional plans addressing natural resources and environmental issues, though there is a higher order of coordination between local and regional plans than seen in Georgia or most other states. In Oregon and Washington, local plans must be consistent with regional priorities, and they are prepared through a development allocation process similar to that outlined earlier.[26]

In our view, RPAs can best defend against cyclical real estate crashes if local governments agree to monitor market demand in concert with their neighboring counties and municipalities. This means that local governments must adopt the same general policy regarding the regional market demand–based development analysis serving as a guide for local review of applications for development approval. This coordination among local governments would be facilitated if a regional plan included consensus allocation of development among local governments. For their part, local government plans would help facilitate market efficiency by allocating sufficient land (through zoning or other land-use controls) served by adequate public facilities now to meet development needs through the near-term planning period, perhaps five to ten years. Once prepared to accommodate its share of the region's development, local and regional governments

---

[26] JERRY WEITZ, SPRAWL BUSTING: STATE PROGRAMS TO GUIDE GROWTH (1999).

may adopt the following decision rules to guide development review over a near-term planning period:

- So long as new development is consistent with projected market demand–based development needs, approval could be fast-tracked.
- If development proposed in one part of a city was less than anticipated but another development elsewhere more than anticipated, the local government could adjust its plans and codes to accommodate both and be consistent with the regional plan overall.
- Regional and local plans could include a market factor adjustment so that more development could be approved than projected; for example, Nelson recommends a 25 percent market factor for twenty-year planning horizons.[27]
- If cumulative development proposals in one community exceed the regional plan allocation, the reason may be that other communities experience less development than anticipated under their allocation. If the affected communities agree, there could be an efficient regional process to amend plans to rebalance the region's development allocations.
- There exists the prospect that one or more developments or proposals exceed market factor thresholds. This should trigger a reassessment of the regional market demand–based development analysis and local government allocations. Assuming that market demand–based development studies occur about every five years, we anticipate this exercise may be rare.

The LDIS is the logical home for market demand–based development analysis. It would be available openly. It would also be updated periodically through a process that would likely vary depending on the nature of the information, such as annual (or more frequent) updates to incorporate new building permits data or every five years or so for new Census numbers.

The end result could be a comprehensive data collection and analysis system on which to base a regional permit coordination process. Successful interjurisdictional permitting systems have been difficult

---

[27] ARTHUR C. NELSON, PLANNER'S ESTIMATING GUIDE: ESTIMATING LAND USE AND FACILITY NEEDS (2004).

to establish.[28] But experts generally agree that permit coordination gives local and state governments the best shot at being effective stewards of local and regional resources. The LDIS could facilitated permit coordination by informing all players in the development decision-making process about what is being developed, where, and when it is completed.

MARKET DEMAND–BASED PLANNING AS A MOSTLY EXISTING TOOL TO MANAGE PERMITTING

Market demand–based development analysis logically leads to market demand–based permitting and as such has a role in the local government's planning and development "toolbox." Market demand–based planning may have a different utility to development professionals working in distinct metropolitan regions. A county commission in metropolitan Atlanta may find market based–demand planning a critical tool to help verify actual market demand and thus, hopefully, to help manage permitting to prevent overpermitting in subareas or of product types. For example, such a system may have been able to prevent overexuberant single-family housing development during the 2000s development approvals in exurban metropolitan Atlanta and in the Miami metropolitan area, where the condominium market was flooded with excess units. In Boston, where significant market demand exists for various types of housing development but where local governments judiciously consider new development proposals due to concerns about traffic congestion, school overcrowding, and infrastructure development, market based–demand permitting may serve a different function. It may help identify the greatest sectors of housing demand so that the local government can prioritize the types of residential development it should encourage. In other words, in considering market demand–based permitting's benefits to a particular metropolitan region, the local development climate will significantly influence how this tool is used.

Local government development permitting presents contrasting realities. In metropolitan Boston, there is a broad need for new

---

[28] PETER A. BUCHSBAUM, *Permit Coordination Study by the Lincoln Institute of Land Policy*, 36 URB. LAW. 191, 193–97 (2004).

housing—particularly affordable housing.[29] Market demand–based permitting in the northeast may serve the purpose of helping citizens, nonprofits, and developers understand whether local governments are approving their fair share of housing to meet regional demand. In Nevada, a state hit hard by the mortgage foreclosure crisis, local governments are mindful of the personal and public fiscal losses inflicted by residential overbuilding. Market demand–based permitting in the southwest and southeast—across the Sun Belt—most likely serves to check local governments' over-exuberant acceptance of requests for development approvals.

Regardless of the geographic region in which market based–demand permitting is implemented, it is based on a local government's review and consideration of an annual metropolitan market study. At a minimum, it enables local governments to take demand into account in making land-use and zoning decisions. At best, it requires that local governments use the market studies to adopt development conditions that protect local governments and their citizens from overbuilding or help developers and housing officials encourage consideration of the most appropriate housing development proposals.

Adopting local and regional reforms to the development approval process will be an important undertaking. Though there will be costs, the prospective benefits in preventing or at least softening the effects of the next real estate crash should be obvious. In the next chapter, we note many important, collateral benefits of the market demand–based planning and permitting system we advocate. Chapter 10 outlines a possible path forward for regions and local governments to adopt this system.

---

[29] Interview with Tim Reardon, Data Services Director, Metropolitan Area Planning Council (MAPC), in Boston, MA (June 17, 2016).

CHAPTER **8**

Smarter Planning through Market Demand–Based Planning and Permitting

▌ OVERVIEW

Thus far, we have posed market demand–based planning and permitting's (MDBPP) benefits. It is a tool that helps to:

- prevent excessive development permitting and thus reduce adverse effects of normal economic downturns;
- protect private property values as well as private property rights; and
- stabilize local government fiscal resources.

It can also serve as a type of insurance against the extraordinarily high monetary and social cost of neighborhood stabilization programs that are needed when there is too much supply relative to demand, as can occur through excessive permitting.[1] These are just a few of the direct benefits to local governments.

---

[1] Insights from Kermit J. Lind, *Strategic Code Compliance Enforcement: A Prescription for Resilient Communities* in How Cities Will Save the World: Urban Innovation in the Face of Population Flows, Climate Change and Economic Inequality 209, 215 & 223 (Raymond H. Brescia & John Travis Marshall eds., 2016).

In review, MDBPP is achieved through local-regional collaboration that generates region-based long-term development-demand projections, allocates projected new development, engages stakeholders to ensure the most informed analysis possible, facilitates periodic updates in considering unforeseen market demands, and allows for flexibility. These activities result in, and then depend on, a land-development information system. This LDIS inventories and assesses land and its development down to the level of the parcel and guides allocation of regional and local market demand–based development, thereby indicating permitting parameters.

Because of its design, grounding in high-quality data, and potential value to both the private and public sectors in making informed market demand–based development decisions, the MDBPP apparatus helps generate many more benefits. As a local government or region develops the ability to focus more carefully on the current supply and emerging demand for new types of real estate development, this can frame other closely associated growth-related concerns. MDBPP's collateral benefits will help support more sustainable, equitable, and inclusive metropolitan regions and localities. This is because market-based demand permitting could also:

- promote more informed investment of local government resources;
- support local government's efforts to comply with Fair Housing Act obligations;
- provide data essential for enabling jurisdictions to use "value capture" to help fund future infrastructure investments;
- stimulate smarter comprehensive planning;
- anticipate infrastructure planning and finance needs;
- bolster a region's resilience to catastrophic disasters;
- enhance environmental protection;
- facilitate mixed-use and transit-oriented development; and
- better inform opportunities for maximizing the use of land banks.

We examine briefly these several collateral benefits of market based–demand permitting.

PROMOTE MORE INFORMED INVESTMENT OF LOCAL GOVERNMENT RESOURCES

Our call for market based–demand permitting springs from the 2008 Great Recession's real estate crash. MDBPP can be viewed primarily as a tool to promote prudent real estate development—a kind of development "speed limit" to pace the flow of development according to market demand. But that view of market based–demand permitting is incomplete; it misses market based–demand permitting's ability to illuminate a range of innovative development opportunities that may have previously been obscured by prevailing biases or prejudices.

From time to time, developers, philanthropists, government agencies, commercial banks, community development financial institutions, and neighborhood activists may wear blinders when considering whether projects are feasible or desirable for their community. Urban development lore is replete with surprising stories of revitalization flowering in places and ways that few anticipated. Several examples include Atlanta's BeltLine, New York City's High Line, and more recently the renaissance of distressed commercial corridors in Birmingham, Alabama, and New Orleans.

Among market based–demand permitting's benefits is that it allows smarter development decisions, and it can uncover previously unappreciated or underappreciated development opportunities. In most U.S. metropolitan areas, there is no comprehensive database for gathering and analyzing demographic, job, and land-use information to inform real estate development decisions. If there is such a database, it is often proprietary and available to relatively few individuals and organizations. MDBPP promises to provide a more transparent, equitable, and readily accessible source of demand information. Through regular, detailed analysis of regional demographic and land-use data and by providing that information in a manner that can be broken down according to local jurisdiction and even neighborhood, market demand–based permitting will increase the likelihood that public, for-profit, and nonprofit real estate investors will recognize development opportunities previously ignored. MDBPP may open the financial spigot so that investment will flow to streets and corridors that once may have been considered "risky or unattractive" locales.[2]

---

[2] See Robin Hacke, David Wood & Marian Urquilla, Community Investment: Focusing on the System 19 (Mar. 2015).

SUPPORT LOCAL GOVERNMENT'S EFFORTS TO COMPLY WITH FAIR HOUSING ACT OBLIGATIONS

The Fair Housing Act mandates that local governments receiving federal funds pledge to take steps to affirmatively further fair housing. This obligation essentially requires that local governments identify and remove obstacles to fair housing. It entails providing affordable housing options for low- and moderate-income families and individuals. These obligations were underscored in the U.S. Department of Housing and Urban Development's new regulations clarifying local obligations under the Fair Housing Act.[3] Equally as important, in June 2015 the U.S. Supreme Court made clear that local governments could be deemed liable for violating the Fair Housing Act if it could be shown through indirect evidence (e.g., statistical analysis) that the governmental entity's *practices tend to have a discriminatory impact.* That is, the local government's practices have the effect of discriminating against a protected class.[4]

MDBPP is about more than just managing the supply of new housing construction to meet needs. It is about gathering vital information about existing housing supply—its character (ownership or rental), its age (new, recently renovated, dated, or dilapidated), and whether the housing is subsidized. That is why market based–demand permitting provides local governments with a tool to help them pinpoint the precise type of affordable housing that is needed (rental or homeownership), the exact strata of greatest economic need (very low, low, or moderate income), and the precise geographic locale where affordable housing may be needed or could be constructed in order to promote desired mixed-race and mixed-income neighborhoods.

MDBPP supplies an important tool to raise consciousness about a metro region's need for affordable housing. If, for example, market based–demand studies establish robust need for workforce housing, then local governments should use that information to work with developers to bring profitable, but also appropriate and needed, units to market.[5] The fact is that most local government officials do not

---

3   Affirmatively Furthering Fair Housing, 80 Fed. Reg. 42272 (July 8, 2015) (to be codified at 24 CFR Parts 5, 91, 92, 570, 574, 576, and 903).

4   Texas Dep't of Hous. and Cmty. Affairs v. The Inclusive Communities Project, 135 S.Ct. 2507 (2015).

5   One former official on the frontlines of California's response to the mortgage foreclosure crisis notes that leading up to the Great Recession, some California

realize the enormous market demand for affordable housing—every metro in the United States has an unmet need—and they have little if any idea of what type of housing its citizens are in greatest need of receiving.[6]

Many American inner cities have experienced a renaissance.[7] That has led to problems not envisioned twenty or twenty-five years ago. Homelessness and widespread displacement of lower-income households through gentrification have rapidly risen to the top of cities' list of concerns, replacing economic development and the need for urban revitalization. Market based–demand permitting gives cities a tool for targeting specific housing needs and then lining up incentives around those needs to help fill gaps.

A thorough market analysis will inform local governments about the demand for market rate, workforce housing, affordable housing, and deeply affordable housing. Even if the local government is not entertaining any proposals to develop an affordable housing product, it is still critical that it understands the existence of demand so that it can encourage rehabilitation of existing housing stock for affordable units and invest limited subsidy dollars in those rehab activities.

PROVIDE DATA ESSENTIAL FOR ENABLING JURISDICTIONS TO USE "VALUE CAPTURE" TO HELP FUND FUTURE INFRASTRUCTURE INVESTMENTS

State and local governments are responsible for planning and constructing critical transportation, water, sewer, and flood-management infrastructure. In certain circumstances, local governments can pay

---

developers were building what was maximally profitable, not necessarily what the local community needed. According to Katherine Porter, the former State of California Attorney General's office independent monitor of banks for a nationwide $25 billion mortgage settlement, there is a very real need for market data that can help local governments understand what kind of housing is actually needed based on the incomes that families are earning. Telephone interview with Katherine Porter, Esq., Professor of Law, University of California–Irvine (Sept. 9, 2016).

6   See TANVI MISRA, *Got an Affordable Housing Crisis? Save the Cheap Housing You Already Have.* CITYLAB (Aug. 26, 2016), www.citylab.com/housing/2016/08/got-an-affordable-housing-crisis-save-the-cheap-housing-youve-already-got/497234/.

7   See JAMES BRASUELL, *Many Cities Now Facing the Challenge of Prosperity*, PLANENTIZEN (Aug. 3, 2016), www.planetizen.com/node/87759/many-cities-now-facing-challenges-prosperity.

for some of these costs from infrastructure-related impact fees, which are paid by developers. However, impact fees do not always cover the government's outlays. To help supplement already tight local and state government infrastructure funds, a tool known as "value capture" is often discussed as a way to recover some part of the so-called government givings or windfalls associated with new public infrastructure investments.[8]

MDBPP will allow local governments to map year-to-year increases in property values and rents. By overlaying major infrastructure improvements such as roads, highways, and parks onto detailed maps showing not just parcel development potential but also parcel value, local governments can track urban development that may, in part, be associated with infrastructure investments. In other words, market based–demand permitting could help local and state governments collect the data that will enable them to realize some part of benefit associated with increased private property values caused by public infrastructure development.

▌STIMULATE SMARTER COMPREHENSIVE PLANNING

We have collectively reviewed thousands of comprehensive plans over careers that started in the 1960s. We have also participated in preparing scores of plans, many of which won major awards. Yet, most plans lack the detail needed to truly understand the nature of future development needs. It is the rare plan that disaggregates housing demand into types of homes in locations serving households. Nor do plans generally project nonresidential development by type and location and the extent to which it will be redeveloped within a planning horizon. Certainly many plans do. Those plans combine information from land development information systems with market demand–based analysis that allocates land that is needed to meet projected needs. They can also better plan for and make investments in infrastructure to meet those needs when they arise. Market demand–based plans will generate the kind of realistic, market-driven information needed to make comprehensive planning smarter.

---

[8] DONALD HAGMAN & DEAN MISCZYNSKI, WINDFALLS FOR WIPEOUTS: LAND VALUE CAPTURE AND COMPENSATION 16-18 (1978).

ANTICIPATE INFRASTRUCTURE PLANNING AND FINANCE NEEDS

Following up on the last point, market demand–based plans that allocate development needs throughout a local government or region can lead to smarter infrastructure planning so that development occurs concurrent with existing or planned facilities. This will also lead to better information about the costs of serving new development. Imagine the difference in development approval decisions if the cost of serving new development five to ten years from now was actually known. Decision makers would then need to find the money to pay for new or expanded infrastructure needs through general taxes or special assessments, grants, infrastructure loans, impact fees, and the like.[9] Closer inspection of costs could reveal (as is often the case) that higher-density, lower-cost areas could end up paying more than its proportionate share of the burden while lower-density, higher-cost areas pay less. This has the perverse effect that lower-cost development subsidizes higher costs, resulting in more higher-cost development and less lower-cost development.

BOLSTER A REGION'S RESILIENCE TO CATASTROPHIC DISASTERS

Just since the year 2000, the federal government has poured hundreds of billions of dollars into rebuilding towns, cities, and counties ravaged by natural disasters. Colorado's 2013 Front Range floods displaced thousands of residents and nearby businesses, making it impossible for many to return to their old home or place of work. Iowa's 2008 floods left thousands of Cedar Rapids homes submerged for days. Superstorm Sandy's storm surge pushed thousands of New York City residents out of their homes, and more than four years later many are just returning.

These recent catastrophic events and others like them share in common an imperative to aid thousands—sometimes tens of thousands—of property owners across a metro region whose homes have been lost or damaged. Disaster assistance and recovery programs require detailed

---

[9] See ARTHUR C. NELSON, JAMES C. NICHOLAS & JULIAN CONRAD JUERGENSMEYER, IMPACT FEES (2008).

information about individual properties, neighborhoods, and cities. Federal, state, and local governments must work together to repair or improve damaged properties, relocate residents and businesses to safer locales, and reestablish entire neighborhoods. Basic ownership information is necessary to proceed with processing applications for federal assistance. Understanding a neighborhood's share of renters or flood insurance policy owners is critical to crafting long-term neighborhood recovery programs to promote resettlement or return. A city or county court's foreclosure records help recovery planners pinpoint the relative strength and weakness of local real estate markets. However, federally funded relief efforts have been slowed by poor access to important parcel-specific and jurisdiction-wide property information.[10] Market based–demand permitting will require that local governments collect and store parcel-level real estate data that is essential to have available when communities are digging out from disaster and as they seek to connect individual homeowners and business owners with appropriate federal, state, and philanthropic disaster-recovery resources. With MDBPP firmly in place, a local jurisdiction will be well positioned with all the parcel-level data needed to receive timely federal disaster relief.

▌ENHANCE ENVIRONMENTAL PROTECTION

A key element of the MDBPP apparatus is the land development information system (LDIS; see Chapter 6). At the regional level, it will generate information on a wide range of environmental concerns down to the individual parcel such as floodplains, wetlands, steep slopes, high water tables, land that is subject to liquefaction in seismically hazardous areas, critical habitats, soil quality, and so forth. Knowing environmental constraints on the regional scale can help inform the local-regional development allocation process about steering development to locations where it has minimal environmental impacts.

---

[10] Disaster recovery experts note that "following a disaster the demand for data escalates as decisionmakers grasp for certainty" amid disorder and chaos. These experts also note that "in the event of disaster, resilience capacity is greater in communities that have a platform that pulls together and presents relevant and reliable data to support crucial decisions that can mitigate damage in the short term and enhance recovery in the long term." ALLISON PLYER & ELAINE ORTIZ, *Building Data Capacity to Foster Resilient Communities* in RESILIENCE AND OPPORTUNITY: LESSONS FROM THE U.S. GULF COAST AFTER KATRINA AND RITA 187, 198 (2011).

FACILITATE MIXED-USE AND TRANSIT-ORIENTED DEVELOPMENT

There is growing market demand–based evidence that a large share of the real estate market desires mixed-use communities. Other studies show a very large mismatch between the market demand for housing that is accessible to fixed-guideway transit such as rail transit, streetcars, and bus rapid transit, and the supply of such housing.[11] MDBPP can be used to determine regional demand for these kinds of developments and to decide how the supply can be allocated most efficiently among local governments.

BETTER INFORM OPPORTUNITIES FOR MAXIMIZING THE USE OF LAND BANKS

One of the consequences of excess supply relative to demand is that properties may be abandoned for long periods of time. Abandoned properties reduce tax revenues, lead to blight, and often attract criminal activity. All of this further depresses a community's property value and ability to recover from economic downturns. As Frank S. Alexander observes:[12]

By rethinking the value and potential of vacant and abandoned properties—seeing them as assets rather than as a disposable commodity—these communities are finding new ways to breathe life into once-forgotten neighborhoods. By using the legal tools a land bank provides, a community can ensure that tax-foreclosed property is sold or developed with the long-term interest of the community and surrounding property owners in mind.

Land banks often provide marketable title to properties previously impossible to develop due to complicated liens and confused ownership histories. While land banks are generally associated with older urban communities that have significant abandonment, they are potentially just as useful to safeguard healthy communities from deterioration, and for smaller

---

[11] See Arthur C. Nelson, Reshaping Metropolitan America (2013).
[12] Frank S. Alexander, Land Banks and Land Banking (2011).

communities seeking to protect land from passing through the slow process of decline so often associated with tax-foreclosed properties.[13]

Through its land-development information system, combined with identifying market demand–based development needs that are then allocated to local governments, the MDBPP can help maximize the use of land banks. The LDIS can identify land-banked properties and their characteristics at the parcel and neighborhood level. Market demand analysis can be used to help determine market opportunities for these properties. And through the development allocation process, land-banked properties can be targeted for redevelopment. Development or other opportunities to use these properties can further be determined through the engagement of stakeholders who are part of the MDBPP planning and implementation process.

▌SUMMARY ASSESSMENT

MDBPP and the LDIS used to help implement MDBPP can do much more than improve the match between development demand and supply. We have offered only a handful of collateral benefits. In Chapter 9 we show that MDBPP represents, at its essence, a tool long-used in making public sector development decisions. Local, state, and federal governments frequently require confirmation of market demand prior to allowing development projects to proceed. Legal considerations surrounding MDBPP implementation follow in Chapter 10.

---

[13] *Id.* at 8-9.

CHAPTER 9

"Old Wine in New Skins": Updating an Existing Tool for Evaluating Development Decisions

■ INTRODUCTION

Assuming there is a market demand–based plan, this chapter focuses on permitting issues. Market demand–based permitting updates a proven tool for prudent government administration. It employs a long-standing but selectively used device for protecting consumers, managing valuable natural resources, and ensuring wise investment of scarce government subsidy. From Massachusetts to the state of Washington, from Louisiana to Michigan, public agencies use evidence of market demand to help protect citizens and ensure sensible public investments.

But this practice of making market demand–based decisions has not been widely used by local, state, or federal governments to inform day-to-day development and growth-management decisions. City councils and county commissions have largely ignored market demand in reviewing proposed real estate development deals. In fact, we maintain this oversight has had negative consequences for many local governments and the regions that encompass them. In this chapter, we explain that, instead, there is a promising and pertinent blueprint for local governments to make smarter growth management decisions.

Leading up to the 2008 crash, local governments seemed to eschew any policy of double-checking a developer's representations regarding demand for proposed homes or new commercial space. This local government lack of oversight almost certainly allowed questionable development projects to proceed. As a result, in jurisdictions where new developments remained only partially occupied or partially complete, vacancy and abandonment had the opportunity to fester. Unoccupied and unattended structures began to deflate surrounding property values, depress the local government's property tax revenues, and require costly government outlays associated with securing and demolishing properties and repairing or maintaining infrastructure.[1] In short, lacking any mandate to "kick the tires" to ensure market demand for new development, many local governments not only failed to check that the development process would result in viable development, but also failed to ensure that adjacent homes' safety and property values would not be greatly jeopardized. To make matters worse, in failing to analyze market demand, these local governments likely exposed themselves to paying the heavy costs associated with maintaining or demolishing under-occupied or insolvent developments.

The 2008 real estate crash dramatically underscored that when privately financed development flops, its failure can have far-reaching financial implications for a city and its residents—even when state and local governments do not have a direct financial stake.[2] That is, even though local governments do not directly make grants or loans in conjunction with projects they review, if those projects fail during or just after development, then the city or county and the homeowners who abut the busted project will almost certainly be left to pick up some of the pieces.

Many local and state governments already have access to a template for a tool that can help them spot, and thus potentially mitigate, the overexuberance that can trigger boom-bust cycles. Cities, towns, counties, and states have for many years protected themselves from investing in or approving activities or projects for which there is insufficient demand. This chapter details how some of MDBPP's essential principles are already in widespread use at the local, state, and federal levels.

---

[1]   Jim Holway, Don Elliott & Anna Trentadue, Arrested Developments: Combatting Zombie Subdivisions and Other Excess Entitlements, 4–8 (2014).
[2]   Id. at 1–2.

MARKET DEMAND STUDIES AS TIME-TESTED TOOL FOR PRUDENT RESOURCE DEVELOPMENT

Market principles have long guided federal and state policy regarding prudent resource development. A broad range of statutes and regulations currently require that market studies inform decision-making or, alternatively, advise that agency actions must be consistent with market demand.

Laws aimed at promoting wise stewardship of natural and human resources include provisions that call for monitoring production to ensure such production levels meet local, state, or national market demand. Federal forest management laws in some cases require that production of timber from specific national forests be consistent with "the annual market demand for timber from such forest."[3] State oil and gas law includes provisions requiring that intrastate production does not exceed "the reasonable market demand."[4] In Massachusetts, statewide apple production goals are tied to meeting "reasonable" or "normal" market demand.[5] Market studies are even used to help states make sure they have sufficient supply of teaching talent. An Oklahoma statute requires that the state conduct a market analysis every three years to "identify areas of teacher shortage and to make recommendations for addressing areas of critical need."[6]

Market principles also help the government make sound decisions before committing money or land to large, specialized development projects. In other words, the government wants to ensure that its loans, grants, and conveyances of real property have the greatest probability of delivering successful results based on evidence that there is demand for the project the governmental entity is being asked to support. This means that the federal or state government might require applicants for government funding supply a market study serving as evidence of sufficient demand. Evidence of such demand is a core part of the

---

[3] 16 U.S.C. § 539d (referring to timber from the Tongass National Forest).
[4] KANS. STAT. ANN. § 55-703 (West 2016); IOWA CODE ANN. § 458A.6 (2016); N. D. CENT. CODE ANN. § 38-08-06 (West 2016); TEX. NAT. RES. CODE ANN. § 86.085 (West 2016); MO. REV. STAT. § 259.090 (West 2016); N.M. STAT. ANN. § 70-2-3 (West 2016).
[5] MASS. GEN. LAWS ANN. ch. 128, § 102 (West 2016).
[6] OKLA. STAT. ANN. TIT. 70 § 6-211 (West 2016).

government decision-making process across a number of different economic sectors. A showing of market demand has been required for the proposed redevelopment of a military base, financing for maritime vessels, and development of airport facilities.[7]

We realize these examples demonstrate state and federal checks on development projects in which a governmental entity has some direct stake. We submit, of course, that requiring evidence of market demand is appropriate and important even when the local or state government has no land, money, or other direct interest in a project. Market demand–based permitting would protect the property and financial interests of citizens who would be directly affected by unwise development, as well as the governmental entities that would have to manage the fallout from failed development. This type of market demand based–permitting safeguard is already in broad use. Virtually all of our states and cities are already affected by market-demand requirements. These requirements shape expansion of our health care and power production infrastructure.

Historically, unwarranted development of hospitals and electrical power infrastructure left hospitals and utilities looking for ways to pay for empty hospital beds and unused electrical-generating capacity. To cover the cost of imprudent development, hospitals and utilities increased their rates. Consumers across cities, states, and even regions were broadly exposed to inflated prices for health care and electricity.[8]

To address repeated overbuilding, federal and state governments began to take steps to protect patients and taxpayers by requiring utilities and hospital developers to produce evidence of demand.[9] States now commonly require that health care and power companies demonstrate need before they purchase expensive medical equipment, expand existing hospitals, erect transmission lines, or construct new

---

[7] 32 C.F.R. § 174.9 (2016) (military base revitalization); 46 C.F.R. § 298.14 (2016) (maritime vessels).
[8] RICHARD CAUCHI & ASHELY NOBLE, CON-*Certificate of Need State Laws* (Aug. 25, 2016), www.ncsl.org/research/health/con-certificate-of-need-state-laws.aspx.
[9] *See, e.g.,* MICH. COMPILED L. ANN. 460.6s(4)(a) (requiring that a utility applying for a certificate of necessity demonstrate need for the proposed for an electrical generation facility); KY REV. STAT. ANN. § 278.020(1) & (5) (West 2016) (requiring a certificate of convenience and necessity, including a showing of "demand and need" before obtaining a "franchise, license, or permit" to operate as a utility); *supra* note 8.

energy production facilities.[10] The great majority of states require hospitals to obtain certificates of need based on a showing of sufficient demand for, say, an MRI machine or an expansion of a hospital's inpatient care facilities.[11] Large energy production facilities also require validation of demand before states will allow companies to proceed with development.[12] States even want to ensure that demand exists for new transmission lines that take electricity from those generation facilities through the electrical grid.[13]

PRECEDENT FOR REQUIRING MARKET DEMAND AS A PREDICATE TO GOVERNMENT SUPPORT FOR REAL ESTATE DEVELOPMENT

The preceding examples of state and federal government entities using market studies to guide decisions about natural resources, critical public services, or unique real estate assets are special cases. But as many city planning officials, developers, and housing professionals already know, it is not uncommon for government agencies to require real estate development project proponents to submit market studies supporting a showing of market demand. These market studies are frequently a predicate for public investment in development projects. A number of federal, state, and local laws specifically require development proponents to show evidence of market demand as part of the public financing and development approval process. For example, the federal low-income housing tax credit

---

[10] The great majority of states require that hospitals obtain a certificate of need (CON) based on a showing of sufficient demand. *See id.* CONs were initially required under federal law as a requisite for obtaining federal funding for health care facilities. This federal law was repealed, but most states have retained the requirement that health care concerns establish need before expanding or developing facilities.

[11] *See* American Health Planning Assoc. (AHPA), *Certificate of Need Coverage Summary by State, 2010,* www.ahpanet.org/images/matrix%201.png (providing detailed matrix of state-by-state certificate of need requirements).

[12] MINN. STAT. ANN. § 216B.243.3 (1), (3) & (6) (West 2016).

[13] *Id. See also* Cassarah Brown, *States Walk the Line: Current State Action Towards More Efficient, Secure, and Cost Effective Electricity Transmission* (July 2013), www.ncsl.org/research/energy/current-state-action-on-electricity-transmission. aspx (discussing generally new and proposed state statutes to facilitate more immediate updating of the nationwide electrical grid but maintaining requirements that companies demonstrate state *and* regional need for new transmission lines).

(LIHTC),[14] publicly backed state and local bond financing,[15] and transferable development rights (TDR) programs,[16] as well as certain types of local government zoning approvals all require a showing of sufficient market demand.

Over the last three decades, mixed-income multifamily housing development has been fueled by federal tax law. The low-income housing tax credit, adopted as part of the 1986 federal tax reforms, helps affordable housing developers raise capital for housing development projects serving low-income families. It does so by creating incentives for corporations to reduce their federal tax liability in exchange for equity investments in private sector affordable housing development. Between 1987 and 2011, an estimated 2.4 million units of affordable housing were placed in service with the LIHTC.[17] Under applicable tax regulations, the availability of these federal tax credits is limited.[18] Affordable housing developers must compete with one another for an award.

The federal government doles out these tax credits to each state based on a formula that is tightly restricted according to a state's population.[19] Demand for these credits always greatly exceeds supply.[20] To qualify for an allocation of tax credits, affordable housing developers must—among other things—demonstrate sufficient demand for the affordable housing units they wish to build.[21] This required

---

[14] Tax Reform Act of 1986, 42 U.S.C. § 4635. Following Hurricane Katrina, the state of Louisiana authorized a market study to determine whether its investment of federal disaster block grant funds and federal tax credits to create affordable housing stock was oversaturating the New Orleans rental market. *See* IVAN MIESTCHOVICH & GCR & ASSOCIATES, INC., NEW ORLEANS MARKET ASSESSMENT: A COMPREHENSIVE ANALYSIS OF DEMAND AND SUPPLY DYNAMICS 11-12 (2011).

[15] KAN. STAT. ANN. § 12-17,162 (West 2016); Innovation and Development Economy Act, 50 ILL. COMP. STAT. ANN. 470/20.

[16] State Transfer of Development Rights Act, N.J. STAT. ANN. § 40:55D-148 (West 2016); *Builders League of S. Jersey, Inc. v. Twp. of Franklin*, 928 A.2d 88, 95 (N.J. Super. Ct. App. Div. 2007) (holding municipalities must do a full market analysis required by the state statute and could not adopt a "streamlined" version).

[17] OFFICE OF THE COMPTROLLER OF THE CURRENCY, COMMUNITY DEVELOPMENTS INSIGHTS, LOW-INCOME HOUSING TAX CREDITS: AFFORDABLE HOUSING INVESTMENT OPPORTUNITIES FOR BANKS (2014).

[18] *Id.* at 10, 24.

[19] MARK P. KEIGHTLY, CONGRESSIONAL RESEARCH SERVICE, AN INTRODUCTION TO THE LOW-INCOME HOUSING TAX CREDIT 2 (2013).

[20] OFFICE OF THE COMPTROLLER OF THE CURRENCY, *supra* note 17, at 21.

[21] Tax Reform Act of 1986 § 4635; N.J. STAT. ANN. § 40:55D-148 (West 2016); LA. ADMIN. CODE TIT. 16 §311 (West 2016); 99-346-016 ME. CODE R. § 2 (LexisNexis 2016); OKLA. ADMIN. CODE § 330:30-4-4 (2016).

showing of demand helps ensure that a relatively scarce and precious affordable housing resource is wisely awarded to developers whose proposed projects will serve well-established demand.

Nonprofit housing developers are not the only development professionals versed in establishing demand for proposed projects. State and local governments sometimes ask commercial developers and for-profit housing developers to establish demand for large community development projects as well as retail, office, and residential projects. This is particularly the case when states support development of convention centers or shopping centers or other catalytic projects to spark community and economic development. These large projects are sometimes supported by equity raised from the sale of state bonds. To secure publicly backed bond financing, developers must satisfy the state agency or state bond commission's requirement by furnishing evidence that sufficient demand exists for the proposed development.[22] The rationale for this requirement is not just that states want to make sure they are committing their limited financial resources to the most deserving development projects. States also want to protect taxpayers from picking up the tab for developers who cannot meet regularly scheduled payments on the state bonds.

Local and state governments do not require a showing of demand only when they play a role in project financing. Some state and local governments also consider evidence of market demand relevant when developers seek to participate in certain growth-management programs or request certain types of land-use and zoning permissions and approvals. TDR is a growth-management tool that helps preserve important environmental or historical conservation areas from additional development by permitting higher-density development in certain areas targeted for growth.[23] TDRs accomplish conservation by allowing the transfer of development rights (e.g., air rights or higher-density residential development) from a "sending parcel" located in the area to be conserved to a "receiving parcel" in the area designated for growth. At least one state-sanctioned TDR program requires that a developer wishing to purchase, for instance, a rural landowner's development rights and send those rights to a

---

[22] Innovation Development and Economy Act, 50 ILL. COMP. STAT. ANN. 470/20 (West 2016); Star Bonds Financing Act, KAN. STAT. ANN. 12-17, 163 (West 2016).

[23] EVANGELINE R. LINKOUS & TIMOTHY S. CHAPIN, *TDR Program Performance in Florida*, 80:3 J. AM. PLANN. ASSOC. 254-55 (2014).

higher-density receiving zone must show evidence of market demand for the proposed development project.[24]

We also think it is important to note that, nationally, a small number of towns, cities, and counties already have requirements to analyze market demand for proposed development. The comprehensive growth management plan of Martin County, Florida, includes a future land use element. This particular plan component is intended to ensure, among other things, that the county manages growth in a fiscally prudent manner, consistent with its "natural and manmade systems," and in a manner that ensures county residents' continued "quality-of-life."[25] Martin County determined that an essential part of meeting the county's goal of planning for its future is making certain that its development approvals are consistent with population projections. As a result, the county has adopted a specific planning objective that requires county planners to monitor biannually applicable development and population data to confirm that the county can accommodate its "projected population needs."[26] We also highlight that recently, and in response to the Great Recession, Maricopa County, Arizona adopted a comprehensive plans requiring that future development proposals include analysis of market demand.[27]

Local governments are also asking applicants who request development approvals in certain types of special zoning districts to demonstrate that market demand exists for the proposed development.[28]

---

[24] State Transfer of Development Rights Act, § 40:55D-148.

[25] MARTIN COUNTY, FL, COMPREHENSIVE PLAN Sec. 4.4.

[26] Id. at Objective 4.1D.

[27] In 2016, Maricopa County adopted a plan provision that specifically calls on the County to "[u]se market feasibility studies as warranted to help identify the need for new urban development in unincorporated areas." Vision 2030: Maricopa County Comprehensive Plan 38, 45 (Jan. 2016), available at https://www.maricopa.gov/DocumentCenter/Home/View/3786.

[28] See, e.g., MANATEE COUNTY, FL, LAND DEVELOPMENT CODE Sec. 349.3.C.4 (applicants for certain large development projects known as "developments of regional impact" are required to furnish the county with "a market study which has been prepared for the proposed commercial development. If such a study has not been prepared, describe in general terms how the overall demand for this project has been determined"); ARROYO GRANDE, CA, CODE OF ORDINANCES Sec. 16.16.030(D)(1)(b) & (c) (applicants for "specific plan" zoning districts, which implement the local government's general plan, may be required to submit "a competently prepared housing market analysis . . . demonstrating the need for housing by price range and number of dwelling units" or, if the project under review proposes a commercial use, a "competently prepared commercial market analysis . . . for any proposed shopping center or major commercial uses, showing

Planned development (PD) or planned unit development (PUD) zoning districts are flexible site plan–controlled zoning districts. These districts often accommodate a mix of uses not generally permitted under the rigid classifications of the typical zoning code. In Abita Springs, Louisiana, the city requires that applicants for PD or PUD zoning approvals establish market demand as part of their application for development approval for their proposed mix of uses.[29] Similarly, one Maryland local government requires that applicants seeking to develop large commercial and light industrial spaces establish demand for the particular proposed use before local approval is granted.[30]

■ GOING FORWARD

Market demand–based permitting represents a significant departure from most local government norms for considering applications for development approval. Even with existing federal, state, and local

---

the need for such uses, in the location requested, and inadequacy of existing district sites to meet this need . . ."").

[29] ABITA SPRINGS, LA., CODE OF ORDINANCES Ch. 8, § 9-804(1)(a). ("Planned unit developments proposed to contain any residential uses shall require submission of at least the following market data: (1) Details about the proposal pertaining to: housing types, floor area of dwelling, estimated price ranges, number of bedrooms, densities, amenities included, etc. (2) An evaluation of the historical market pattern for the types of units proposed. Building permits issuance trends and/or surveys of existing recently constructed residential developments shall be used in this evaluation. (3) Total anticipated demands in the town for the type of units proposed shall be estimated for the immediately subsequent five-year period. The percent of that *demand* which would be absorbed by the proposed planned unit development shall be identified. Methods used in determining the five-year *demand* shall be indicated") (emphasis added).

[30] LA PLATA, MD, CODE OF ORDINANCES Sec. 191-25.1(B)(1)(B)(11) (project applicants are required to submit a report that includes a "preliminary market study demonstrating the viability of the development concept and estimating the general rate of absorption of the proposed development program land uses within the stated development time frames. The study should take into consideration assumptions about market changes over the course of the development projected build-out time frame. These assumptions may include estimates of new development and population growth in the surrounding market area in conjunction with the timing of development phases on this site"). *See also* PLANTATION, FL., CODE OF ORDINANCES Sec. 27-282(b)(1) (requiring that applicants seeking to develop a mixed office and retail space ["OB-C Office Business-Combined Zoning District"] and who wish to devote more than 60 percent of their project's gross square feet to retail uses must furnish a "market study which evaluates the present need for uses which are candidates for the subject property's office use component within the market area defined by such study . . .").

precedent for market demand–based permitting, we understand that the idea of grafting a market demand–based permitting requirement into local comprehensive plans and zoning ordinances may cause anxiety for some city attorneys and planning directors. They know that the well-established examples discussed in this chapter will not stop certain landowners and development professionals and putative private property rights advocates from lodging legal challenges to a market demand–based permitting requirement. They also know that simply sprinkling the terms *market demand* and *market study* throughout state and local land-use and zoning laws will not affect the changes necessary to soften the blow of cyclical real estate crashes.

Designing and implementing our suggested approach to reviewing requests for development approvals necessitates confirmation of the legal basis for local code provisions authorizing market demand–based permitting. Mindful that real estate markets generally cut across city and county boundary lines, adoption of market demand–based permitting will also require careful consideration of how local governments within a metropolitan region coordinate its design and implementation. We believe that the neighborhood debris and decay associated with the recent real estate crisis—and the costs local governments have incurred in cleaning up this decay—furnish substantial basis for local governments to require confirmation of market demand in conjunction with development approvals.[31] And Chapter 10, which follows, outlines a possible strategy for local and regional implementation of a new market demand–based permitting requirement.

---

[31] In the Great Recession's wake, there have been general calls for demonstration of market demand in conjunction with local development approvals. See HOLWAY ET AL., *supra* note 1, at 38-40; JAN G. LAITOS & RACHEL MARTIN, *Zombie Subdivisions in the United States and Ghost Developments in Europe: Lessons for Local Governments*, 4 WASH. J. ENVTL L. & POL'Y 314, 352-53 (2015). These scholars and experts, whose work provides a detailed analysis of particular national and international experiences with excessive permitting and entitlements, do not specifically address the legal basis or the economic and planning rationale for local governments to require evidence of market demand prior to issuing development approvals.

CHAPTER **10**

Implementing Market Demand–Based Planning and Permitting: Legal Considerations

▌INTRODUCTION: THE FOUNDATION ALREADY EXISTS ▌FOR MDBPP

Market demand–based planning and permitting (MDBPP) does not require substantial changes to current planning and permitting systems, but some enhancements may be needed to enable MDBPP. As we showed in Chapters 2, 6, and 7, local and regional governments already have substantial planning powers, and local governments have permitting authority. For their part, most regional governments in most states already have the power to employ market demand–based planning and then often work informally with local governments to allocate regional development needs. All metropolitan planning organizations (MPOs), for instance, are required by federal law to:[1]

- carry out cooperative, continuous, and comprehensive planning processes for making transportation investment decisions in the metropolitan area with program oversight from the Federal

---

[1] Adapted from FEDERAL TRANSIT ADMINISTRATION, METROPOLITAN PLANNING ORGANIZATION (MPO), OVERVIEW, www.transit.dot.gov/regulations-and-guidance/ transportation-planning/metropolitan-planning-organization-mpo.

Highway Administration, the Federal Transit Administration, and the state Department of Transportation;

- prepare and maintain a long-range (including often multimodal) transportation plan;

- prepare a transportation improvement program to provide for transportation investments to meet metropolitan transportation needs; and

- perform other duties as required to comply with state and federal regulations.

MPOs thus have at least the implicit federal authority to engage in market demand–based planning, as outlined in Chapter 7, to adequately address transportation needs. Moreover, MPOs receive federal planning funds. This means that the resources may exist to create a regional land development information system (LDIS; see Chapter 5), which is critical for guiding and monitoring development, and to facilitate preparation of a regional market demand–based plan. As we noted in Chapter 7, nearly half of all councils of governments (COGs) are the MPOs for their regions. The other COGs also have a range of planning functions "such as regional and municipal planning, economic, and community development, pollution control, transit administration, transportation planning, human services, and water use. Councils of governments also play a role in regional housing, hazard mitigation, and disaster planning and in the gathering, analysis, and distribution of demographic and GIS data."[2] In short, many of the powers needed to engage in regional market demand–based planning as a collaboration between local and regional governments already exist. Further, through local government permitting, the authority to match development permitting with market demand exists at least implicitly (see Chapters 2, 6, and 7).

For example, some regions, such as many of those in California, Florida, Georgia, Hawaii, New Jersey, Oregon, Washington, among others, have developed a system of intergovernmental regional cooperation,

---

[2] DAWN JOURDAN, SHANNON VAN ZANDT & NICOLE ADAIR, *Meeting Their Fair Share: A Proposal for the Creation of Regional Land Banks to Meet the Affordable Housing Needs in the Rural Areas of* Texas, 19 J. AFFORDABLE HOUS. & CMTY. DEV. L. 147, 158 (2010); JOHN KINCAID, *Regulatory Regionalism in Metropolitan Areas: Voter Resistance and Reform Persistence*, 13 PACE L. REV. 449, 468–73 (1993); WIKIPEDIA, *Council of Governments*, https://en.wikipedia.org/wiki/Council_of_governments.

grounded in state statutes, which address the need to project long-range market demand for development. Other regions base their cooperation on nonbinding agreements. These agreements, such as the Mile High Compact, bring together local governments in the metro Denver's region under a council of governments. And some local governments rely on informal professional networks of city and county planning directors to communicate about regional growth and growth management.[3] Many local governments coordinate regionally to satisfy requirements for receiving federal transportation funding for local transit projects.

Implementing policy ideas looms as a challenge for most state and local governments because they already operate above and beyond the capacity suggested by their limited staffing or funding. To introduce MDBPP at the local, regional, and state levels may require clarifying existing legal authority or advancing statutes to create new powers. For instance, though there are no explicit mandates to do so, there are no restrictions against MPOs creating land development information systems (see Chapter 6) or engaging in market demand–based planning as part of their transportation planning powers. MPOs may also be able to allocate development among local governments but only in an advisory capacity, since mandating collaboration may not be enabled. Other forms of regional development agencies (RDAs) may have similar ability to create LDISs and conduct market demand–based development analysis.

For their part, local governments in most states already have the authority to create LDISs, engage in market demand–based analysis, prepare market demand–based plans, and implement them through market demand–based permitting. But they would have little ability to restrict other local governments in the same region from engaging in permitting practices that undermine local government plans. As a first step, regional authorities and local governments should consider the extent to which they are already enabled to conduct MDBPP.

To manage growth in a manner that effectively softens the boom-and-bust cycle of real estate development, a region should consider agreeing to strict limitations to each of its jurisdiction's annual development order approvals. However, if a state or region lacks consensus on whether to require local governments to adhere to limitations on

<hr>

[3] Telephone interview with Frank Duke, FAICP, Director of Planning, East Baton Rouge Parish, Louisiana (Aug. 5, 2016) (regarding the strong communications network that existed between and among planning directors in Durham, Chapel Hill, Wake County, and Orange County, NC).

development approvals, there may be a way to take a positive step toward raising consciousness regarding demand for real development. A region may wish to consider an approach that encourages—or even "nudges"—local governments to adhere to their fair share of a region's anticipated growth.[4]

Though we argue below that it may be most effective to mandate local government adherence to a regional market demand–based plan, it may not be crucial in practice to achieve the ultimate goal of preventing excessive permitting. If the region prepares the kind of market demand–based analysis we recommend and that regional analysis informs infrastructure investments, especially transportation, it would behoove local governments to make their own plans in a manner that takes full advantage of those investments. Moreover, the level of detail of the regional plans as we propose serve as notice to all decision-makers about the parameters of market demand–based development needs throughout the region. Jurisdictions choosing to ignore their reasonable allocation of demand risk criticism from their residents regarding the dangers of over-permitting as well as public shaming from sister jurisdictions who, as regional "team players," choose to honor the regional allocation.

ENHANCING LOCAL-REGIONAL COLLABORATION IN THE CONTEXT OF MDBPP

In researching for this book, we learned from planning officials, local government attorneys, and development sector professionals that there are few metropolitan regions whose local governments would be willing to adopt new planning and zoning restrictions that limit local discretion to approve development. But under MDBPP all development approvals remain at the local government level. We note that local government staff and developers have expressed genuine interest in an MDBPP system driven by accurate and informative market data that gives local governments a range of flexible options for protecting

---

[4] A market demand-based planning and permitting system need not necessarily use a "stick" to mandate local government compliance with the regional plan. MDBPP may check imprudent local government development approvals by highlighting a local government's failure to abide by the regional limitations designed to protect metropolitan economic vitality. *See generally* Ryan Calo, *Code, Nudge, or Notice?*, 99 Iowa L. Rev. 773, 783–84 (2014).

their welfare and that of its citizens. Local staff know that it is the availability of quality information that will drive most prudent decisions by all engaged in the development process.

We remind readers that local government development applications must comply with applicable state and local law. This frequently means that new development must, at a minimum, satisfy requirements of the jurisdiction's comprehensive plan and its code of ordinances. Further, a consideration that all local governments should keep in mind is whether MDBPP is supported by state law. In some states, the state legislation authorizing local governments to handle land use and zoning matters may need to be amended to allow local governments to make decisions based on evidence of sufficient market demand. This possibility is discussed briefly next.

STATE ENABLING LEGISLATION

Does a state's zoning enabling legislation grant local government authority to adopt a demand-based permitting ordinance related to its enabled planning function powers? A state zoning enabling act based on the Standard Zoning Enabling Act arguably supports local adoption of MDBPP without further statutory amendment (see Chapter 2). However, it is worth considering that the safest foundation for MDBPP may involve amending state zoning enabling legislation to clearly tie market demand–based permitting with market demand–based planning. State enabling legislation or administrative rules may also address such issues as:

- organizational structure;
- plan preparation;
- procedures for plan review and adoption;
- relationships and agreements with other units of government.

The American Planning Association offers guidance in these and related respects.[5]

---

[5] STUART MECK, *Chapter 6: Regional Planning*, GROWING SMART LEGISLATIVE GUIDEBOOK, (2016), www.planning.org/growingsmart/guidebook/six01.htm.

REGIONALISM AND HOME RULE

In states that give municipalities home rule powers, cities and counties already have the basic authority to adopt and amend zoning codes. But not all states vest local governments with this authority.[6] Under a legal doctrine known as Dillon's Rule, certain states grant to local governments only those powers that the state constitution or state legislature gives explicitly to the local government.[7] This means that adopting a regional MDBPP system will involve working with the state legislature or with individual jurisdictions across a metropolitan region.

In Chapter 1, we noted that a local government's home rule powers—or their absence—do not necessarily present an obstacle to local adoption of market based–demand permitting. We add only that metropolitan regions considering MDBPP must study how home rule might influence the way a region adopts market based–demand permitting.[8] Home rule powers can potentially circumscribe a state legislature's ability to create a market based–demand permitting scheme that restricts the local exercise of land use and zoning powers.[9] Further, it is important for local governments to consider whether home rule powers authorize a local government to act and plan regionally.[10]

STATE STATUTE ENABLING A REGIONAL, COLLABORATIVE MARKET DEMAND–BASED PLAN

MDBPP holds greatest promise for limiting overbuilding where a state creates an integrated implementation and oversight approach. In other words, state and regional agencies provide data and analysis to support and guide local implementation of MDBPP. Local governments would seek to coordinate their permitting decisions in accordance with state and/or regional market analyses.

---

[6] Frank S. ALEXANDER, *Inherent Tensions Between Home Rule and Regional Planning*, 35 WAKE FOREST L. REV. 539, 540 (2000).

[7] *See id.* at 543.

[8] *See id.* at 577–78.

[9] *See id. at* 558–59, 561

[10] FRANK S. ALEXANDER, LAND BANKING AS METROPOLITAN POLICY (2008) at 9, 14–16.

Many states already have regional planning agencies in place. We believe RPAs likely have the authority to create an LDIS and engage in market demand–based planning at the regional scale. However, local governments' conformance of their plans to the region's is often merely voluntary, and RDAs cannot influence local permitting decisions. Perhaps this is enough in many cases both politically and practically. Politically, there may be little support for elevating regional plans to the status where local government plans need to be consistent with it even if the regional plan is a composite of local plans as is the case in Florida and Georgia, for instance.[11] As a practical matter, the existence of a high-quality LDIS combined with market demand–based analysis with informal allocations to local governments (based on insights from the market analysis) may lead to a kind of self-fulfilling prophesy whereby local plans are substantially informed accordingly.

Nonetheless, we advocate for state statutes that mandate RDAs prepare LDISs and market demand–based analysis, thus leading to collaboration by local governments. The general purpose of those statutes mandating regional market demand–based analysis would be:

- to prevent excessive development, which can lead to vacancy, abandonment, public health risks, and public and private costs associated with remediating blight; and
- to prevent the duplication of new commercial and residential development.

Local governments would work together to agree on the allocation of development generated by the regional market demand–based analysis. RDA plans would become a composite of local government plans so that the sum total of all development within those plans would equal the total of development needed based on the regional market demand–based analysis. As we noted in Chapter 7, there would be a market adjustment factor allowing for more development than projected to ensure sufficient supply is available to meet unforeseen needs[12] and to ensure a competitive marketplace. Through a combination of general statutory guidance and administrative rules, the

---

[11] JERRY WEITZ, SPRAWL BUSTING: STATE PROGRAMS TO GUIDE GROWTH (1999).
[12] ARTHUR C. NELSON, PLANNER'S ESTIMATING GUIDE: ESTIMATING LAND USE AND FACILITY NEEDS (2004).

regional market demand–based plan would be comprised of at least these elements (adapted from Chapter 2) applied to the regions:

- The amount of land required to accommodate anticipated growth, including the prospective need for affordable and market rate housing;
- The projected permanent and seasonal population of the area;
- The character of undeveloped land;
- The availability of water supplies, public facilities, and services;
- The need for redevelopment and land banking, including the management and renewal of blighted areas and the elimination of nonconforming uses that are inconsistent with the character of the region;
- The compatibility of uses on lands adjacent to an airport;
- The need for job creation, capital investment, and economic development that will strengthen and diversify the region's economy;
- Encouraging the location of areas of employment, shopping, gatherings, and schools proximate to urban residential areas to the extent possible;
- Coordinating future land uses with the topography, soil conditions, and the availability of facilities and services;
- Ensuring the protection of natural and historic resources;
- Providing for the compatibility of adjacent land uses;
- The amount of land designated for future land uses in the region should allow the operation of real estate markets to provide adequate choices for permanent and seasonal residents and businesses (this is the "market factor" adjustment); and
- A regional land development information system will be created and used to assist in market demand–based analysis, including tracking development approvals and permitting (see Chapter 6).

The statute and rules would ensure that this would not be a top-down process but a collaborative one. The RDA would generate overall, region-wide projections and assessments of need that can include the projections and assessments of individual local governments; then all units of government would negotiate the allocation to local governments. The result would be a regional market demand–based plan that would be a mosaic of local market demand–based plans that sum to the region's total based on a regional market demand–based analysis.

LOCAL MARKET DEMAND–BASED PLANS

In states that mandate regional market demand–based plans, local government plans need to be consistent with them. But even in the absence of state mandates, a local government could design its plan around regionally determined market demand–based analysis. In either case, the local comprehensive plan memorializes guiding principles for all future development. In jurisdictions where comprehensive plans have the force of law, a local government's plan is often viewed as its land-use constitution (see Chapter 2).[13] That means, among other things, a jurisdiction's development approvals must be consistent with that comprehensive plan.

In any event, development permitting remains the province of local governments. The local government market demand–based plan guides all future development. Plan amendments would ensure that the overall development parameters contained in the market demand–based plan are not exceeded, including compliance with any market factor adjustment.

Every five to ten years, the region's market demand–based analysis should be updated. At this time, the region would also reassess its development needs over the next planning horizon and work with local governments to allocate anticipated growth accordingly. Local

---

[13] *See also* EDWARD J. SULLIVAN & JENNIFER BRAGAR, *Recent Developments in Comprehensive Planning*, 46 URB. LAW. 685, 685–702 (2014) (explaining that there are three general ways of describing the status of a local government comprehensive plan: the "unitary" view, the "planning factor" view, and the "planning mandate" view. Each of these views is based on courts' interpretation of applicable state comprehensive planning law. The "unitary view" characterizes comprehensive plans as neither required nor binding for consideration in local government land-use decision-making; only the local zoning code is considered dispositive for determining the legitimacy of land-use decisions. According to the "planning factor" view, the comprehensive plan is a factor to weigh when determining the legitimacy of land-use decisions. The "planning mandate" view interprets state law as giving comprehensive plans the significance of a local government land use constitution. That is, the comprehensive plan is considered a binding document that must guide land-use decisions).

governments may decide to undertake wholesale changes to their plan or account for updated regional needs through the plan amendment process.

It is important to understand, however, that though plans include overall development parameters built on market demand–based analysis, this does not mean every development proposal must be approved.[14] For example, the mere evidence of market demand does not give carte blanche to the local government to approve any given development project. While new development should be supported by evidence of sufficient market demand, it still needs to address the community's broader needs and goals for sustainability, equity, efficiency, and infrastructure sufficiency. Thus, state, regional, and local governments should provide incentives for local governments to develop in a way that is consistent with market demand and with these other foundational development goals as expressed in comprehensive plans.

It is in the nature of the development industry to measure or perceive demand and then to pursue approvals and financing to meet that demand. However, it is common for several developers to perceive the same demand and seek to meet that demand. Each proposed development could well be pursuing the same customers, with the result being overproduction. It is the nature of market studies to analyze past demand and then project that demand into the future, typically with little to no regard to what other developers may be proposing. Taken individually, each proposed development could be sound, but taken collectively the result could well be the type of calamity we have recently seen.

Reviewing agencies will have to be on the lookout for such situations. There is no easy answer here. There will need to be some type of rational criteria to decide among competitive applications—perhaps as simple as date of application, or more encompassing, such as considering the applicant's inclusion of affordable housing or economic opportunity. It is the nature of the free market to tend toward overproduction. On the one hand, this is good in that it provides competition and thus lower prices, but on the other hand, overproduction can lead to the consequences discussed herein.

---

[14] Interview with Ezra Rapport, Esq., Executive Director, Association of Bay Area Governments (ABAG), San Francisco, California (July 19, 2016).

LOCAL ORDINANCE AUTHORIZING PARTICIPATION IN REGIONAL MARKET DEMAND–BASED PLAN PROCESS AND IMPLEMENTATION

Most regions are comprised of numerous general and special purpose local governments. Not only must a state enable a regional planning entity to create a regional market demand–based plan, but also local governments must adopt ordinances memorializing their participation in the process.[15] This ordinance can also serve as a basis for compacts or interlocal agreements between the RDA and other local governments. It would further recognize the RDA's responsibility for periodic updates also requiring local government participation.

MARKET DEMAND–BASED PERMITTING AND THE LOCAL LAND DEVELOPMENT CODE

Market demand–based plans are implemented through market demand–based permitting. This is the province of local land development codes, including zoning, subdivisions, special use permits, building permits, and other similar approvals.

The local government's land development code establishes the requirements and procedures applicable to consideration of all applications for development approvals. Anyone involved in the development process should be able to review the development code and applicable administrative procedures to understand the local development process. Projects generally enter the development pipeline with the developer's preapplication staff meeting and move to submission of an application for development approval, staff review of that application, and then public hearing. Ultimately, building permits are issued.

Once a market demand–based plan is adopted, land development codes need to be amended to facilitate development toward meeting demand. In Chapter 7, we noted that there should be sufficient, buildable land available for development in accordance with the market demand–based plan during the period until the next scheduled plan update, in about five to ten years. We also posed a development

---

[15] *See e.g.*, MASON COUNTY, WA ORDINANCES, § 2.08.010 (county participation in a regional air management program).

decision process implying that so long as development proposals are in accordance with the plan, they would be approved, though subject to development-specific concerns (e.g., drainage, access, site plan). It would even be possible for the accumulation of new development to be in excess of development need projections provided it is within the market factor adjustment.

It is when new development for an area is not in accordance with the plan that special evaluations would be needed. To elaborate, these can include:

- Amending the plan to reduce development parameters elsewhere to allow more development at the proposed location but thereby keeping total development within the parameters of the market demand–based plan. This can be triggered when refined analysis of other sites reveals they are incapable of being developed at the level designated.

- Amending the plan to recognize that prior development assumptions have changed—such as increased demand for townhomes and reduced demand for detached homes on large lots—and that the proposed development is consistent with emerging market demand. This does not necessarily require changing the current designation of detached home areas immediately but rather during the scheduled plan update period.

- Amending the plan, recognizing there is more growth than projected. If the region is growing more than the plan assumed, then the regional market demand–based plan may need to be updated sooner than scheduled. The update process can lead to new development allocations to local government.

The preparation of market demand–based plans should be done by regions in collaboration with local governments, and the market analysis paid for by those entities. This does not preclude other interests from funding their own market analyses and sharing them with governmental units during the planning process—in fact, we recommend it. But once the market demand–based plan is adopted and implemented by local governments, there is the presumption that the projected need exists, at least until the next plan update. Subject to site planning and design, and other public policy concerns noted earlier, developments meeting projected needs should be approved, though perhaps with conditions.

If development proposals call for more development than is presumed to be needed, the burden falls onto the developer to demonstrate the new or additional need. If the change is accepted by the local government, perhaps after RDA review and comment, and if it is covered by the first two situations bulleted on page 182, approvals (with conditions) would seem prudent. It is only when the situation discussed in the third bullet is triggered that an amendment to the regional market demand–based plan would be needed.

▌SUMMARY OBSERVATION

This much is sure. The next real estate crisis is coming to a city, town, or county near you. The Great Recession's real estate crash and the cyclical real estate crashes that preceded it, such as the 1980s savings-and-loan (S&L) crisis, reflect more than a one-time failure of developers and financial institutions to adequately assess real estate market demand. Periods of exuberant real estate development, in which developers, bankers, and other key players in the real estate sector misjudge a market's appetite for new supply, have previously gone unchecked in multiple instances, leading to disastrous results. The time has come for more proactive, collaborative regional and local efforts to:

- determine the long-range development needs of the region, leading to a regional market demand–based plan;
- allocate those needs through a negotiated and deliberative process to local governments, resulting in local market demand–based plans;
- create a market demand–based permitting process to approve development that is in accordance with those plans (subject to site planning, design, and other planning policy concerns that do not substantially reduce the ability of the proposed development to meet development needs); and
- include provisions to amend plans as needed to meet unforeseen or emerging market needs.

In our epilogue, we speculate on the benefits America would have received had MDBPP been in place before the events leading to the S&L crisis and certainly the events leading to the Great Recession.

EPILOGUE

Looking Back and Looking Forward: How Market Demand–Based Planning and Permitting Can Lead to a Wealthier Nation

To stimulate the economy in the early 1980s, President Reagan and Congress signed the Economic Recovery Tax Act (ERTA) into law, which used financial regulatory tools to induce real estate development. The ERTA was so successful that local governments permitted far more development—mostly nonresidential—than the market could absorb, as we showed in Act 1 (Chapter 3). An entire financial industry—savings and loans—mostly collapsed. In our view, the main lessons of 1980s are (1) financial regulation can lead to overdevelopment when used to stimulate the economy, and (2) the forgotten role of state and local governments is to provide oversight of their own economies regardless of federal actions. Those states that used market demand–based planning and permitting to match new development supply with demand saw fewer losses but also subsidized states that allowed development in excess of need.

In Act 2 (Chapter 4), we fast-forwarded to the 2000s to see that the lessons of the 1980s were not heeded. There are some who argue that sufficient federal regulatory oversight alone could have prevented the oversupply of residential development. We believe the evidence presented in Chapters 3 and 4 refutes this. All states enable local governments to plan and to use those plans to guide development permitting. If those plans are based on realistic market-demand assessments, and if development permitting is made in accordance with a comprehensive plan, the magnitude of the Great Recession may have been reduced. Our analysis suggests that if all states used market demand–based planning and permitting to guide their development in ways roughly equivalent to the states that exhibited such discipline, the number of foreclosures may have been reduced by half. Moreover, trillions of dollars in equity and economic productivity that were lost because of overbuilding could have been saved. The Great Recession might instead have been just a garden-variety recession.

If we can "right-size" development permitting so that it meets market demand and no more, America's economy will flourish. In this epilogue, we assess what would have been had our market demand–based planning and permitting (MDBPP) approach been in place since at least the early 1980s. Looking ahead, we find that only through market-based permitting will America's economy sustain its greatness.

▌LOOKING BACK

Since the presidency of Ronald Reagan, the United States has gone through two real estate-driven recessions. They each cost the American economy dearly.

The events leading up to the savings-and-loan (S&L) bailout, including the recession of the early 1990s, cost the American economy in two ways.[1] First, the gross national product of the nation from 1981 to 1990 is estimated to have been reduced by nearly $400 billion (in 2016 dollars). But the Congressional Budget Office also estimates that the economy was reduced by nearly another $600 billion. The estimated total cost to the economy of the S&L crisis was about $1 trillion.

Though not trivial—indeed, it is more than the 2015 budgets of the ten largest states—the figure is dwarfed by the cost of the Great Recession. The Dallas Federal Reserve Bank[2] asserts that the Great Recession cost the American economy between $15 and $30

---

[1]   We base our assertion on Congressional Budget Office, The Economic Effects of the Savings and Loan Crisis (1992).

[2]   Tyler Atkinson, David Luttrell & Harvey Rosenblum . How Bad Was It? The Costs and Consequences of the 2007–09 Financial Crisis (2013).

trillion (in 2016 dollars).[3] This is a range of about four to eight times the total federal budget in 2015.

The damage inflicted on Americans is legion:

- Nearly 9 million jobs were lost and unemployment more than doubled from less than 5 percent to about 11 percent.[4]
- Even among those who were employed, those who wanted a full-time job had to settle for part-time jobs if they could find work, and many millions simply became so discouraged seeking employment that they dropped out of the labor force, thus making the official unemployment rate seem less worse than it was. In total, about 27 million workers or about one of six were either unemployed or underemployed during the height of the Great Recession.[5]
- Among workers over age fifty-five and nearing retirement age, many lost their jobs and thus the ability to accumulate pensions. For others, the value of their pensions was reduced, forcing them to work longer or accept less income when they retired.[6]
- A wide range of adverse social outcomes was seen, such as the reduced ability of parents to transfer wealth to their children or support them in college; compromised parental relationships; reduced personal health, especially that of minority persons; increased criminal behavior; reduced ability of younger generations to accumulate wealth and be able to buy homes or finance college from their own funds without going into debt; reduced wealth among all households but disproportionately greater

---

[3] *Id. See also* Atkinson et al. offer several ranges based on individual analyses. In all cases, they discounted future estimated costs by a rate that turns out to be several times higher than seen in the latter 2010s. In cash flow analysis, the present value of a future sum is discounted by an assumed rate of investment return. The higher the discount factor, the lower the present value; conversely, the lower the discount factor, the higher the present value. Given actual rates of return in the latter 2010s compared to the early 2010s, we surmise the economic cost of the Great Recession is at the high end of their estimates.

[4] See http://stateofworkingamerica.org/great-recession/job-loss/.

[5] See http://stateofworkingamerica.org/great-recession/unemployment-and-underemployment/.

[6] See ALA L. GUSTMAN, THOMAS L. STEINMEIER & NAHID TABATABAI, THE GREAT RECESSION, RETIREMENT AND RELATED OUTCOMES (2015).

losses among minority households; and delayed household and family formation, among many others.[7]

- The Great Recession also reduced federal, state, and local government services, including education, public transit, public safety, and public health and welfare services,[8] resulting in the loss of more than 500,000 jobs.[9]

In short, while the economic costs can be estimated and are considerable, the social costs are perhaps more considerable, though incalculable. This waste of America's resources was caused substantially by permitting development in excess of market demand.

LOOKING FORWARD

Imagine a United States without the S&L crisis or the Great Recession. The United States—and all economic systems—certainly has cycles of expansion and contraction, and perhaps a recession may have been due around the time of both the S&L bailout and the Great Recession. Since 1945 they have occurred roughly every five to ten years, and they last an average of less than one year.[10] We see from Chapter 5, however, that the length and severity of the Great Recession was clearly anomalous, being many times more severe than the average of all recessions since 1945. Literature seems conclusive that the reason for the difference is excessive development permitting during the 2000s. Even if there should have been a recession in the late 2000s, the evidence suggests:

- It would have led to the layoffs of 2 to 3 million workers over about a year instead of 8 million jobs lasting nearly two years;
- Recovery to prerecession employment levels would have taken about two years compared to nearly ten;

---

[7] See numerous papers published by the Russel Sage Foundation accessible from www.russellsage.org/research/social-effects-great-recession-description.

[8] See https://www.brookings.edu/articles/state-and-local-budgets-and-the-great-recession/. See also ADAM H. LANGLEY, *Local Government Finances During and After the Great Recession* in LAND AND THE CITY (George W. McCarthy, Gregory K. Ingram & Samuel A. Moody, eds., 2015).

[9] See www.brookings.edu/blog/jobs/2012/08/03/a-record-decline-in-government-jobs-implications-for-the-economy-and-americas-workforce/.

[10] See www.nber.org/cycles.html.

- It would have reduced the gross domestic product by a few hundred billion dollars compared to perhaps up to $30 trillion;
- Federal, state, and local government services would have been much more resilient to a small and short-lived recession compared to the deep and long-lived Great Recession; and
- Social and personal costs would have been negligible compared to having impacts on generations of persons who were forced to change their life circumstances, perhaps forever.

Can recessions of the future be prevented? Perhaps not. But through market demand–based planning and permitting we may assure that they will not be artificially created by the overdevelopment of real estate relative to market demand.

References and Selected Bibliography

Advisory Commission on City Planning and Zoning, Standard City Planning Enabling Act (1928).

Advisory Committee on Zoning, A STANDARD ZONING ENABLING ACT (1926).

Alexander, Frank S., *Inherent Tensions Between Home Rule and Regional Planning*, 35 WAKE FOREST LAW REVIEW 539 (2000).

Alexander, Frank S. LAND BANKS AND LAND BANKING (2011).

Atkinson, Tyler, David Luttrell & Harvey Rosenblum, HOW BAD WAS IT? THE COSTS AND CONSEQUENCES OF THE 2007–09 FINANCIAL CRISIS (2013).

Auxier, Richard C. (2010). *Reagan's Recession* (2016), www.pewresearch.org/2010/12/14/reagans-recession/.

Barsky, Robert B. & Lutz Kilian, A MONETARY EXPLANATION OF THE GREAT STAGFLATION OF THE 1970S (2010).

Berke, Phillip R., David R. Godschalk & Edward J. Kaiser, URBAN LAND USE PLANNING (5th ed. 2006).

Bollens, Scott A., State Growth Management: Intergovernmental Frameworks and Policy Objectives, J. AM. PLANN. ASSOC. 58(4), 454–466 (1992).

Bosselman Fred and David Callies, The Quiet Revolution in Landuse Control (1971), http://eric.ed.gov/?q=The+Quiet+Revolution+in+land+use+control&id=ED06727.

Buchsbaum, Peter A., *Permit Coordination Study by the Lincoln Institute of Land Policy*, 36 URB. LAW. 191 (2004).

Burby, Raymond J. & Peter J. May, MAKING GOVERNMENTS PLAN: STATE EXPERIMENTS IN MANAGING LAND USE (1997).

Callies, David L., REGULATING PARADISE: LAND USE CONTROLS IN HAWAII (1985).

Cauchi, Richard & Ashely Noble, *CON-Certificate of Need State Laws* (Aug. 25, 2016), www.ncsl.org/research/health/con-certificate-of-need-state-laws.aspx.

Chapin, Tim, Harrison Higgins & Evan Rosenberg, COMPARISON OF FLORIDA'S APPROACHES TO LARGE-SCALE PLANNING (2007).

City of Corvallis, Oregon, CORVALLIS LAND DEVELOPMENT INFORMATION REPORT (2015).

Clawson, Marion, *Urban Sprawl and Speculation in Suburban Land,* LAND ECON. 38, 99–111 (1962).

Coase, Ronald H., *The Problem of Social Cost,* J.L. & ECON. 3, 1–44 (1960).

Congressional Budget Office, THE ECONOMIC EFFECTS OF THE SAVINGS AND LOAN CRISIS (1992).

Congressional Budget Office, FANNIE MAE, FREDDIE MAC AND THE FEDERAL ROLE IN THE SECONDARY MORTGAGE MARKET (2010).

Cox, Wendell, *Florida Sheds Its "Smart Growth" Dunce Hat: Land-Use Laws Meant to Limit Urban Sprawl Instead Prompted One of the Nation's Biggest Housing Bubbles,* WALL ST. J. (October 18, 2013), www.wsj.com/articles/SB10001424052702304864504579143371449924220.

Davidoff, Paul & Neil Newton Gold, *Exclusionary Zoning,* YALE REVIEW OF LAW AND SOCIAL ACTION, 1(2), 57–63 (1971).

Dawson, Mary, *The Best Laid Plans: The Rise and Fall of Growth Management in Florida,* J. LAND USE & ENVTL LAW 11(2), 325–374 (1996).

DeGrove, John M., LAND, GROWTH AND POLITICS (1984).

DeGrove, John M., PLANNING AND GROWTH MANAGEMENT IN THE STATES: THE NEW FRONTIER FOR LAND POLICY (1992).

DeGrove, John M., PLANNING, POLICY AND POLITICS: SMART GROWTH AND THE STATES (2005).

Diamond, Henry L. & Patrick F. Noonan, LAND USE IN AMERICA (1996).

DiMento, Joseph, THE CONSISTENCY DOCTRINE AND THE LIMITS OF PLANNING (1980).

Dowd, Kevin, *Moral Hazard and the Financial Crisis,* CATO J. 29(1), 141–166 (2009).

Downs, Anthony, *Have Housing Prices Risen Faster in Portland Than Elsewhere?* HOUS. POLICY DEBATE, 13:1, 7–31 (2002).

Downs, Anthony, NIAGARA OF CAPITAL: HOW GLOBAL CAPITAL HAS TRANSFORMED HOUSING AND REAL ESTATE MARKETS (2007).

Downs, Anthony, REAL ESTATE AND THE FINANCIAL CRISIS (2009).

Federal Reserve, FINANCIAL ACCOUNTS OF THE UNITED STATES (2016).

Fender, Ingo & Martin Scheicher, *The ABX: How Does the Markets Price Subprime Mortgage Risk?* BIS QUARTERLY REVIEW 67–81 (September 2008).

Fernando, Ferreira & Joseph Gyourko, *A New Look at the U.S. Foreclosure Crisis: Panel Data Evidence of Prime and Subprime Borrowers from 1997 to 2012* (2015), www.nber.org/papers/w21261.

Fischel, William A., THE ECONOMICS OF ZONING: A PROPERTY RIGHTS APPROACH TO AMERICAN LAND USE CONTROLS (1985).

Fischel, William A., THE HOMEVOTER HYPOTHESIS HOW HOME VALUES INFLUENCE LOCAL GOVERNMENT TAXATION, SCHOOL FINANCE, AND LAND-USE POLICIES (2005).

Freilich, Robert H., Robert J. Sitkowski & Seth D. Mennillo, FROM SPRAWL TO SUSTAINABILITY: SMART GROWTH, NEW URBANISM, GREEN DEVELOPMENT, AND RENEWABLE ENERGY (2nd ed. 2010).

Gale, Dennis E., *Eight State-Sponsored Growth Management Programs: A Comparative Analysis*, J. AM. PLANN. ASSOC. 58:4, 425–439 (1992).

Gardner, Max III, *Mortgage Securitization, Servicing, and Consumer Bankruptcy*, LAW TRENDS & NEWS (September 2005), www.americanbar .org/content/newsletter/publications/law_trends_news_practice_ area_e_newsletter_home/mortgagesecuritization.html.

Godschalk, David R., Scott Bollens, John S. Hekman, & Mike Miles, LAND SUPPLY MONITORING (1986).

Graham, Bob, Communication provided to the authors via e-mail on October 29, 2013.

Gustman, Ala, L., Thomas L. Steinmeier & Nahid Tabatabai, THE GREAT RECESSION, RETIREMENT AND RELATED OUTCOMES (2015).

Haar, Charles M., *In Accordance with a Comprehensive Plan*, HARV. L. REV. 68(7), 1154–1175 (1955).

Haar, Charles M., *The Master Plan: An Impermanent Constitution*, LAW & CONTEMP. PROBS. 20, 353–418 (1955), http://scholarship.law.duke .edu/lcp/vol20/iss3/2.

Hacke, Robin, David Wood & Marian Urquilla. COMMUNITY INVESTMENT: FOCUSING ON THE SYSTEM (2015).

Hagman, Donald & Dean Misczynski, WINDFALLS FOR WIPEOUTS: LAND VALUE CAPTURE AND COMPENSATION (1978).

Harris, Benjamin & Brian Moore (2013). RESIDENTIAL PROPERTY TAXES IN THE UNITED STATE (2013).

Haughwout, Andrew, Richard W. Peach, John Sporn & Joseph Tracy, THE SUPPLY SIDE OF THE HOUSING BOOM AND BUST OF THE 2000S (2012).

Hills, Roderick M., Jr. & David Schleicher, CITY REPLANNING (2014).

Hutchinson, Martin, *Scrap Heap for Financial Models* (2008), www .silverbearcafe.com/private/2.08/scrapheap.html.

Immergluck, Dan, *The Cost of Vacant and Blighted Properties in Atlanta* (2015), http://45tkhs2ch4042kf51f1akcju.wpengine.netdna-cdn.com/wp-content/uploads/2016/02/Cost-of-Vacant-and-Blighted-Properties-in-Atlanta.pdf.

Institut d'aménagement urbain, ABÉCÉDAIRE DE LA FUTURE MÉTROPOLE DU GRAND PARIS (2014).

Jourdan, Dawn, Shannon Van Zandt & Nicole Adair, *Meeting Their Fair Share: A Proposal for the Creation of Regional Land Banks to Meet the Affordable Housing Needs in the Rural Areas of Texas*, 19 J. AFFORDABLE HOUS. & COMM. DEV. L.147, 158 (2010).

Juergensmeyer, Julian C. & James C. Nicholas, *Loving Growth Management in the Time of Recession*, URB. LAW. 42(4)/43(1), 417–423 (2010).

Juergensmeyer, Julian Conrad & Thomas E. Roberts, LAND USE PLANNING AND DEVELOPMENT REGULATION LAW (3d ed. 2012).

Kent, T. J., THE URBAN GENERAL PLAN (1964).

Kincaid, John, *Regulatory Regionalism in Metropolitan Areas: Voter Resistance and Reform Persistence*, 13 PACE L. REV. 449, 468–73 (1993).

Knaap, Gerrit J., ed., LAND MARKET MONITORING FOR SMART URBAN GROWTH (2001).

Knaap, Gerrit J., LAND SUPPLY AND INFRASTRUCTURE CAPACITY MONITORING FOR SMART URBAN GROWTH (2003).

Knaap, Gerrit J., MONITORING LAND & HOUSING MARKETS: AN ESSENTIAL TOOL FOR SMART GROWTH (2004).

Knaap, Gerrit J. & Lewis D. Hopkins, *The Inventory Approach to Urban Growth Boundaries*, J. AM. PLANN. ASSOC. 67(3), 314–326 (2001).

Knaap, Gerrit J. & Arthur C. Nelson, THE REGULATED LANDSCAPE (1992).

Kushner, James A., *Comparative Urban Governance: Why the United States Is Incapable of Reform*, FORDHAM URB. L.J. 61, 20–28 (2014).

Langley, Adam, H., *Local Government Finances During and After the Great Recession*, in LAND AND THE CITY (George W. McCarthy, Gregory K. Ingram, & Samuel A. Moody, eds., 2015).

Lee, Douglass B., *Land Use Planning as a Response to Market Failure*, in THE LAND USE POLICY DEBATE IN THE UNITED STATES 149–164 (Judith I. deNeufville,1981).

Lind, Kermit J., *Strategic Code Compliance Enforcement: A Prescription for Resilient Communities* in HOW CITIES WILL SAVE THE WORLD: URBAN INNOVATION IN THE FACE OF POPULATION FLOWS, CLIMATE CHANGE AND ECONOMIC INEQUALITY (Raymond H. Brescia & John Travis Marshall, eds., 2016).

Linkous, Evangeline R. & Timothy S. Chapin, *TDR Program Performance in Florida*, J. AM. PLANN. ASSOC. 80(3), 253–267 (2014).

Logan, John R. & Harvey L. Molotch, URBAN FORTUNES: THE POLITICAL ECONOMY OF PLACE (1987).

Daniel Mandelker, *The Role of the Local Comprehensive Plan in Land Use Regulation*, 76 MICHIGAN LAW REVIEW 899 (1976).

McKenzie, Evan, PRIVATOPIA: HOMEOWNER ASSOCIATIONS AND THE RISE OF RESIDENTIAL PRIVATE GOVERNMENT (1994).

Meck, Stuart, GROWING SMART LEGISLATIVE GUIDEBOOK (2002).

Mian, Atif & Amir Sufi, Household Debt and the Great Depression (March 2014), http://houseofdebt.org/2014/03/15/household-debt-and-the-great-depression.html.

Misra, Tanvi, Got an Affordable Housing Crisis? Save the Cheap Housing You Already Have. CITYLAB (Aug. 26, 2016), www.citylab.com/housing/2016/08/got-an-affordable-housing-crisis-save-the-cheap-housing-youve-already-got/497234/.

Moudon, Anne & Michael Hubner, MONITORING LAND SUPPLY AND CAPACITY WITH PARCEL-BASED GIS (1999).

Moudon, Anne & Michael Hubner, MONITORING LAND SUPPLY WITH GEOGRAPHIC INFORMATION SYSTEMS: THEORY, PRACTICE AND PARCEL-BASED APPROACHES (2000).

Murphy, Edward V., WHO REGULATES WHOM AND HOW? AN OVERVIEW OF U.S. FINANCIAL REGULATORY POLICY FOR BANKING AND SECURITIES MARKETS (2015).

Musgrave, Richard A. & Peggy B. Musgrave, PUBLIC FINANCE IN THEORY AND PRACTICE (1973).

National Commission on the Causes of the Financial and Economic Crisis in the United States, THE FINANCIAL CRISIS INQUIRY REPORT (2011).

Nelson, Arthur C., The Design and Administration of Urban Growth Boundaries, REAL ESTATE FINANCE 8(4), 11–22 (1990).

Nelson, Arthur C., Comment on Anthony Downs's "Have Housing Prices Risen Faster in Portland Than Elsewhere?" HOUS. POLICY DEBATE, 13(1), 33–42 (2002).

Nelson, Arthur C., PLANNER'S ESTIMATING GUIDE: PROJECTING LAND-USE AND FACILITY NEEDS (2004).

Nelson, Arthur C., Reducing Financial Risk Through Needs Certification, J. URBAN PLAN. D., 126(1), 39–54 (2000).

Nelson, Arthur C., RESHAPING METROPOLITAN AMERICA (2013).

Nelson, Arthur C. & Casey J. Dawkins, URBAN CONTAINMENT IN THE UNITED STATES: HISTORY, MODELS, AND TECHNIQUES FOR REGIONAL AND METROPOLITAN GROWTH MANAGEMENT (2004).

Nelson, Arthur C. & James B. Duncan, GROWTH MANAGEMENT PRINCIPLES AND PRACTICE (1995).

Nelson, Robert H., ZONING AND PROPERTY RIGHTS (1978).

Nolon, John R., Zoning's Centennial: A Complete Account of the Evolution of Zoning into a Robust System of Land Use Law, 1916–2016, in LAND USE AND SUSTAINABLE DEVELOPMENT LAW, CASES AND MATERIALS (John R. Nolon et al., eds., 9th ed. 2017).

Office of the Comptroller of the Currency, COMMUNITY DEVELOPMENTS INSIGHTS, LOW-INCOME HOUSING TAX CREDITS: AFFORDABLE HOUSING INVESTMENT OPPORTUNITIES FOR BANKS (2014).

Pelham, Tom, *Florida's Retreat from Planning and Growth Management*, PRACTICING PLANNER, Vol. 9 (online) (2011a).

Pelham, Tom, FLORIDA COMPREHENSIVE PLANNING SYSTEM ENCOUNTERS STORMY WEATHER, Chicago, AM. BAR. ASSOC. (2011b).

Richmond, Henry R., *Metropolitan Land-Use Reform: The Promise and Challenge of Majority Consensus* in REFLECTIONS ON REGIONALISM (Bruce Katz, ed., 2000).

Samuelson, Paul A., ECONOMICS (1948).

Singer, Joseph William, *Foreclosure and the Failures of Formality, or Subprime Mortgage Conundrums and How to Fix Them*, CONN. L. REV. 46, 497–559 (2013).

Smith, Adam, *An Inquiry into the Nature and Causes of the Wealth of Nations* (1776), https://www.ibiblio.org/ml/libri/s/SmithA_WealthNations_p.pdf

Steinemann, Anne, MICROECONOMICS FOR PUBLIC DECISIONS (2nd ed. 2011).

Stroud, Nancy, *A History and New Turns in Florida's Growth Management Reform*, 45 J. MARSHALL L. REV. 397 (2012).

Sullivan, Edward J. & MATTHEW J. MICHEL, *Ramapo Plus Thirty: The Changing Role of the Plan in Land Use Regulation*, URB. LAW., 35, 75 (2003).

Tiebout, Charles M., *A Pure Theory of Local Expenditures*, J. POLIT. ECON. 64, 416–424 (1956).

Tomàs, Mariona, METROPOLITAN GOVERNANCE IN EUROPE, CHALLENGES & MODELS. (2015).

U.S. Census Bureau, INTERIM STATE POPULATION PROJECTIONS (2005).

Walker, John R., *Depression-Era Bank Failures: The Great Contagion or the Great Shakeout?* ECONOMIC QUARTERLY 91(1), 39–54 (2005).

Weiss, Marc A., THE RISE OF THE COMMUNITY BUILDERS: THE AMERICAN REAL ESTATE INDUSTRY AND URBAN LAND PLANNING (1987).

Weitz, Jerry, SPRAWL BUSTING: STATE PROGRAMS TO GUIDE GROWTH (1999).

Whitaker, Stephan & Thomas J. Fitzpatrick IV, *Deconstructing Distressed-Property Spillovers: The Effects of Vacant, Tax-Delinquent, and Foreclosed Properties in Housing Submarkets*, 22 J. HOUSING ECON. 79 (2013).

Index

Featured Publications from the Section of State and Local Government Law

Section of State and
Local Government Law
AMERICAN BAR ASSOCIATION

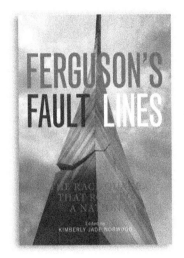

Ferguson's Fault Lines
The Race Quake That
Rocked a Nation
Kimberly Jade Norwood

The Zoning and
Land Use Handbook
Ronald S. Cope

To order 🌐 visit www.ShopABA.org
or call 📞 (800) 285-2221.

Featured Publications from the Section of State and Local Government Law

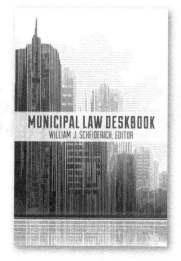